THAT PUNK JIMMY HOFFA!

COFFEY'S TRANSFER AT WAR WITH THE TEAMSTERS

MARILYN JUNE COFFEY

UNITED COMMUNICATIONS PRESS

OMAHA, NEBRASKA

Paperback ISBN: 978-0-9989018-1-7
Kindle ISBN: 978-0-9989018-2-4
EPUB ISBN: 978-0-9989018-3-1
Audio ISBN: 978-0-9989018-4-8

Library of Congress Control Number: 2017905321
Cataloging in Publication Data on file with publisher.

www.MarilynCoffey.net

Omega Cottonwood Press
c/o CMI
4822 South 133rd Street
Omaha, NE 68137

Production, Distribution and Marketing: Concierge Marketing Inc.

Front cover: Two delivery trucks used by Coffey's Transfer in Omaha in the 1950s.
Back cover: Coffey's Transfer trucks: a big over-the-road truck and, behind it, smaller square delivery trucks. In the background is Tom Coffey's main office building in Alma, Nebraska.
Page 321: Photo of Frank Sheeran courtesy of Charles Brandt, author of *I Heard you Paint Houses: Frank "The Irishman" Sheeran and Closing the Case on Jimmy Hoffa.*
Page 367: Photo of Marilyn Coffey courtesy of Suzanne Luttig.

Printed in the United States
10 9 8 7 6 5 4 3 2

"It's rare when an opportunity arises to read a gem like *That Punk Jimmy Hoffa!* This is an historically accurate, nonfiction account of the author's father, Tom Coffey, and his battle with Jimmy Hoffa and the Teamsters.

"In the Teamsters' humble beginnings and throughout their formative years, union reps convinced individual employees to unionize. Hoffa changed all that by coercing transportation owners instead. Those who refused to sign union contracts, like Tom Coffey, were harassed, or worse, driven out of business with hard-core interference strategies and scare tactics.

"There has been a lot written about Hoffa. Many can't decide whether he was a criminal or hero. However, everyone agrees Jimmy Hoffa wielded incredible power and political influence. He was a bigger-than-life figure in American history, and Coffey captures his ruthless ego, brilliance, and fury against his enemies from a perspective she shared with her father.

"This book is a fun and desirable read, because Coffey elaborates on the voice of Jimmy Hoffa and her father, while retaining the full accuracy of the historical facts and events of the Teamsters' movement. This lends to the realism of the characters, who jump off the pages. The book is loaded with well-researched history, and moves at a brisk pace. Highly recommended."

—Dan Reynolds
Author of *Dangerous DNA*

"When a short, stout bully and a midwestern, small town businessman clash, it turns personal. No one predicted that it would change the huge labor union's practices and public law. Coffey's superb research and compelling storytelling create a must-read tale with implications for life in today's age."

—Wayne M. Anson,
Author and President of the Nebraska Writers Guild

"Marilyn Coffey's entertaining new book about her father's battle with the notorious, powerful, and mob-connected Teamster boss Jimmy Hoffa is a page-turning true story that only a daughter could tell.

"Coffey's father, Tom, the mayor of his Nebraska town, owns a highly successful trucking business that draws Hoffa's attention as he seeks to consolidate his power. Despite Tom's reputation for fairness, Hoffa threatens a Teamster takeover that includes visits from a 350-pound, gun-toting bruiser from Brooklyn and other strong-arm strategies. Tom's drivers are bribed and intimidated, while Tom's middle daughter, Marilyn, delights in her father's heroics as well as his raucous sense of humor.

"When U.S. Attorney General Robert F. Kennedy steps in to fight the Teamsters, Tom is finally forced to yield. And even RFK cannot defeat Hoffa.

"Yet the last laugh becomes Tom Coffey's, and later, Marilyn's, as Tom's story is nationally circulated through Congressional hearings. The older, wiser author looks back on this period of embattled family interlude and recreates it in this highly readable memoir."

—Carole Rosenthal

TO MY FATHER,
JUNE THOMAS COFFEY,
WHO LIVED IT.

CONTENTS

INTRODUCTION

It seems as though I've always written about Tom Coffey, my father. In my childhood journal, I wrote about him all the time: how he gave me a live rabbit for Easter; how he became mayor of our little town of Alma, Nebraska; how he built me a tree house.

In 1956, Dad knuckled under Jimmy Hoffa's six-month-long Teamsters strike. He sold his twenty-seven-year-old truckline, Coffey's Transfer Company, rather than sign Hoffa's contract. Nineteen years old, I wrote Dad a sympathetic letter, a letter so passionate it appeared, eight years later, in a major national magazine, *Saturday Evening Post*.

In 1958, now a University of Nebraska journalism student, I met Robert Kennedy in Washington, DC. I'd gone to the Capitol to see Dad testify against Jimmy Hoffa before John F. Kennedy, then just a senator, and Robert Kennedy, the Rackets Committee's counsel who had sworn to put Hoffa behind bars. My journalism professor assigned a paper about the experience, so I wrote about my dad again.

The following year, for my senior research paper at the university, I chose to write about executive, or secret, sessions in Nebraska's Unicameral legislature. I was against them. So was my dad, although we didn't see eye-to-eye. My research soon revealed that my father (earlier a state legislator in the Unicameral) had led a debate about these sessions.

Of course I had to interview him.

Before I did, I asked him at dinner if he remembered anything about the 1953 Unicameral fight. Dad, a natural raconteur, mocked other senators and the radio broadcaster involved in the debate. He kept me in stitches. But on the day of the interview with me, he became formal as we set up two folding chairs on the front porch.

"Before we start," he said, "I have to know whether this is on the record or off the record."

"On the record." That meant I could print anything he said.

The raconteur disappeared. I couldn't get my dad to fess up to anything he'd said at the dinner table. And, thereby, I learned a good lesson about the nature of politicians.

When Dad died in 1977, I inherited his papers: reams of pages of his testimony in front of the National Labor Relations Board (NLRB), in various courts, and before the Kennedy brothers, plus photographs, recorded radio interviews, and two copies of the *Saturday Evening Post* that published my letter and his story.

But I didn't think about writing this book until 1992 when I was teaching at Fort Hays State University in Hays, Kansas. There I mentioned, in passing, that my dad had tangled with Jimmy Hoffa. When he heard this, my boss, the English department chairman, Clifford Edwards, lit up. He plied me with questions and insisted that I write a book about my dad's war with Jimmy Hoffa.

One morning after that, I awoke with a working title in mind: *I Watched My Dad Beat Jimmy Hoffa.*

Research began. Copious research, for I knew little about Jimmy Hoffa or the Teamsters Union. Along the way, I interviewed Carl Curtis, the Nebraska senator who had served on the Rackets Committee with the Kennedy brothers. Curtis gave me his records of that experience, to be placed with my papers in the Marilyn Coffey Collection in the Archives of the University of Nebraska library in Lincoln.

Then I wrote. I spun out a promising beginning for a hundred or so pages, only to abandon it and start a new, more promising version. Don't be alarmed. I just write this way. I typed out version two, version three, and so on to this version seven. This one lived up to its promising beginning. Here it is for you.

PROLOGUE

Mama snipped her scissors. The knot on top of the big, brown package sprang apart. I grabbed the rough string and tugged.

"No no," Mama bent to pry open my fingers. "Wait!"

But I couldn't wait! Uncle Glen had sent me and my sister this package from way across the ocean where he fought Japs. Good-looking Glen, Dad's youngest brother, was my favorite uncle. I jumped up and down. It was July 1942.

Mama pushed the package into the middle of the dining room table so I couldn't reach it. The string slithered off onto the floor. I grabbed the edge of the table and pulled myself up on tiptoe.

"Just hold your horses."

Brown paper rustled as Mama opened the package.

"Oh, look!" She lifted a cluster of flowers—red, yellow, white, blue. Behind me, I heard my sister, Margaret, eight, oooooing. I, now four, ooooed, too, but our sister, Margery, in diapers, said nothing. Daddy wouldn't let me play with her anymore, not after I upset her in her carriage.

Uncle Glen, left, with his army buddies.

Mama worked some magic with her hands, and the cluster of flowers turned into a garland. She dropped a beautiful ring of flowers around Margaret's neck, then around mine. Flowers hung way past my belly button.

"They are leis." Mama smiled. "When you go to Hawaii, they greet you and put one of these around your neck."

I didn't know what Mama meant, but I didn't care. I lifted the lei up to my face and sniffed the stiff flowers, but they smelled like fresh paper.

"Oh, look at this, girls!" Mama shook out what she called a skirt, but it didn't look like any skirt I'd ever seen. Long strings of grass hung from the waist. "Here. Take off your shorts. Let's put these on." She handed a skirt to Margaret, old enough to dress herself, and helped me tie the string on mine.

"Oh, no, Margaret. Not so high." Mama dropped the skirt below Margaret's waist. Now both our belly buttons showed.

"Let's dance!" Mama began to sway, undulating her hips and waving her hands. I shuffled back, amazed at my mother. Then I waved my hands, too, and shook my behind.

"Oh, look, Tom." My mother's voice rang out. "Hula girls!"

Dad unfolded himself from his living room chair and entered the dining room. His laugh ricocheted around the room.

"I've got to get this." Dad rummaged for his movie camera, and we all went outdoors. There, in our front yard, in our small town of Alma, Nebraska, I wiggled my hips for posterity.

THE JAPANESE SURRENDER

"Oh, my lord!"

Mama swear? I perked right up.

She stood by the buffet, listening to some man talking on our little brown box of a radio.

"Tom!" She dashed into the living room. "They've surrendered! The Japanese have surrendered! The war is over! The war is over!"

Dad leaped to his feet and hugged her. He wiped tears off her cheeks and kissed her. "Sweetheart, we got to celebrate this." His voice sounded warm and low.

Mama giggled and wiggled out of Dad's embrace. She rummaged around in the buffet, pulled out her old school bell—Mama taught school before she married Dad—and handed it to me. I grabbed the bell's clapper so it wouldn't ring. I knew Mama thought it made too much noise.

"Go ahead. Ring it. And say the war is over. Like this." She grabbed the handle, shook it and shook it and cried, "The war is over. The war is over." Then she handed the bell to me. "Can you do that?"

I certainly could. And did. The bell made an awful racket.

Mama squatted and looked at me right in my face. "Here's what you do. You walk all around the block— twice—ringing and shouting. Let all the neighbors know the war's over."

I headed toward the front door.

"Where are the other girls?" Dad asked.

"Margaret took Margery to Grandma's house."

Mama headed up the stairs first, and Dad put a little pop on her behind just as I opened the front door.

"You're Such a Big Girl Now!"

Soon my uncles, handsome Glen and teddy bear Lyle, came back from the war—Glen from Christmas Island and Lyle from the European front.

My Uncle Lyle in WWII uniform.

"Look at you," Glen ruffled my hair. "You're such a big girl now, I can't toss you in the air anymore." That made me feel both proud and sad.

Glen brought a fistful of gifts: a bracelet of New Zealand coins for Mama, a money clip with a silver dollar on it for Dad, and handkerchiefs for us girls. I loved mine, with a beautiful white eagle embroidered on it. Glen decided to live with us and drive one of my dad's Coffey's Transfer trucks.

Lyle arrived empty-handed. He'd changed. He never talked much, but now he sat silent as a stone, shifting only to drink his bottle of beer. Soon he went to Colorado where he joined his brothers, Ray and Vic.

Years later Dad told me that Lyle had been shot out of the Sherman tank he drove in the war; he alone of his whole crew survived. I wondered if that trauma explained

Dad's office crew. From left, DeWayne Cary, Don Cary, Harold Bennett, Ross Andres, Arnold Peterson, and Tom Coffey.

his drinking, his awesome silence, and his death as an old man: when the Memorial Day parade passed below his window, he blew his head off.

More than 400,000 American boys failed to return home from World War II, including Dad's prize employee, DeWayne Cary. Before the war, DeWayne had worked as a bookkeeper in Alma's Coffey's Transfer office until my father promoted him to manage the new Omaha terminal.

When the draft caught up with DeWayne, he served in the navy on a rapid attacking PT (patrol torpedo) boat. He no doubt saw his death coming, felt its divine wind. A Kamikaze pilot, one of those suicidal Japanese aviators who fought by diving straight into their targets, plummeted out of the sky and exploded on the deck of DeWayne's boat.

I learned about DeWayne's death after the Sunday church service where his parents unveiled an immense painting, hung in honor of their son. The monumental painting of Christ in Gethsemane stunned me.

As we left, I tugged on Dad's suit jacket. "Why didn't DeWayne come?"

"He couldn't."

I frowned. "Why not?"

"He's dead."

I drew back. Dad's voice caught. "They buried him at sea. They wrapped his body in the American flag and lowered him into the ocean."

DeWayne had a younger brother, Don, not drafted because of an ear problem. When Dad asked Don to work for him, Don demurred. He had plans to become a mortician.

"A mortician!" Dad scoffed. "Hang around dead bodies the rest of your life?"

Don relented. He became Dad's right-hand man, staying by my father's side for eleven years, until Coffey's Transfer folded.

However, Don never worked in the Omaha terminal. That job went to hot-tempered Glen, who would face armed Teamsters, slashed truck tires, and equipment dynamited during the 1955-1956 Jimmy Hoffa war with my dad.

THAT "RUM RUNNER'S" KIDS

Our living room fan whirred, a slight comfort against Nebraska's sweltering heat. Mama wiped her brow and looked at Margery and me, curled in our cubbyhole, a tiny space under the stairs.

Mama turned her eagle eye on me. "Seven years is too old to play under there, isn't it?"

I didn't answer; I just crawled farther under the cool stairs, unwilling to yield the cubbyhole to Margery, who could scoot, at two and a half years, much deeper than I.

Mama sighed. She sat on the couch, picked up a newspaper, folded it in half, and scrutinized it. She loved to read. She read all the time. She read to us girls at bedtime until we fell asleep; she read long articles to Dad in the evenings. Sometimes she even read while she cooked, stirring white sauce on the stove with one hand and holding a book in the other.

"Oh, no!" She spoke to herself.

I heard Dad's car pull into the drive. Soon, all jaunty, he walked into the living room. "Hi-ya, honey." A pause. Then, "What's wrong?"

"Joe Kennedy." Mama choked up.

"The old man?"

"No, the son. The firstborn. Dead."

I knew what upset Mama. She adored royal families. She absorbed every word printed about British royalty. She even named my older sister after Princess Margaret, then an adorable two-year-old.

Mama seemed to regard the wealthy Kennedys as an American royal family. Which it was, even though Joe Kennedy's money supposedly oozed with alcohol bootlegged from Europe and Canada during Prohibition. "Rum runner," Dad called him.

Newspaper reporters swarmed around Joe Kennedy's father-in-law, John F. Fitzgerald, mayor of Boston. "Mark my word," he told them as he viewed the swaddled baby that was Joe Jr., "this child will be the United States' first Irish Catholic president."

So Joe Jr.'s grandpa and father groomed the boy for that fate. He excelled in private schools and Harvard, impressing many with his eager zest for life, with charm and gusto.

When war broke out, Joe Jr. joined the navy. He became a pilot and served in Britain as a land-based bomber. On August 12, 1944, over the English Channel his plane exploded midair, killing him instantly.

On that day, neither of my parents could have guessed the impact Joe Jr.'s death would have on Dad. The presidential mantle, designed for the Kennedy firstborn, dropped on the next son: John Fitzgerald Kennedy. He and his sidekick, brother Robert, as they worked their way to a JFK presidency, encountered Jimmy Hoffa. They swore to stop Hoffa, imprison him, and toss away the key. In so doing, the Kennedy brothers would provide national support for my father.

TRIGGERING HOFFA'S APPETITE

World War II transformed both my dad, Tom Coffey of Coffey's Transfer Company, and Jimmy Hoffa of the International Brotherhood of Teamsters. Neither man fought in the war; the government exempted both for the same reason: their ties to the vital transportation business. Wartime shifted manufacturing into high gear, which, in turn, required trucks to ship the new goods.

The union we commonly call "the Teamsters," Jimmy's group, formed in 1903 from men who drove teams of horses, oxen, or mules. In its early days, it functioned primarily like a criminal organization. Its first president, Cornelius Shea, lived in a brothel, flaunted a mistress, and hosted parties during Teamsters' strikes.

By World War II, thanks to rapid organizing during the Great Depression, the Teamsters Union had almost a million members. It had become one of the nation's most powerful unions—and also the most corrupt.

The Teamsters, like the country's other unions, didn't benefit from the war until the fighting ended and the government lifted its wartime control. Then unions bucked like Brahma bulls, kicking up more strikes in 1946 than in any earlier year. The United Auto Workers struck. So did steel workers, oil refiners, rubber workers, and meat-packers. Even railroad workers walked out, threatening to halt national transportation. That made President Harry S. Truman say, "If you think I'm going to sit here and let you tie up this whole country, you're crazy as hell."

Dad, by contrast, made a bundle from the war. After President Roosevelt wrote to truckline owners about the essential role America's five million trucks would play in the war effort, the trucking business took off. Even though buying a new truck became almost impossible and securing needed repairs difficult at best, still Coffey's Transfer prospered.

By May 1946, Dad owned the biggest business in our small town of Alma, Nebraska. His fleet of sleek red trucks picked up goods from customers in dozens of towns in south central Nebraska and in Kansas. His drivers carried those goods to terminals in Lincoln and Omaha to be shipped out of state by other trucklines. Then Coffey's Transfer trucks fetched big-city goods back into the Corn Belt.

Dad's drivers each wore this Coffey's Transfer Company patch.

Dad felt understandably proud of his business. He had built it out of sweat and smarts, since 1929 when he borrowed a battered four-wheeled truck, loaded a neighbor's cattle in it, and drove 250 miles to Omaha's stockyards over roads graveled at best.

Now thirty-six years old, he no longer hauled livestock. Instead, he shipped a variety of general commodities: paper, Campbell's chicken soup, soap, John Deere tractors. Plus loads of butter.

Dad's tank truck for hauling Campbell's chicken soup.

Unfortunately for my father, Coffey's Transfer Company had grown large enough to catch Jimmy Hoffa's eye. Dad's prosperity whetted Jimmy's appetite. "What that trucker needs," he decided, "is a Teamster contract."

And so, in May 1946, my dad's war with Jimmy Hoffa began.

1

IN THE
BEGINNING, BUTTER

The day that Jimmy Hoffa came after Dad, May 16, 1946, started like any other day. Mama still slept in their big double bed, as usual. She hated it when Dad woke like a rooster, crowing at dawn, but she just grumbled and went back to sleep.

"Some day, I swear," she told me, "I'm going to fill a cattle trough with ice water and put it alongside your father while he sleeps." Her laughter sounded light and giddy. "We'll see how cheerful he is when he leaps out of bed crowing."

But she hadn't yet.

Eight years going on nine, I fixed my breakfast in the kitchen, Cheerios and milk, and I tried to forget my embarrassment about last night at school when the parents all showed up and stared at us. Mama and Dad came, Dad still in his business suit and Mama looking so pretty, which she always does. The teacher asked questions, and when it came my turn, she turned on the record player.

"What instrument is this, Marilyn?"

I said, "Oboe."

I knew that was right, but she said, "No, it is a bassoon."

Now how could I mix them up? I felt so ashamed. I didn't mind Daddy teasing me so much, but I knew Mama would pinch my ear lobe and say, "What's wrong with you, Marilyn. Don't you pay attention in class?"

I leafed through Mama's *Saturday Evening Post*, trying to forget about the bassoon. I loved the new cartoon about a maid, Hazel. Vines on the screened-in back porch filtered the morning sun. It dappled Mama's magazine.

Dad, I knew, sat in Alma's popular Bud's Cafe with a few coffee-guzzling friends. After the waitress dropped their breakfast check on the table, Dad pulled a worn silver dollar out of his pocket. Twenty years old, it was the first dollar he ever earned. "Who's gonna match me today?"

His tall, skinny friend Henry grinned. "I'll take ya on, you and your silver charm."

"Feelin' lucky?"

Henry nodded. The waitress cleared the coffee cups.

"So what'll it be?" Dad jiggled the dollar in his palm.

"Heads."

All eyes focused on Dad's hand as he pinched his coin straight up and down. When his fingers snapped, the silver dollar whirled around itself and spun in larger circles on the table top.

The spectators released their breaths as the coin fell flat. "Tails!" someone called, and laughter rose.

"Damn!" Henry scooped up the check. "I don't know how ya do it, Tom."

"It's that cursed Irish luck of his." Don Cary, Dad's assistant manager, raised an eyebrow.

Cute Red Trucks

Everybody in town knew my dad. Half of Alma, Nebraska, worked for him, well, maybe not quite, and the other half did business with him. Every day Dad's men loaded merchants' goods on his big red Coffey's Transfer trucks. They sped out of town on Highway 183, a major route that runs a thousand miles from South Dakota to Texas. It sliced Alma in two.

Dad housed his truckline in a small rectangular brick building that faced Alma's Main Street. Out back, fronting the alley, stood the high flat loading dock, sometimes gray and empty and other times piled high with boxes and bins.

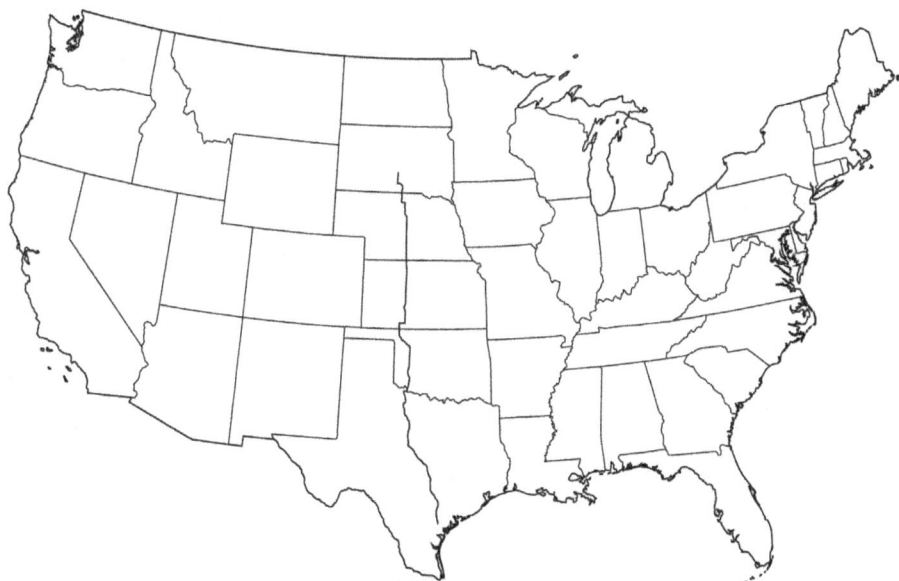

Highway 183 runs from South Dakota to Texas. Alma is about a third of the way south, where Nebraska meets Kansas.

From the dock, my dad's huge red trucks with their white-winged "Coffey's Transfer Company" logos raced halfway across Nebraska's flat plains, transporting goods to Lincoln and Omaha. Meanwhile, in Alma, cute little red delivery trucks waited to be loaded with boxes from Omaha or even Chicago. Those little trucks would growl south taking goods to stores and other businesses in Nebraska and nearby Kansas.

Dad's red trucks. How I loved them!

My father sometimes let me scramble up onto the high leather passenger seat. There I peered out the huge windshield and hung onto the door as he revved up the engine, an awful bawling and growling, and cruised out of the dock. He drove us around the block, the truck bellowing at every curve, and into the dock again. There he shifted gears and drove in reverse. His hands, massive when he grasped mine, looked tiny on the huge steering wheel.

As Dad made that final turn, I looked out my window to watch the tail end of the trailer fold up almost alongside me. How did he manage to turn that big old rackety truck up that way and then back right to the loading dock, time and time again, without ever smashing the truck or the dock?

I knew better than to ask him.

"Got eyes in the back of my head," he'd say, grinning, one big eyelid dropping in a wink. I knew better than to believe *that*. One day when he got down on all fours to play with our electric train, I'd ruffled the back of his hair up good, but he had nothing under that hair but head.

5,000 Pounds of Butter

On Wednesday, May 15, 1946, one Alma truck driver on his way to Omaha stopped in Minden, about fifty miles away. There, at the Minden Creamery, he picked up a load of butter that weighed 5,518 pounds. It took up almost a quarter of his truck's full load.

Minden's not much bigger than Alma, a couple hundred more folks, maybe, but it's much more famous. Besides the big Minden Creamery, in business for dozens of years, it had Carl Curtis, a member of the House of Representatives in Washington, DC. Even though Dad wasn't in Mr. Curtis's voting district, still Mr. Curtis knew my father.

Senator Carl T. Curtis helped my dad fight Jimmy Hoffa.

When the Coffey's Transfer driver got to Lincoln, he pulled into Dad's terminal there and unloaded the butter. My father had arranged for another truckline, Watson Brothers, to pick it up and ship it to Chicago. Dad's trucks didn't go out of state, except to nearby Kansas, so he often scheduled other trucklines to ship for him.

What's Eating Them?

On the Thursday morning of May 16, while I was at school, the big, black rotary dial telephone in Dad's office jingled and jangled. Three heads popped up at their desks. Eyebrows raised. Pale spring sun spilled through a big square window and speckled their shoulders. The men watched Vera, Dad's secretary, pick up the receiver, speak a few words, and hang up.

Then their boss, Tom Coffey, could be heard whistling "Zip-a-dee-doo-dah" as he entered the office with Don.

Inside an early Coffey's Transfer office—Don Cary, left, and Tom Coffey.

"Can't get that durn tune out of my head." My father plopped his gray fedora on its hat hook, turned and grinned. "Marilyn got me started." Marilyn, his second daughter, me. The ornery one.

Dad turned toward his secretary. "And what do you say, Vera. It *is* a wonderful day, isn't it?" Dad chuckled, plucked his silver dollar out of his pocket, and jiggled it.

Vera's eyes widened. "Don't tell me you won your breakfast check again today!"

Dad smiled and slipped his lucky dollar back in his pocket.

"Would you look at that!" Vera's eyebrows raised. "Oh, by the way, before you came in, Tom, your Lincoln manager called."

"Delbert?" Dad's face closed. "What did he want?"

"Didn't say. Just said call back. Shall I dial him for you?"

Dad nodded.

Long-distance calls gave him the willies. Even I knew that. He talked about those calls at dinner, how they often meant that one of his trucks had broken down or crashed, stranding its driver on some remote highway, waiting for Dad to get him.

Dad picked up the call from his Lincoln, Nebraska, office, some two hundred miles away. "Delbert, how's things?"

"Not so hot, Tom."

"What's up?"

"You know that big load of creamery butter from Minden?"

"Yah."

"Supposed to go to Chicago early this morning, but it's still sitting on the dock."

Dad rubbed the back of his neck. "So what happened? Watson Brothers didn't pick the butter up?"

"Right. I called, but they didn't say much. And Tom, it's hot here. Almost eighty degrees already today. Due to hit eighty-seven."

The thought of 5,518 pounds of butter slowly softening on his dock, from spreadable to rancid, drained the blood from my father's face, lifted the hair on his arms.

"I'll get back to you, Delbert." Dad handed the receiver to Vera. "Get Watson Brothers for me." He visibly cursed under his breath so he wouldn't redden his comely secretary's ears. Don, his right-hand man, stifled a giggle.

"What the devil do you suppose is eating Watson Brothers?" Dad walked to the office's picture window, looked out on Main Street, then turned. "How many loads you suppose we've shipped through them—to Chicago, St. Louis, Kansas City, Denver—and they'd always been so dependable."

"Dozens. Maybe hundreds." Don motioned toward Vera. "I think she's connected." Dad picked up the receiver.

Frank McKay, Watson manager, answered.

"How come you guys didn't pick up my five thousand pounds of butter today?"

"Well, it's the Teamsters, Tom. They came by here, said you were nonunion, and told us to stop picking up or delivering your freight."

"Just like that? And you agreed?"

"Ah, come on, Tom. Give us a break. That contract of theirs has got us hog-tied. It's not like the old days when an owner was boss."

Dad handed the receiver back and exploded. "The Teamsters! The Teamsters! I've run Coffey's Transfer Company for seventeen years without Jimmy Hoffa and his Teamsters, so why is he all of a sudden hungry for my butter?"

He went to his desk, grabbed his briefcase. "Call Zelma, will you Vera, and tell her I've gone to Lincoln, might not be home tonight." He snapped his briefcase shut.

"I don't get it, Don. I don't see any pickets out front, do you? It's not as if we're engaged in a labor dispute."

But Dad was. He just didn't know it yet.

WATSON BROTHERS

Those damned Teamsters, Dad thought. *If they hadn't risen up to clobber the Watson boys in that 1937 strike, Watson Brothers never would have caved in about my butter.* His nostrils flared.

Dad had known the five Watson boys—strong, honest people—for fifteen years, almost as long as he'd been trucking. Hell, he even knew their mama: Mrs. Helma E. Watson. She'd put up her own money so Ray, Thomas, and Fay could buy their first three trucks.

By 1937, Watson Brothers had snowballed into one of the major lines in Nebraska, operating big vans throughout the Great Plains, servicing Chicago, St. Louis, Kansas City, Denver, and Sioux Falls. But large as the line was, the Watson boys still prided themselves on running a family outfit. They participated in day-to-day operations, and they knew each of their drivers by name.

No one feared the Teamsters in those days. At least not in Nebraska. Their biggest outfit, Teamsters Local 554 in Omaha, barely cast a shadow.

"That local's been decrepit since the 1920s," Fay Watson maintained. "They're nothing but a bunch of wimps."

Then eleven Watson Brothers drivers decided to strike. They could no longer tolerate their pitiful twenty-five-cents-an-hour pay and long eighty-hour workweeks.

The drivers argued about whether to join Teamsters Local 554. Those against joining held no hope for help from such a pitiful organization; those for joining argued that its protection would reduce their risks of striking alone. At last they flipped a coin and joined the union.

A startled local 554 woke up to find itself with eleven new members and a strike on its hands.

The strike surprised the Watson brothers too. The Teamsters had tried to woo Watson drivers two times before, to no avail. Twice their drivers remained loyal to the company. But in 1937, the rest of Watson's drivers followed the first eleven and joined the Teamsters too.

The strike spread like wildfire to dozens of Omaha trucking firms and to Kansas City carriers as well. When those drivers joined the union, its membership skyrocketed. Soon the roster of members rose beyond 500. "Give me an adding machine," the secretary pleaded, "so I can keep up with folks joining." That wimpy local didn't even have a room big enough to hold its new members, so it rented the Omaha Labor Temple's dance hall and carted in chairs to seat the turnout, by that time 4,000 strong.

When Daniel Tobin, longtime leader of the International Brotherhood of Teamsters (IBT), got wind of the strike, he sent national organizers from his headquarters in Indianapolis, Indiana, to Omaha to help out. They found strikers ringing the city, in open defiance of Nebraska's antipicketing law. Pickets imprisoned any moving freight. They halted all of Watson's shipments, leaving 300,000 pounds of freight sitting in warehouses or trucks.

Of course, the Watson brothers agreed to talk. What option did they have? But Fay had the good sense to insist that his striking drivers return to work. Most did, but some kept busy hauling large trucks off the highway. They turned back a Watson Brothers truck heading to Kansas City with a load of meat. The *Omaha World-Herald* reported that Ray Watson said, "Okay, I won't send out any more trucks. I'll just let them sit, along with the three-hundred-thousand pounds of my freight you've already stopped."

Watson Brothers sat down with the eleven original strikers backed up by Teamster members from local 554 and from the national office. Talks stalled, then lurched forward until Watson and the Teamsters signed a contract.

Local 554, no longer a wimp, now represented all the drivers who worked for 205 commercial truckers. And Watson Brothers, now beholden to the Teamsters, no longer could act as a free agent. If the Teamsters said, "Don't pick up Coffey's butter," then Watson could not.

Loose-Lipped Gus

Dad still stood in the office holding his briefcase when Don cleared his throat. "Look out the window, Tom."

Dad stepped to the window, dismayed by the sight of little "Gus" Strickland strutting up the street: Gus, head of a nearby Teamsters local, maintained that he represented all of Dad's drivers, but Coffey's Transfer drivers wanted nothing to do with him, the brown noser.

Dad felt contempt for Gus, a short guy who dressed in brown. Looked like a beetle. Worse than his looks was his mouth. Gus liked to gossip, and he had a loose lip. Dad knew exactly what Gus thought of him: "typical small-town operator, likes to be a big shot." Dad knew, because those words had traveled via the grapevine from Gus's mouth into my father's ear.

No one spoke to Gus as he entered the office. He stood, his head tilted, regarding the impassive faces. "Oh, there you are, Tom. I'm glad I caught you in. Thought you might be on the road."

Dad looked up, his face a mask. "Driving? I don't drive my trucks anymore. I've got plenty of guys to do that for me." As he stood to greet Gus, Dad's eyes narrowed. "What brings you here?"

"Your contract." Gus blinked as he fished into his attaché case.

"What contract? I don't have any contract."

"Oh, here it is." Gus pulled out a stack of papers and handed them to Dad who stiffened, then backed away.

"I don't have any Teamster contract."

Gus capped and uncapped his pen. "Well, it's yours, Tom. A standard CSDC contract, the same that Jimmy negotiated for 125,000 Midwestern drivers, men just like your drivers. I thought you'd like to sign it, get that butter on the road."

Just my luck, Dad thought, *to be saddled with Teamsters.*

"Jimmy really knows what he's doing, Tom. All his experience. You can't go wrong signing with him."

"Well, you tell your Mr. Jimmy Hoffa he can shove this contract up his— (Dad, suddenly aware of Vera, swallowed "wazoo") upside his Detroit office, if you get what I mean?"

Gus's high-pitched laughter lingered a bit too long. "Don't worry, Tom. I'll keep it buttoned up. So shall I tell him you weren't quite ready to sign today?"

Dad's brow furrowed. He sidestepped the Teamster, put his hand on Gus's elbow, and steered him toward the door. "Tell him whatever your busy brain conjures up. Just don't say it came from me."

Gus stuck out his hand for a good-bye shake. Dad ignored it, so the little Teamster offered a thumbs-up instead. "Oh, Tom. You're such a joker."

Dad closed the door on Gus and locked it, then thought better of it and unlocked the door. He stood awhile, then turned and announced to his office mates, "There ought to be a law against folks like these."

"Maybe there is." Don Cary said. "Why don't you call Ace?"

So Dad called his Lincoln lawyer, "Ace" Jackson. Ace thumbed through his law books and took Dad's claim to court. Eventually District Judge Wilson heard the case.

Later that spring when we heard Dad's brand new Buick Roadmaster turn into the drive, Mama rushed to the kitchen to heat up our late supper while I raced outside to welcome Dad home from Lincoln.

He got out of the car and took big strides across the backyard with his long grasshopper legs. When he saw me, he cried, "We dood it!" and pitched his fedora at me. I jumped and caught it, clapped it on my head, and barreled into him for a hug.

We walked to the house, his big arm draped across my shoulders. "By golly, Junebug, I made those Teamsters eat butter! Wait until I tell your mom."

In the square kitchen, filled with supper smells, I listened. "My luck's hot, Zelma. That district judge gave Ace and me a restraining order on that old Jimmy Hoffa. Judge prohibited the Teamsters and Watson Brothers from interfering with my butter shipments. Now the Teamsters got to accept my freight. They've got to drop their boycott, and they can't force my drivers into their old union. The judge said so. Whoopee!" And he began to dance into the dining room.

I loved to watch Dad win. He whooped and hollered, his face beamed, and he twirled me round and round. The sun was about to set when we got around to eating.

2 BEFORE BUTTER–JIMMY

Jimmy Hoffa, only sixteen, lied and said he was eighteen and signed up for the night shift at Kroger Grocery's warehouse in Detroit. Al Hastings, the foreman, paid Jimmy thirty-two cents an hour, but only when he loaded or unloaded railroad cars or trucks full of produce.

Still, Jimmy felt lucky to be lifting crates. It was 1930. As he walked to work, he passed lines of men looking for work. Many had been looking since last October when the bottom fell out of the stock market.

Hastings, the foreman, loved to scream, curse, and fire workers without notice. Then he dramatically replaced them, slowly choosing from long lines of unemployed prospects.

One day, Sam Calhoun, an older guy, sat next to Jimmy and said, "What this place needs is a union."

Jimmy jumped. Michigan outlawed strikes. Then he winked. "Damn right!"

Together with some others, Calhoun and Jimmy plotted a Kroger strike.

Jimmy excelled at recruiting men. "He stood right up close to you and looked right at you," William Crow remembered. "He was the sincerest little guy I've ever seen. Jimmy gave me confidence to join a union. He made me feel it was the right thing to do."

The warehousemen didn't find a reason to strike until spring of 1931. Then one night the hot-tempered Hastings fired two warehousemen who left Kroger for a midnight meal at a food cart—a standard practice. That galvanized Jimmy and his angry coworkers.

Several days later a truck pulled in from Florida, loaded with delicate strawberries, the fruit so ripe it would rot if not unloaded quickly and stored in warehouse iceboxes.

The men unloaded about half the truck, then called a work stoppage.

They chose their moment well.

Hastings ranted in vain, but the warehouse manager agreed to meet with union leaders.

Several days of negotiation later, Kroger recognized the 175 coworkers as a union. It elected Jimmy vice-president. He was now really eighteen, and understood, without a doubt, the negotiating power of perishables.

ORGANIZING WAREHOUSE WORKERS

Twenty-four hours after Jimmy Hoffa stomped out of Kroger's warehouse in 1932, the Teamsters hired him.

He went to work as a full-time organizer for two Detroit locals, one as weak as the other. The International Brotherhood of Teamsters or IBT, headquartered in Indianapolis, wasn't in great shape either. It had lost 5,000 members in the last decade.

The Teamsters paid Jimmy no salary. Instead, he received a modest percentage of each new recruit he signed up.

With Jimmy from Kroger came his union. All 175 dockworkers joined Teamsters Local 674. Those dockworkers included the "Strawberry Boys," four tough workers who'd helped pull off the strawberry strike at Kroger. They became Jimmy's permanent staff members.

Jimmy's first assignment: go back to Kroger and organize the rest of its warehouse workers, about 400 men. But though Jimmy and his Teamsters struck Kroger for eighteen months, they did not organize the grocer.

THE PADDY WAGON

Kkkkker-whack! Sergeant Clancy's nightstick parted Jimmy Hoffa's mop of thick brown hair and raised a red welt on his scalp.

Jimmy spun and hiked up his fists. "What the f—?" At the sight of the police badge on Clancy's visored cap, Jimmy shut up.

"You!" the sergeant pointed to the United Storage and Warehouse dock. "What you doing here?" Pickets circled in the parking lot. Their stiff signs, "UNITED employees on STRIKE," wobbled in the morning breeze.

"Whadda you think I'm doing?" Rage inflamed Jimmy's face. He'd quit trying to organize Kroger's workers, but he hadn't given up on other Detroit warehousemen.

Clancy stood with his feet apart, twirled his stick, and glared at the stocky young organizer. "Ain't you a Teamster?"

"Yes, sir."

"Then you're bound to be up to something." He grabbed Jimmy's jacket sleeve and marched him to the black paddy wagon. "Get in."

Jimmy sat down, muttering, "Goddamn dumbfuck paddywhack."

Clancy turned in the driver's seat. "What j'ou say?"

"Nothin', sir."

"No funny stuff now." The sergeant revved the engine and bounced four miles downtown to the police station.

Karl Russow, the desk captain, shuffled a few papers at the counter. He glanced at Clancy and Jimmy. "What did he do?"

"He was about to cause trouble," Clancy said. "I got him just in time."

"Sergeant, you gotta wait until he does something. Then I can charge him." Russow looked at Jimmy. "Dismissed."

Clancy and his successor pulled Jimmy into the station house for a total of eighteen times during the twenty-four-hour period that the Teamsters picketed, but the desk captain repeatedly dismissed charges.

THAT OUTSIZED BILLY CLUB

The strike got rougher the next day.

The United boss hired a dozen ruffians who rushed the picketers. One mountain of a man, muscular and armed with an outsized billy club, lunged at Jimmy and swung at his head. Jimmy, furious, stooped to avoid the blow. He lit into the ruffian, pummeling with his fists, until the thug dropped, blood gushing from his nose and mouth.

Two cops grabbed Jimmy and twisted his arms so high behind his back he thought they would crack. Another cop bent over the mugger, dabbed a clean white cloth on his face, and helped him up. The cops held Jimmy upright and let that ruffian work Jimmy over. That huge billy club laid Jimmy's scalp open and nearly knocked him cold before a third cop finally ousted the thug.

That scalp injury required a trip to the hospital and ten stitches.

"That was nothing." Jimmy's sore arms hung limply at his sides. "Seems like there's a Teamster strike every day, and every fuckin' strike turns into a fight." Jimmy rubbed the back of his neck. "The scuzzballs."

Sylvia Pagona tossed her thick black hair aside as she sat down in Jimmy's office later that week.

Jimmy thought it natural to turn to his ex-lover. Their affair had been brief, but it managed to convert them from lovers to close friends. Besides, Sylvia worked as Teamster clerk by day and Detroit's most notorious gun moll by night.

"What's up, goofus?" she said.

Jimmy grinned and shuffled a few papers on his desk. "Hey, I want to ask you a damned favor."

"Shoot."

"Well, the bosses are importing thugs to bust our heads open. I'm fuckin' sick of it."

The afternoon light waned. Jimmy clicked on his gooseneck desk lamp. The light pooled on his cluttered desk. "I want to import a few goddamn thugs myself, bring in some Sicilian Mafias from the Purple Gang, maybe a couple Mustache Petes. And especially Santo Perrone."

Sylvia's eyebrows raised. "The Shark? But why would you want to meet him? He's the number one union buster in the city."

"I'll meet any motherfuckin' mobster you care to introduce me to." Jimmy pushed up his sleeves. "But winnin' Perrone over would be sweet. If I could talk him into protecting Teamsters instead of breaking strikes all over town, we'd win twice. I think the Teamsters could fuckin' well afford him. So let's start there."

Long-Distance Truckers

The Teamsters promoted Jimmy, in 1934, to business agent of truck drivers' local 299, the largest in Detroit. It had more debt than dues-paying members.

Jimmy earned a weekly salary of $25. When he could collect it. Few of his 250 members paid dues, so Jimmy felt lucky to squeak $5 a week out of his unit's empty coffers.

His only hope was to increase membership. But how?

Long-distance trucking, with more than three million drivers on the nation's roads, seemed promising. Since these car haulers worked mostly on the road, a determined Jimmy decided to go to them. He cruised from Detroit toward Cleveland on the up-to-date gravel highway, intent on corralling new Teamster members. If he spotted a parked car-hauler rig, he'd pull over, wake the sleeping driver, and pitch him.

Catnapping drivers rarely welcomed Jimmy's wake-up call. Since they often roused with a tire iron grasped in one fist, Jimmy discovered the virtue of a speedy introduction: "Hi-I'm-Jimmy-Hoffa-Organizer-for-the-Teamsters-and-I-wonder-if-I-could-talk-to-you." Then he ducked out of range.

A typical anti-union driver, Woody Sylvester, fired off argument after argument, which Jimmy rebutted, one after another.

"Anyway," Woody reached down to start the truck. "I just plain don't like unions. You union guys are always causing trouble. I want to be my own man, decide what to do, not cotton to some union boss."

"So, sir, that's exactly why you should join the Teamsters. In the Teamsters, the members call the shots. You attend every meeting, you vote on every decision. The union bosses are directly responsible to you and the dues-paying membership, and to no one else."

"You have an answer for everything, don't you, Mr. Teamster?"

"Jimmy's the name. Just try me. What else do you want to know?"

"God! You never let up!"

Jimmy grinned his wide toothy smile and handed the driver a membership card. "It's your call."

Woody looked it over, laughed, and said, "By cracky, if I don't sign this card, we'll still be here jawing when the sun goes down."

Jimmy pulled a pen out of his suit's breast pocket and watched the new Teamster member write.

STRIKEBREAKERS GALORE

Because he had an answer for everything, and because he never let up, Jimmy signed up many drivers. Soon local 299 collected dues all the way down to Evansville, Indiana, 479 miles southwest of Detroit.

Then one day, Jimmy parked on the highway behind a car hauler that had stopped for a break. He walked to the cab and knocked. "Hey! You awake?"

Before Jimmy could grasp the handle, the door burst open and out leaped two burly thugs. They wielded flexible billy clubs strengthened with lead weights.

Whop! Jimmy got a taste of the nasty little club, then lit into a strikebreaker, knocking him down. But the other thug crawled all over Jimmy, beating him into the edge of the highway. There the bruiser grabbed Jimmy by his throat and pulled him up, face-to-face. "Stay away from our trucks!" He shook Jimmy. "This is just a warning. Next time it'll be first class." He threw Jimmy to the ground where he passed out.

But the plucky organizer didn't quit. Soon he and others had signed up enough car haulers to strike. Shortly after, a contract was signed.

Bright Blue Eyes

When Jimmy arrived to help out at a striking laundry that March 1936, he found it topsy-turvy. The boss had run the women workers out with a shotgun. Then they ran off the scabs sent by the boss and set up a picket line. The boss called the cops.

Jimmy set up a standard picket line, with strikers parading in two circles. The outer circle walked clockwise, and the inner circle, counterclockwise. Then he joined the marchers, walking in the outer circle, facing inner circle marchers, mostly women.

"I was looking," he recalled, "into the brightest damn pair of blue eyes I'd ever seen. Geez, but they crinkled in the corners when she smiled back at me. Her goddam hair was shining blond, and although she was small and looked frail, she walked erect and proud. I felt like I'd been fuckin' hit on the chest with a blackjack."

The next time they passed, Jimmy grinned. When the blonde smiled back, he jumped in line behind her. "Better watch out. There's a man on your heels," he said.

And there was.

Jimmy talked her into a movie date that evening, but he blew it when he pulled up to her home in his recent model Chevrolet and honked the horn. Josephine Poszywak broke their date.

The next day marching in the line, Jimmy asked, "Jo, for crying out loud, what the hell happened last night?"

Her voice sounded chilly. "You tooted."

"Tooted?"

"Yes. You blew your horn. Nobody honks for me, not on that street."

"Gosh, Jo. I meant no disrespect."

"The neighborhood's Polish, Mr. Hoffa. Traditional. You can't just do things like toot your horn."

"Damn, I didn't mean to be coarse, Jo. But what's the harm, anyway?"

"Oh! Can't you see? Everybody and his cousin would know a new fellow was picking me up."

"So?"

"So I'm not the sort who comes running for every Tom, Dick, and Harry who honks."

But Jo did agree to try again that night. Jimmy didn't toot. He came to the door (she'd coached him "by the book"), rang the front bell. Jo met him and introduced him to her mother. They chatted for a few polite minutes until Jo said, "Coming?"

In the dark of the theater, Jimmy picked up Jo's hand.

She whispered, "We Polish girls don't hold hands until we mean it."

But she didn't pull away, so Jimmy tightened his hold.

"Boy, Jo," he whispered back, "do I hope you mean it, because I'm sure dead serious about you."

HITCHED IN A JIFF

Six months later Jimmy and Jo drove to Bowling Green, Ohio, a town well-known as a place where a couple could get hitched in a jiffy. It featured a judge who'd accept anyone, even someone off the street, for a witness. There the justice of the peace married them on September 24, 1936, a Saturday. They spent that night in a Cleveland hotel. The next day, they returned to Detroit, so Jimmy could be back at work on Monday. Jo claimed Jimmy still owed her a honeymoon.

Their marriage, despite a few infidelities, proved to be strong. Jimmy and Jo doted on each other. He even upgraded his sloppy dress—cheap suits, old ties, and white socks—for her. All but the white socks. He never changed those for anyone.

3
BUTTER AGAIN—DAD

My dad waited for his Hastings (Nebraska) College psychology class to start. He flipped open the cover to his biology text and finished drawing the flapper he'd started there. She pleased him, right down to the t-bar strap across her high heels.

He looked up to see his drawing standing in the aisle, looking for a seat in the crowded classroom. Slender in a nice loose dress with hardly any breasts. He raised his hand and waved, then pointed to the empty seat beside him. She ran down the aisle, her marcelled hair bouncing, and plopped down.

"So what's your name?" He smiled.

"Zelma." She shifted her books on her lap; he noticed her knees. "But my friends call me Pete. What's yours?"

"June."

"June! That's an odd name for a man."

"That's what my frat buddies say."

Zelma put her books on the floor. "Where'd you get a name like that?"

Zelma "Pete" Kemper and June "Tom" Coffey

"My mom really wanted a girl, so she named me June for my birth month."

The two whispered as the professor entered the class.

"But don't you hate being called June?"

"Nah, Pete. I'm used to it. That's what everybody calls me."

Pete and June sat side-by-side in psychology class that semester of 1925. About a month had passed, when my dad announced, "Don't call me June anymore. I'm Tom now."

"What happened?"

Dad stroked his mustache, a rectangular boxcar mustache, thick and black.

"They said only men wear mustaches. If I kept on calling myself June, they were going to shave it off."

"Oh, Tom!"

"They had a razor and hot water ready too."

"How awful!"

"So I decided to use my middle name, Thomas. Do you like it?"

"Yes, I like your mustache. Very handsome."

Dad, the first among his large, predominantly Irish kin to attend high school, then college, continued on into his junior year. Initially, he'd planned to be a doctor, but he lacked the money, even though he'd bailed hay and worked with a combining crew and with a paving gang to pay for school.

So he decided to become a math teacher. Having passed all the required courses, he snagged an offer from a Layton school in western Nebraska to teach eighth grade for $800 a year. For the interview, he traveled 300 miles, mostly by train, and walked to the country school.

Mr. Rosemart, a drab man whose glasses rested heavily on his cheeks, examined Dad. That went well. Dad picked up a pen to sign the contract, when Mr. Rosemart said, "Let me go over our rules." He recited, "No smoking, no drinking, no dancing." Plus nightly curfews and church on Sunday. Mr. Rosemart's list went on and on and on.

When it stopped, Dad stood and held up his hands. "I might be able to do without dancing, but as for the rest…" He shrugged and picked up his hat. "I wouldn't live up to your rules for eight hundred dollars, let alone teach school."

"You're making a mistake, young man." Mr. Rosemart stared over the rims of his glasses. "Our rules are typical. I'll wager you can't find a school that doesn't have requirements like ours."

On the ride back to Hastings, my father considered. He couldn't afford to be the doctor he wanted to be. And now, if Mr. Rosemart was right, he'd never be the teacher he planned to be. So why should he finish college? There seemed to be little point in it. So in 1928 after he completed his junior year, Dad, now almost twenty-one, quit.

A BUMPER CROP

In March 1929, Dad and a half-dozen neighbors sat on Joe Howard's farmhouse porch shucking corn. Joe turned to a neighbor. "I know it's a bumper crop, but how we going to get it from Harlan County to Omaha?"

"Beats me, Joe. Didn't you take it last year?"

"I did." Husks rattled as Joe tore them off. "But I can't spare the time this year. Get up before dawn, drive until dusk, get to that burg at night, city folks crawling all around. Took a hotel for safety, get up before dawn, drive until dusk."

Dad, twenty-one, at the time he drove his first truck.

Dad tilted his head to one side. "Did you see city folks everywhere you looked?"

"Ain't you ever been to Omaha?" Joe's face lit up.

Dad shook his head and grabbed another ear of corn.

"Tell you what," Joe said, "I'll loan you my truck if you haul this corn to Omaha for us."

Dad beamed and grabbed Joe's hand and shook it.

Before dawn, Dad showed up at Joe's farm. Joe's truck looked like a Model T, which it might have been. Ford had been converting cars into trucks since 1917.

Together the men loaded the corn. "Gotta lift this seat up to check the fuel," Joe hoisted the front seat to reveal a big fuel barrel. Next Joe crawled under the truck to show Dad how to check the oil.

The sun illuminated trees along Sappa Creek when Dad pulled out, the truck bucking a bit under his rookie hands.

After he returned the truck, Dad felt Joe nudge him. "Well," Joe asked, "how was life in the big city? Did you see folks everywhere you look?" He chuckled and handed Dad more cash than he'd expected.

A Far Cry from Hauling Corn

Then one day, Joe asked Dad to haul cattle to Omaha's big stockyards, second largest in the nation. He agreed. Together they loaded up.

Dad hadn't driven far when the cattle in the back end of the truck shifted left. He straightened the truck, but then the back end of the truck shifted right.

This is a far cry from hauling corn, he thought. *Here I am half driving, half sliding along this dirt road, and inside that truck, those beasts are mooing and shuffling back and forth, dancing the hootchy-kootchy.*

Dad put his body weight on the wheel to keep the truck moving straight. He thought he'd never make it to the Union Stockyards, and when he did, he was stunned.

Hundreds of pens spread as far as he could see, covering an acreage bigger than his dad's farm. He waited hours in the long line to unload his cattle.

On his way home, Dad dreamed about trucking full-time. *If, on my return trips, I could bring goods to folks in Harlan County, I could make money both ways.*

Of course, being a trucker doesn't have the prestige of a doctor. He laughed. On the other hand, a trucker, unlike a teacher, could cuss whenever he pleased.

ON HIS KNEES

Dad hauled enough corn and cattle to make a down payment on a used truck designed to haul livestock. The converted Model T, complete with running boards and tall exposed tires, cost more than he could afford, so he borrowed money from The Stamford Bank.

"It was a rickety old truck," he told me later, "but I knew it would make it to Omaha and back."

Dad then established Coffey's Transfer Company with business headquarters in Stamford, Nebraska. He waited and waited, but no customers showed up, not even any browsers.

This concerned both Dad and the banker, Brian Bowles. When farmer Herman Ehrke sauntered into the bank to run an ordinary errand, Brian intercepted him.

After a brief chat about the weather, the banker remarked, "I loaned Ben Coffey's oldest boy some money to buy a used truck. You know Ben, don't you?"

Herman nodded. "Big strapping fellow."

"Well, Tom bought a truck, but he can't find anything to ship in it. Any chance you might have some cattle ready for the Omaha market that he could haul down there for you?"

Herman didn't take long to answer. A farmer doesn't have a much better friend than a banker. He agreed to do the favor.

The next day, Dad pulled into Mr. Ehrke's driveway, helped load the heavy cargo, and pulled out.

The engine grunted and groaned, struggling to haul the cattle up the hill. The truck barely crested the first hill, but the next one proved too steep. The truck stalled and stopped.

Unable to change gears from inside his cab, Dad got out, dropped to his knees, crawled under the truck, and changed to a lower gear. Then he jumped in the cab. Tortuously, the truck mounted the second hill. At the top, Dad stopped again to crawl under the cab and rechange gears so he could continue.

On his way home, my father stopped at Mr. Ehrke's farm. The place looked quiet, so Dad honked. Then Mr. Ehrke edged around the corner of the house. When he saw Dad standing by the truck, Mr. Ehrke tilted his head. "Why, look what the cat dragged in!"

Dad chuckled. "Bet you thought I'd never make it."

"Right. I was worried about my stock."

"They did fine." Dad didn't mention crawling under the cab to change gears. He just handed over the stockyard papers. Mr. Ehrke dipped in his side pocket and counted out cash for Dad, who headed home, happy with his first customer. It was November 1929.

After that, Dad just kept on trucking, picking up little jobs, and driving himself.

Courtin' Pete

The world turned a pristine white. *Just right for our wedding*, Dad thought as he pulled his father's buckboard in front of Pete's palatial home. He knocked the glistening snow off his boots and rang the bell.

Pete answered, to his relief. *So the Kempers hadn't closeted her, so she could make a grand entrance.*

"Tom! Where's your father?"

Dad stomped on the porch mat. "He said to tell you he's sorry, he couldn't come."

"But why not?"

Dad entered and gave Pete a quick squeeze. "He didn't have any clothes good enough to wear here."

"But he could have worn his overalls! That would have been all right."

"I know, I know, but he didn't see it that way."

Pete slid open the parlor doors, revealing a formal room set with wine-colored armchairs, delicate tables, and painted globe lamps.

Walking down the aisle on Christmas Day was a Kemper tradition, so Dad and Pete married in her mother's parlor on Friday, December 25, 1931.

Afterward she turned to him and shook his arm. "Now when anyone asks me why I chose to get married on Christmas, I can laugh and say, 'So Tom will remember our anniversary.'"

My Father's Son

After Zelma and Tom married, he moved Coffey's Transfer Company from Stamford to Alma. The young couple lived in the second-story apartment above his mother-in-law's Racket Store, an early version of a five-and-dime store.

Their first child, a girl, was born February 16, 1933. Zelma named her "Margaret" after Britain's Princess Margaret, then two and a half years old. Dad liked his new daughter, although he had hoped she would be a boy.

By 1937, Coffey's Transfer flourished enough so Dad had a truck terminal in Omaha as well as in Alma. He bought a car and divided his time between the two branches, letting other people drive his trucks and manage his two offices.

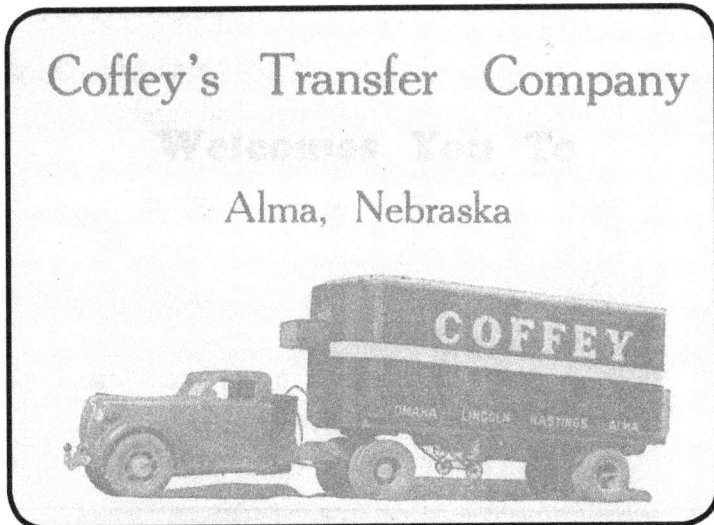

An early Coffey truck with no wings used on the logo.

December 1937. I'm the baby, with sister Margaret and our parents.

My folks moved out of their apartment and rented a small, square house. There in the bedroom at midnight on July 22, 1937, Zelma gave birth to her second child: me.

"I delivered you myself," she told me later, "while your dad and the doctor sat in the living room arguing politics, the doctor shaking his mass of curly hair and your father pounding his fist in his palm."

When Dad saw I was a girl, he cursed his bad luck.

Mama picked "Marilyn" for my first name; she wanted a name to match my sister's Margaret. Dad agreed.

"You pick her middle name, Tom."

Still smarting that he had another daughter, he said, "I think I'll name her for me."

"Thomas?"

"No, not Thomas. June."

So I became Marilyn June, my mother's daughter, Marilyn, but my father's son, June.

He taught me how to be a brave boy, how to put mercurochrome on a cut without crying.

He taught me how to swallow pills instead of eating them squashed up in a teaspoon with water, such a nasty taste.

He built me a tree house and gave me cars and trucks and railroad sets to play with.

He stood with me on the back porch in rainstorms, showing me how to inhale the storm.

He taught me how to ride a bike and how to walk on stilts and how to belch at will.

He showed me, in the bathtub, how to stick my head underwater and hold my breath.

He even taught me how to win every time when flipping a coin by calling, "Heads I win, tails you lose."

KEEPING AN EYE ON DADDY

After I turned eight, my father had a freak accident behind his office's dock. He'd gone to work on a Sunday morning, as usual. Dad never went to church in those days, but Mama took me and my sister, dressed to kill, to the big old Methodist church and stuck us in the basement with the other kids while she worshiped upstairs.

At the dock, Dad decided to link a truck and a large semitrailer, getting them ready to roll. The uncoupled truck had been repaired, and the trailer loaded to capacity.

When Dad backed the truck into the trailer, its supporting wheels gave way. The heavy trailer dropped its weight on the truck's cab, flipping it into the air. The cracked steering wheel crushed Dad into his seat and broke his back.

What to do?

No one would miss him, he knew, until after church. Then Pete and the girls would wait for him to eat the noon meal (roast beef timed in the oven, so nice not to ration meat anymore). Main Street lay quiet. Not even an occasional car rumbled by. Dad hit the damaged horn, but it didn't honk. No one could hear him holler. His office building hid him.

So he twisted out of the cab, half stepping, half falling flat. Panting and halting, he pulled his body to the street, using his elbows to inch along.

His strategy worked. Once he reached the sidewalk, a passerby discovered him. Soon he lay in the Mary Lanning Memorial Hospital at Hastings.

Preparing for his return, Mama installed a real hospital bed in the living room. It lay under the long flight of stairs to the second floor.

How good it felt to have Dad home, even though he just lay awful quiet in his bed.

"Now whatever you do, don't disturb him." Mama's eyes narrowed. "He can't even sit up yet: doctor's orders."

Later, I stood at the top of the stairs, stroking the shiny banister and debating. I loved to throw a leg over the banister and glide down, although I knew I shouldn't. Mama called it dangerous, but I couldn't see why. The newel post stopped me every time. Whenever she caught me sliding down, she threw a conniption fit. But Dad just laughed. "Don't fall off face first. You'll lose your two front teeth and never be able to gnaw corn off the cob."

I wanted to slide down, but Dad lay in bed right below me, so I decided not to throw my leg over the banister as usual, but to slide down on my belly, head first. My long skinny legs could reach the stairs and serve as brakes; I hung my head and arms over the rail so I could keep an eye out for Daddy. I didn't want him to see me.

Halfway down the handrail, I still couldn't see Dad. So I stretched farther and farther forward until, whoomp, I fell straight down past the end of my father's bed and struck the floor. I twisted to see if Daddy was okay. I heard a crack and felt astounded to see him sitting straight up in bed.

Mama ran in from the kitchen. "You lie down," she scolded Dad. She sounded mad, even though he said, "Don't worry, Pete. I'm okay." Which he was. The crack I heard was me.

I checked my teeth. They were okay, but when I tried to stand up, one of my arms didn't work right. Just like Dad, I had to go see the doctor. Broken collarbone, he said.

Mama made me a pretty sling covered with birds and flowers and clouds, but before she helped me into it, she made me promise to never ever, ever, ever slide down that banister again.

So I promised I never ever would, but I crossed my fingers, so what I said didn't count. Dad taught me how to do that so I won't have to go to hell for telling lies.

4 JIMMY'S WHOPPING DOUBLE CROSS

"Hey, Hoffa. Dobbs wants to see you." Jimmy's boss, Teamster Ray Bennett, ran thin fingers through his brush haircut.

"What for?"

"He didn't say, but I bet he's got green eyes for your long-distance truckers."

Jimmy laughed. The brilliant Farrell Dobbs jealous? Only three years ago, he, then twenty-six, led the most violent strike in Minnesota history. It turned Minneapolis into a union town and skyrocketed Teamster membership.

But Dobbs did want Hoffa to come to Minneapolis, so Bennett took Jimmy there, even though Bennett disliked Dobbs's pinko politics. *The man's a card-carrying communist.*

Sometimes two people click, for no known reason. That happened between Dobbs, twenty-nine, and Jimmy, not quite twenty-four.

Dobbs became Jimmy's mentor, teaching him how to claw his way up the Teamster ladder. Jimmy, fascinated, listened to Dobbs by the hour. "His ideas," Jimmy later said, "had an impact on my mind."

"But, Jimmy," Dobbs frowned, "these long-distance truckers are a pain. When I have a contract ready to sign, I have to jog around to each little truckline to negotiate it. So I've been dreaming. Why can't the Teamsters write just one contract for all those Midwest truck operators?"

Jimmy stared. He'd never heard of such a thing. One contract for hundreds of trucklines? But Dobbs's idea would enable Jimmy, twenty years later, at the apex of his career, to be the first union leader in US labor history to sign a single contract between the Teamsters and the nation's trucking companies, all 15,000 of them.

"I'm working on it." Dobbs paused. "Last month, I set up a conference with Teamsters from six Midwestern states. It's a first. If it works, we can negotiate one contract to cover thousands of over-the-road drivers."

As a test, Dobbs decided to see if he could negotiate a single contract for 300 trucklines headquartered in Chicago and another 300 from the adjoining area. He, Jimmy, and Chicago's Teamsters sat down with the representative of 600 over-the-road truckline operators, John Bridge. He looked seamless, in his sleek dark suit.

Curiously, Bridge, spokesperson for the operators, worked hand in hand with the Teamsters. Even so, talks lasted more than a week. Jimmy watched Dobbs's every move.

On August 23, 1938, Bridge signed, for the truck owners, the Teamsters' first area contract, a one-year agreement covering 600 trucklines.

What a victory!

But it didn't satisfy Dobbs. "Chicago's just the big boys. We haven't won until hundreds of little lines in all eleven Midwestern states have signed."

Jimmy's mouth fell open. His voice rose. "So what now?"

"Well, first we've got to get as many trucklines as we can to voluntarily sign our contract." Dobbs's foot jittered against the floor, then stopped. "As for the rest, we'll have to knock them into line."

They went to work.

Before long, using the same contract, they'd signed up 1,700 trucklines in seven of the eleven states. That contract covered more than 100,000 drivers, but Dobbs wanted more. Jimmy stared as his mentor told Teamsters' locals in reluctant states—Iowa, Missouri, South Dakota, and Nebraska—to get those unsigned operators to sign up immediately. Or else.

TOBIN PUTS A MATCH TO THE FIRE

In Indianapolis, IBT President Tobin endorsed Dobbs's plan to organize the remaining Midwestern truckers. And why not? Teamster membership had leaped by 202,000 from its low of 78,000 members in 1932, and Tobin knew that most of this impressive growth had been Dobbs's doing.

So on Wednesday, September 7, 1938, Tobin's office contacted Teamsters locals in defiant Nebraska, South Dakota, Iowa, and Missouri and told those locals to demand that unsigned over-the-road operators sign up at once.

Here's what happened in Nebraska.

Thursday, Omaha Teamsters Local 554 asked the Nebraska Commercial Truckers Association and its backer, the BMA, to sign the area contract for its members, 200 commercial trucklines. Friday morning, the trucklines locked some 3,000 Omaha Teamsters out of their jobs.

The showdown began.

Teamsters deliberately broke Nebraska's antipicketing law. They patrolled highways and stopped nonunion trucks, driven by "scabs." The pickets let farmers bring produce to market, so the BMA hired men to stone the farmers' trucks; then it blamed the strikers. Pickets worked around the clock until they'd stopped all scab trucks.

"To all intents and purposes," Dobbs wrote later, "we laid siege to Omaha and the state of Nebraska."

But not entirely. Omaha freight kept sliding out of Nebraska, helped by Kansas City trucklines.

Then Dobbs fell so ill he went to a Minneapolis hospital. J. M. "Red" O'Laughlin, Detroit Teamsters head, rushed to Omaha with Jimmy to fill in for Dobbs. Red, no longer young, bragged about sparring with the world's heavyweight champ, curly-haired Jack Dempsey. "What a puncher Jack was!" Red told Jimmy. "Jack couldn't sing and he couldn't dance, but he could lick any SOB in any bar in town."

In Omaha, police made mass arrests. "If you suspect anybody is going to start trouble, throw them in jail," the chief told his cops. Police picked up carload after carload of cruising pickets, arresting more than sixty. Judges held pickets in jail without bail as long as possible. A public clamor rose as pickets threw their food into jail corridors, banged tin cups on the bars, and raised hell. Judges freed most of them.

On November 15, the truck operators asked the Teamsters to negotiate, but the truckers' list of demands ran so long that the Teamsters refused to take the truckers seriously.

Meanwhile, the noose around Omaha tightened. Sixty small Nebraska firms and South Dakota and Des Moines truckers had signed with the Teamsters. Now only Sioux City, Kansas City—and Omaha—remained obstinate.

LEAPFROGGING

Kansas City's roundabout shipping connections kept sliding Omaha freight out of Nebraska, letting Omaha operators thumb their noses at the Teamsters.

"We gotta force those assholes to stop." Red O'Laughlin tightened his fists. "Let our pickets go after them."

"I think this calls for leapfrogging." Dobbs, no longer ill, had returned.

Leapfrogging! The very word excited Jimmy.

"Takes two trucklines," Dobbs said, "a main line to be leapfrogged over and a second line to boycott the first one. That's why Congress calls it a 'secondary boycott.'"

"And outlaws it?" Jimmy raised his eyebrows.

"That's right. It's illegal." Dobbs scowled. "Okay, so we could leapfrog over Omaha, go to Kansas City. Of course they won't boycott Omaha unless we can get them to sign the area contract."

"And if they won't?" Jimmy smirked.

Dobbs pushed up his sleeves. "We strike!"

"But what about Tobin?" Red tugged at his ear. "He ain't gonna like this."

This meant a trip to Indianapolis to see if Tobin could be persuaded.

The Siege of Nebraska

Tobin greeted Dobbs, Red, and Jimmy cordially. "What's the latest Omaha news?"

"The Kansas City guys are helping Omaha lines ship stuff out of the state." Red crossed his arms.

"What?" Tobin backed away.

"Show him the map, Red."

Red pulled out the map of Kansas, Missouri, and Nebraska that Dobbs had marked to show how the KC operators worked.

The men moved to the president's desk and unfurled it.

"Why, look at this!" Tobin leaned over the map. "You flagged those points just like a general would do."

That map did the trick. Tobin agreed to support Dobbs all the way.

Here's what happened.

Dobbs, Red, and Jimmy arrived in Missouri's Kansas City and checked into the Muehlebach Hotel, dubbed "White House West" because so many presidents had stayed there.

Negotiations with the Kansas City over-the-road operators took place in the hotel on November 28. The KC men sported a cocksure attitude, bold, cheeky, boastful, their thumbs in their tooled leather belts.

"Under no circumstances," their leader said, his chin jutting out, "will we sign your area contract." He crossed his arms. "And we won't negotiate with you at all on that contract, only on the proposals we've drafted." He rocked back on his heels.

Unflappable Dobbs lifted their proposal, riffled through its many pages, and nodded. "We'll need some time to look this over." He spoke gently. "Please grant us a recess until, say, 4 p.m."

The leader waved his cigar and granted Dobbs's request.

Dobbs found a pay phone and called Tobin, as they had planned.

Tobin chortled. "I'll poll my board members and get back to you."

When Dobbs returned to the negotiation table at 4 p.m., he held Tobin's wired approval of a strike of Kansas City operators. The wire also guaranteed payment of benefits to Teamsters involved in the strike.

Dobbs handed the wire to the leader and watched him stiffen. He shook his head. "A recess." He raised one hand to stop the other truckline operators from speaking. "We'll need a recess to deal with this." And the truckers piled out of the room.

Three weeks later, on December 14, 1938, after some stiff bargaining, the Teamsters signed the area contract with the Kansas City employers in Missouri and Kansas.

The Teamsters won a major victory without a strike, which pleased Tobin and made him willing to help defeat the remaining holdouts—Omaha and Sioux City trucklines, now completely isolated.

Nebraska employers refused to yield. They hounded strikers verbally, financially, legally, and physically, until finally, they could tolerate the strike no longer. On January 23, 1939, contract talks began. Three weeks later, the strike ended. The siege of Nebraska was over.

That marked the end of Jimmy's apprenticeship with Dobbs, who accepted Tobin's offer of a job as national staffer.

By now, Jimmy called Dobbs his "master." Before the two men met, Jimmy had been an opportunist. Dobbs transformed the stocky young organizer into a strategist. Now that Jimmy could use his head, he no longer had to rely so heavily on his fists.

Dobbs's idea of leapfrogging especially delighted Jimmy. He was impressed with what a powerful tool it could be. He would choose that tool to bring my father to his knees in their six-month battle in 1955 and 1956.

THOSE DAMN COMMIES

President Dan Tobin sat scowling behind his solid oak desk, longer and leaner than Franklin's desk in his Oval Office at the White House, and waited for Jimmy. The IBT president rolled his miniature semitruck back and forth on his desk top, taking care not to spill its load of paper clips. He'd glanced at his little round clock, when the door opened and in bounced Jimmy Hoffa. Tobin beamed. He stood and pointed to the chair in front of his desk, then sat again.

"How's Jo doing?" Tobin leaned forward.

"Swell." Jimmy sat straight and alert. "We're expecting number two in about a month, but we got a long fuckin' way to go to beat you!"

Tobin's laugh boomed. He had six kids—five boys and a girl. "Just don't give up, Jimmy. Don't give up."

Then Tobin shifted in his chair, grew solemn. His jaw set. "You know about the goings on in Minneapolis?"

Jimmy looked away. "Rumors."

"Your Dobbs is becoming an embarrassment."

Jimmy raised an eyebrow but said nothing.

"You know, here I am, my friend the president is preparing America for war, and I'm drawing up a 1941 war-readiness program for the IBT. But instead of supporting Franklin like good citizens, Dobbs and his rebels oppose him. Shrilly, I might add. Highly embarrassing."

Neither man spoke. Tobin twirled and looked out the office window, then returned.

"I do respect Dobbs for what he's done for us, but that can't last forever. Not with his latest shenanigans. He and his rebels left the Teamsters, you hear?"

Jimmy nodded.

"And then who did they join? The CIO, our biggest competitor." Tobin's fist came down on his desk; the little semitruck jumped. "And now they have the gall to organize a new union for truck drivers!"

Jimmy cleared his throat, glanced sideways at Tobin, then back.

"Now, Jimmy, I think you could help me with this. You and your Detroit boys could go to Minneapolis and wipe out that red bed of communism. See that Dobbs and his rebels have to leave town, go back to Russia where they belong. What do you say?"

"I can't do it, Pop." Jimmy's nostrils flared. "It's none of my fuckin' business."

"Oh, but it is your business, Jimmy. It's affecting the IBT, all of us, including you. It's only a matter of time before they set up a CIO truckers union in Detroit."

Tobin came around his desk, pulled up a chair, and sat facing Jimmy. "You aren't soft on communism, are you?"

"Naw." Jimmy snorted. "Those damn screwball commies are a bunch of nuts."

Tobin nodded. "Well, it's an intolerable situation, Jimmy. Someone's got to step into Minneapolis and clean it up."

"Pop, you know how fuckin' much Dobbs meant to me." Jimmy's face tightened.

"I know, I know. He meant a lot to lots of us, but he's not the same man he was when you knew him. He's running wild with those Dunne brothers now."

"And one of those fuckin' Dunne brothers, Vance, he and I are friends." Jimmy looked down at his hands, curled into fists.

"Vance Dunne? He's one of the ring leaders."

"I can't do this, Pop." Jimmy crossed his arms.

Tobin began to talk about how much he'd done for Jimmy, how he'd let Ray Bennett hire Jimmy as an organizer, how Tobin hadn't interfered with Jimmy's decision to organize over-the-road drivers, how Tobin had okayed Jimmy taking time off to study with Dobbs, to go to Chicago, to Nebraska.

Jimmy didn't move.

Tobin changed the topic. "How much are you making these days?"

"Not quite seventy-five fuckin' bucks a week."

"Well, if you clean up Minneapolis for me, I'll see that you make double that." Tobin thrust his chest out. "You could go in like a field marshal, leading the troops. You know that I'll be grateful to you, and in a monetary way."

When Jimmy still said nothing, Tobin pulled closer, almost knee to knee. "No?" Tobin's voice quavered. "Well, then, I'm going to ask you to do this for me, Jimmy, as a personal favor."

Jimmy looked up at his old Irish boss, sixty-six, his jaws slack with age. He'd been IBT president for thirty-four years, and Jimmy, at twenty-eight, only nine years a Teamster. The man was, after all, the top dog. So Jimmy said okay.

JIMMY'S STRAWBERRY BOYS

Teamster Ray Bennett, Jimmy's boss, agreed to oversee Tobin's fight with the Minnesota communists. He named Jimmy his field marshal. Jimmy enlisted his Strawberry Boys plus a hundred other crack fighters, and they headed from Detroit to Minneapolis.

Declaring open war, they descended on the city. They took over Dobbs's office and clashed time and again with Dobbs, the Dunne brothers, and their communist allies. They fought mostly on the streets with fists and sticks. Finally, they defeated them.

"We won every battle," Jimmy bragged. "We took their union over."

But Dobbs taunted Jimmy. "Now it's true Jimmy was among the goon squads Tobin sent into Minneapolis. But Jimmy claims he whipped us. With a little help, I might add. The police helped him, and the city, county, and state courts. So did the mayor and an antilabor law hustled in by the governor. Not to mention the FBI, the US Department of Justice, and FDR as president of the United States. Jimmy exaggerates when he says *he* whipped us. The man does exaggerate."

And it's true that the Teamsters had some help. The Justice department indicted Dobbs and twenty-seven other communist union leaders on charges of sedition, or stirring up people to rebel against the government. The department found eighteen guilty. It sentenced Dobbs to twelve to eighteen months in prison.

Jimmy, however, quickly received, from Tobin, the job that Dobbs once held, negotiating chair for the eleven-state Midwestern council that Dobbs had formed, now called the Central States Drivers Council (CSDC).

Some say that Jimmy's Minneapolis fight with his mentor must have traumatized him. And it is true that the fight did not curb Jimmy's admiration for Dobbs. For the rest of Jimmy's life, he credited Dobbs with a vision "enormously beneficial" to the labor movement and repeatedly called him the "master architect of the Teamsters' over-the-road operations."

But others argue that turning on his friend just strengthened Jimmy's ruthlessness, a characteristic that would grow as Jimmy aged.

5

OH, NO! BUTTER AGAIN

The wind whipped Teamster Jimmy Hoffa's dark brush cut. He caught his breath as he stepped down out of the airliner, hat in hand. Back in bush-league Nebraska after nine fuckin' years. He saw an empty paper cup streak by as he strode across the tarmac.

Think of that, a damned greenhorn then. But no longer. Now a Big Cheese. Jimmy ran his hand through his hair, donned his hat as he entered the terminal. *Got every Detroit Teamster riding in my hip pocket. Plus most of Michigan state's locals, for cripes sake.* He jutted his chin out. *And now it's me negotiatin' a single contract for 125,000 fuckin' drivers in twelve Midwestern states.*

Includin' these bumble-fuck Nebraska truckers.

Except for this Coffey's Transfer Company. Coffey just don't get it.

James "Jimmy" Riddle Hoffa.

Jimmy looked around, his eyes narrowed. *Where the hell is everybody?* He pushed his way through the airport. *Ah!* There they stood, the whole gang, hanging around the fuckin' baggage claims. He pegged his fellow Teamsters in an instant, thanks to his extraordinary memory. Dick Kavner, good old boy from St. Louis now dodging charges of dynamiting; weird Karl Keul from Des Moines, the spitting image of Adolf Hitler; the chief big wigs from Omaha and Lincoln, like Bobbsey twins in their button-down suits, plus little Gus Strickland, head of a large rural local but just a class one toady.

Jimmy pressed forward, shaking hands and patting the big shoulder pads in their 1940s business suits.

DOWN WHITE POLE ROAD

Tom Coffey, thirty-nine-year-old owner of Coffey's Transfer Company, slipped his 1946 Buick Roadmaster in gear and took off down US Route 6 on his way to Lincoln to hear what Jimmy Hoffa had to say. Tom snorted. *He'll say a lot, no doubt. Folks say he never shuts up. Probably doesn't have to. Not with that trigger-happy crowd behind him.*

Route 6 rode pretty well, now gravel, not the rutted dirt Tom drove on when he started trucking in 1929. But he couldn't get used to those new US signs, numbers on a shield. To him, Route 6 remained the White Pole Road, marked by utility poles painted white.

Tom gripped the steering wheel. His hands felt clammy. He knew why. Hoffa no doubt wanted him to sign a Teamsters' contract. Same as last year.

But pen to paper would turn Tom's twenty drivers into Teamsters whether they wanted or not. Most didn't. Tom's nostrils flared. He hated the way Hoffa worked from the boss down. The domino effect. Faster, cheaper, more effective than sweet-talking drivers, one by one, to join the union.

Tom rolled the car window down a bit. Warm for May, warm enough to melt that butter sitting on the Lincoln dock. Just as it sat last year, 1946, the first year the Teamsters had come after him.

Now they had cropped up again, and last year's court order no longer held. Now May had reappeared, and so had butter, all 5,518 pounds of Minden Creamery butter, slowly softening from spreadable to rancid on the dock.

Only this time the Teamsters had brought in its big gun: Jimmy Hoffa.

SPLITTING THE TABLE

Tom shot up Tenth Street and swung around to Lincoln's popular meeting spot, the classy ten-story Cornhusker Hotel on Thirteenth Street. Its brown-and-white twin towers shadowed the street. He parked under the awning, nodded for the valet, then glanced at his watch. Cutting it close. Don't want to be late for Hoffa. He picked up his pace.

Inside, he stopped at the desk to confirm the meeting room number, then bolted across the large, airy lobby, two stories high. When he reached the ample, winding staircase, he slowed down to enjoy the thud of his heels on the plush carpeted steps and relish the smooth hardwood banister sweeping beneath his palm.

The carpeted second-floor conference room held an elongated table and a dozen chairs, all empty. Good. Tom could pick his spot. First he switched on the plump, cone-shaped overhead lights. The room came to life. He opened the heavy wine-colored drapes, but closed them when the sun hit his face.

By then, he knew where he wanted to sit. He pulled out a chair across the table from the door and sat on the leather seat.

Sunlight from the window sliced a long thin line down the middle of the table, like a line in the sand, separating them. Didn't close those drapes tightly enough, so he stood to go back. Just then, the door cracked open and "Ace" Jackson, Tom's lawyer, entered. Tom decided not to fix the drape. Let the line split the table in two.

Ace sat to Tom's right. Together, they shot the breeze, fidgeting as minutes passed.

"Think Hoffa's standing us up?" Tom checked his watch again.

"Naw. He's just trying to get on your nerves." Ace chewed the inside of his lip. "Let's give him ten more minutes."

ENTER THE TRIBE

A commotion in the hallway filled the room as Hoffa's tribe spilled into it, circling, shaking hands, settling into chairs. The men varied, some short, others tall, some skinny, others portly. But they looked like carbon copies in their "larger than life" summer-weight business suits, double-breasted, wide-legged pants, padded shoulders, a square of white silk folded in their pockets. And on each head a fedora. Tom heard matches scratch and whiffed sulfa as the men lit up.

Little Gus Strickland sat so close to Tom that he could smell Brylcreem on Gus's hair. "How you been, Tom?"

Tom snorted. "Busy." His jaw tightened. "A bit too busy for my druthers. Where's Hoffa?" He looked at the empty chair across the table.

"Now, Tom, don't get all rattled, he'll be here soon. Little boys' room snatched him." Gus snickered.

Just my luck, Tom thought, *to be saddled with Gus. I know he thinks we're buddies because his local includes my drivers, or so he maintains, but I never do business with him. He makes my skin crawl.*

Then short, stocky Jimmy, now thirty-four, burst into the room, grinning his big, toothy, butter-eating smile. It split his baby face in two. His black bristly hair glistened like patent leather. He whipped off his jacket, hung it on the back of his chair, loosened his tie, and rolled up his sleeves, flaunting heavily muscled forearms and wrists.

"A barbells-and-calisthenics nut," Ace whispered.

Looks tough as nails, Tom thought. And young.

Tom stood and reached across the table to shake hands. At six foot two, he rose like a beanpole above Hoffa, who stood only five and a half feet. No wonder Teamsters nicknamed him the "Little Guy."

Jimmy gave a vigorous handshake. Tom glanced at Hoffa's calloused hand and flinched at the sight of a whopper of a scar along the Little Guy's knuckles.

Jimmy's smile faded. He drew his hand back. "Fuckin' freakin' accident, goddamn it."

His high-pitched voice startled Tom. *Damn! Why did I have to notice his scar?*

"But you was just a kid, right?" Gus leaned forward, his voice loud. "Isn't that what you said?"

"Yeah. Eight fuckin' years old." Jimmy sat down and gripped his right hand. "Mothafuckin' ax blade sliced my knuckles."

Gus squealed. "How horrible!"

Jimmy shifted in his chair. "But thank God for Mom. A goddam corker. Ripped a sheet, wrapped my hand real tight. Slowed my fuckin' bleeding until we could get to a doc." Jimmy clenched his fist to expose his scar. "Scumbag doc swore I'd never use it."

Then Jimmy's voice rose higher. He thrust his chest out. "And now," he shook his scarred fist at Tom, "now I can shake anybody's friggin' hand."

The room fell silent, then everyone talked at once, some to Jimmy, some to each other. Tom, his back to Gus, turned to Ace who dragged on his cigarette. "Someone ought to soap out that dirty mouth of his."

"You first." Tom snorted and lit up too.

DICKHEAD COPS

The coffee wagon lumbered into the room, pushed by what looked like a coed wearing a red satin vest and a white apron. The Teamsters tumbled out of their seats and surrounded the wagon, joshing with each other as they waited for the young woman to pour coffee and hand out sweets and napkins.

Tom and Ace joined them, but not Jimmy. Tom had heard that the Little Guy was puritanical in his personal habits: no caffeine, no cigarettes, no alcohol, plus strenuous daily workouts. Gus brought a tall glass of ice water to "the boss."

By the time everyone settled down, Jimmy had adopted a serious air. He raised his scarred fist high. "This," he shook his fist, "was nothin' as to what those dickhead cops did to me when I started a strike. Shithead cops and asshole goons ridin' shotgun for the boss. I slugged it out with billy clubs or blackjacks or tire irons or whatever."

Ace scribbled on a napkin and pushed it in front of Tom. It read, "Think he's going to brag about his Mafioso friends?" Tom smirked and wadded up the napkin. He and his lawyer exchanged knowing looks.

Jimmy's high-pitched voice got louder. "Shithead strikebreakers hit me so often, I can't count the goddam bruises. Goddam knock-down-drag-out fights." Jimmy crossed his arms. "Split my scalp so wide open had to get freakin' stitches a dozen times."

He looked at Tom and snarled, "But those dickhead guys who tried to break me up, they got it worse." Jimmy stopped, looked somberly around the table at the silent faces, then smiled until his cheeks dimpled. "I took my fuckin' lumps, but I always gave as good as I got."

Tom believed him. Solid muscle wrapped Hoffa's short, stocky frame, thanks to those strenuous daily calisthenics. Indeed, he looked like the roughneck he claimed to be.

Not that Hoffa's musculature scared Tom. He was himself physically imposing and knew how to settle matters with his fists, but he felt lucky he'd never been tested the way Hoffa had been.

"The Odds Have Shifted"

"Hey, Brock!" Jimmy's high-pitched voice rang down the room. "You got those fuckin' contracts?"

At the far end of the table, "Brock" Gardner, head of Teamsters Local 608 in Lincoln, stirred and reached inside his jacket. "Sure, Jimmy. I'm gonna send down three and keep one for myself."

"Got ya." Jimmy's fingernails clicked the table as he watched Brock count the contracts, then pass three down. Each thick contract had been folded twice to form a long, narrow volume. Jimmy splayed the three like a deck of cards. "For you." He slid a contact across the table to Tom. "And your lawyer." Ace grabbed his.

"It's our CSDC three-year contract."

Tom raised his eyebrows and glanced up. "CSDC?"

"Central States Drivers Council." Jimmy scowled. "Covers 125,000 drivers in twelve Midwestern states, includin' Nebraska. Only not you, not yet. What's the pussyname of that podunk town your main office is in?"

Tom stiffened. "Alma."

"Alma. Jeez." Jimmy smirked. "Sounds like a fuckin' girl's name."

Tom frowned. "Well, somebody did name the town after his daughter."

"Right." With a slight smile, Jimmy flipped open the contract. His eyes brightened. "You know, before CSDC, I'd sign up truckers like I'm doin' today—one outfit at a time. You remember those days, Tom. Before gravel highways. Nobody traveled long distance then."

Tom fingered his contract and braced himself to listen to Hoffa.

"But gravel highways changed that. Truckers shipped fuckin' new cars from Detroit to dealers all over North America.

"And who was drivin' them? Long-distance drivers." Jimmy grinned. "And who was organizin' them first? Me. That's who." He slammed his fist on the table, setting a coffee cup to chattering.

Tom turned his contract over, laid it back down. Hoffa wasn't telling Tom anything he didn't know. He glanced down the table at Karl Keul from Des Moines, the crazy Teamster who looked just like Hitler with his funny little toothbrush mustache, that tiny patch of hair under his nose. Keul had been one of the first Teamsters keen on signing up long-distance drivers. He had come to Omaha from Des Moines some ten years ago before Hoffa was on the scene. Tom remembered what a fuss Keul made about winning over Omaha's Watson Brothers, then full of drivers taking cargo to Chicago, St. Louis, Kansas City, and Denver.

Tom flipped the contract again but didn't open it. It didn't seem to apply to him. Tom hired none of those over-the-road drivers Hoffa bragged about. Coffey's Transfer drivers ran smaller runs, not just terminal to terminal but terminal to dozens, even hundreds, of customers scattered over the Great Plains of Kansas and Nebraska.

But Hoffa kept right on—about signing up long-distance drivers from Detroit to Evansville, Indiana, nearly 500 miles away, about jerking wages up 20 percent for 125,000 long-distance drivers by signing just one master contract.

"This here contract." Jimmy slapped it across his palm. "Take a look at it. Yooze guys meet me back here tomorrow."

THE EXIT

Chairs rattled as Teamsters lunged for the door. Gus stuck so tightly behind Tom that they walked around the big table together.

"Tom, you know you're dealing with a man on his way to the IBT presidency."

"IBT?" Tom asked as they navigated the door. He picked up speed.

"International Brotherhood of Teamsters." Gus kept up the new pace. "Now, Tom, I'm surprised you didn't know that."

They padded down the two-story high staircase, one behind the other. When they arrived in the lobby, Gus powered up again. "Why, any fool can see what he's up to, building his power base here in the Midwest, extending his domain, then using this base to rise to the presidency."

So Hoffa's heading toward the top, so what? The idea didn't frighten Tom then.

When they reached the entrance, he turned, grabbed Gus's hand, and shook it. "See you tomorrow." Tom pirouetted on one foot and hailed a valet before Gus could answer.

Tom slid into his Buick and headed home. Alma. The town with a girl's name. *What a slap! That Hoffa, boy, he's sure greedy to be in control. A little Hitler.*

Miles slipped away; at Holdrege, Tom turned south onto Highway 183. That straight-as-an-arrow road from South Dakota to Texas shot right across Alma's business section. Thirty minutes later, Tom turned right onto Main Street and parked in front of his square brick building. He grabbed his CSDC contract and entered his now empty office. He was hungry, but that could wait until he digested this Teamster atrocity.

He'd read halfway down the contract's second page when his phone rang. He picked it up. Ace. Good. And their connection not bad for 200 miles away.

"It's written for long-distance drivers, Tom. Did you catch that?"

"Yeah. And me with only a couple. None full-time."

Ace's voice softened. "I wonder what he's up to."

"Beats me." Tom frowned. "Can't we just take him to court again, like we did last year?"

"If only it were that simple. Last year, when we took those guys on, we were just fighting Brock's Teamsters Local 608 in Lincoln." Ace's voice seemed strained. "But this year, if we hauled the Teamsters into court, we'd be fighting the Midwestern Teamsters with Hoffa and his 125,000 drivers. Or maybe the whole shebang."

Tom fingered his silver dollar. "The odds have shifted."

"That's right." Ace raised his voice. "Those Teamsters would run your court costs so high you'd wish you'd settled."

Tom sighed.

"Not that I wouldn't like to go to bat for you," Ace's low-pitched voice held steady, "but I think your best bet is to negotiate Hoffa down on that CSDC contract."

After they hung up, Tom, hoping for a late supper, walked over to the Alma hotel to see if Mr. Mahoney could still muster up a Salisbury steak for him. He could, and covered it with those tiny mushrooms out of a can. Tom's favorite. Mr. Mahoney served the meal with a smile, a bit of conversation, and a white towel draped over one arm. Who could ask for more?

"I Can't Sign Your Contract"

The next day, Tom and Hoffa arrived at the conference room door together. Tom wore his best dark-vested suit, a white shirt, and a patterned burgundy tie. Jimmy's garish tie dangled under his collar.

Both grabbed for the doorknob. Each retreated. When Tom opened the door, he spotted the Little Guy's white socks in black shoes beneath his blue pants legs. He'd heard about those famous white socks from Gus. "They're Jimmy's trademark. He wears them everywhere. Colored socks make his feet sweat."

The early birds sat at the table, as before: Jimmy and Tom faced each other and Gus snuggled in at Tom's left.

"You know, Jimmy, we both started driving rigs and worked our way up." Tom hoped to break the ice. "We're on opposite sides of the table now, but we still want the same things for the industry."

"Wrong twice," Jimmy said. "There's no fuckin' room in the industry for a two-bit operator like you. One of these days, we're gonna negotiate a goddamn nationwide contract with just ten big-line truckers."

Those words struck like a blow between Tom's eyes.

Jimmy went right on. "And I never drove no truck, neither."

Tom stiffened. He cleared his throat. "So how did you wind up in the Teamsters Union?" The moment the words left his mouth, he regretted them. Just opening the Hoffa dike again.

"Strawberries!" Jimmy whooped. "Fresh fuckin' strawberries."

Gus tugged on Tom's suit sleeve. "He means it too."

Tom scowled, brushed Gus away, and stared at Hoffa. "All right, all right. I'll bite." His voice rose. "How did strawberries make you a Teamster?"

"Well, let me ask you this first." Jimmy punched a finger at Tom. "What the fuck were you doin' in 1929 when the blasted stock market came crashin' down. Were you truckin' then?"

Tom shrugged. "That's easy." He leaned back in his seat. "I was driving a borrowed truck to Omaha, my first run. Hauling cattle. The rickety old lattice-sided truck still had running boards."

"Bet you stood in no bullshit breadlines during the Depression, did you?" Jimmy asked.

"No. Didn't have to. I could always eat at my dad's farm."

"And today?" Jimmy leaned forward. "You haul no shithead cattle these days, do you?"

"No. I quit in '36 and went into those mechanically refrigerated trucks developed by the ice cream industry. Now I haul stuff like Campbell's chicken soup and," his voice rose, "like that five thousand pounds of Minden Creamery butter you got melting on my dock."

"Butter, strawberries. Strawberries, butter," Jimmy chanted. "All tastes the same to a Teamster."

Tom crossed his arms across his chest. "What about that butter. Let's talk butter."

"Well, we can't talk butter until we talk strawberries." Jimmy stretched and leaned back in his chair. "Kroger Grocery in Detroit, those old bastards, taught me that when I was sixteen. Put me to work unloadin' trucks fuckin' full of lettuce, carrots—and strawberries.

"They paid shit for long hours, and the dickhead foreman was the world's worst."

Jimmy spread his legs wide; his arms hung at his sides. "That solid gold son of a bitch would scream and threaten to fire you if you didn't jump to his fuckin' tune."

Keul, Brock, and the other Teamsters slipped into the room, one at a time. Jimmy paid no attention to them except raising his squeaky voice a notch. "So when the stupid-fuck foreman fires a couple of cocksuckers, a bunch of us decide to strike.

"But not right away."

Jimmy licked his lips and smiled. "We wait for the right moment. When the shithead boss can't say no. Then in pulls a truck, loaded with juicy ripe strawberries! Jerkoff strawberries. Easily spoiled. Might as well been butter." Jimmy grinned at Tom.

"We unload half the fuckin' truck, then strike. And get our motherfuckin' way."

Jimmy thrust his chest out and glowered at Tom. "So that's how shithead Kroger's showed me how to use perishables—like strawberries or butter—to get the top dog to talk.

"And see, here you are." Jimmy beamed. "Have you looked at our contract?"

Tom reached in the inside pocket of his suit jacket and pulled out the thick folded contract. Ace leaned over and spoke behind his hand. "Hang in there, Tom. He's just a bully, trying to wear you down. An old horse-trading tactic."

Jimmy scowled. "So, you ready to sign up?"

"I can't sign your contract." Tom's face reddened. "Not with that dual-wage provision."

"Dual-wage? Oh, you mean peddle drivers." Jimmy's eyes narrowed. "But you got plenty of peddle drivers, don't you?"

Tom nodded. He relied on them. His peddle drivers picked up goods from big city shippers at his Omaha or Lincoln terminal, then delivered them to little towns in south central Nebraska and north central Kansas. "They bounce between dozens of rural communities, delivering door to door. They're like mail carriers. They pick up and deliver along an established route.

"So I pay them for an eight-hour day." Tom's brow wrinkled. "But if I signed your contract, I'd have to pay my peddle drivers by the mile for driving and by the hour for unloading."

Jimmy shrugged. "So?"

Tom's voice turned quiet and deliberate, as though he were explaining something to a child. "My Coffey's Transfer Company has twenty trucks now, and we ship everything from soap to tractors."

Dad felt proud of his fleet of trucks.

Gus interrupted, face flushed. "I know your red trucks, Tom, with those white wings spread on the sides. Yours is a big outfit, I can vouch for that."

"Big? Nowhere big as Watson Brothers."

"No, but you're the largest operator of your kind in the whole state." Gus shook a finger at Tom. "And you know it. We can't ignore you."

"Maybe not." Tom swept an arm across the table and turned back to Hoffa. "Bosses for long-distance drivers supervise their drivers at either terminal, picking up or dropping off, but under this contract, I have no way to supervise my peddle drivers. Oh, I could calculate how many miles my drivers drive, but how could I figure how much time they'd spend unloading?" He glared. "There's no way I can figure how much I'll have to pay under this contract of yours."

When Tom stopped, he heard the sound of men shifting to light a cigarette; their movement sounded like leaves crackling underfoot.

Silent, Jimmy just looked at Tom.

"I'm telling you, this contract can't work." Tom's nostrils flared. "This special wage scale for peddle drivers just invites padding and featherbedding."

Jimmy rose.

My luck has run out, Tom thought. *Maybe because I've been trucking eighteen years without a Teamsters contract.*

Jimmy grabbed his suit jacket off the back of his chair and tossed it over his shoulder.

Or maybe Gus is right, my business had grown too big for the Teamsters to overlook.

Jimmy started toward the door, then turned to Tom. "I'll check in with you tomorrow mornin' at eight before I catch my fuckin' Alabama flight." And he left.

"Damned If I Do, Damned If I Don't"

On the long drive to Alma, Tom ruminated about the past two meetings. He had expected Hoffa to be tough and aggressive, perhaps even brutal, but the man proved to be such a windbag. Tom hadn't foreseen that. Hoffa's high-pitched voice still battered Tom's ears, and the little guy's profanity! *Lord, eliminate Hoffa's cuss words, and the man couldn't talk.* Tom flashed on Hoffa sitting there, coat off, tie open, shirt sleeves rolled back…and his mouth going.

But one view of the Little Guy perplexed Tom. He'd been warned that Hoffa would be a formidable negotiator. *What a laugh! Negotiation isn't Hoffa's specialty.* "You don't negotiate with him," Tom had told Ace. "You listen." Ace agreed.

At home, Tom tumbled into his La-Z-Boy, blew a kiss to his wife, and napped until suppertime. When he took his place at the head of the table, he tipped his head back for a moment and closed his eyes. Just hearing the clatter of cutlery against the plates and Zelma's chatter with their daughters made him tear up.

Tom's low spirits deepened as he climbed into bed that night. Hoffa's big achievement, that area-wide CSDC contract covering 125,000 drivers in twelve states, had turned into a nightmare. Tom felt trapped. What could he do?

If he signed that three-year contract, the featherbedding, or adopting pointless work procedures, would wreck his company, but if he didn't sign it, then he'd have to face a Teamsters' strike.

Damned if I do, damned if I don't.

A fight with the Teamsters might be like those two bitter Teamsters' strikes he'd witnessed in the late 1930s and early

1940s with shootings, bombings, and head busting. He had seen truck windshields smashed with railroad spikes, and he saw how a tablespoonful of sugar in the gas tank could devastate a truck engine.

I dare not buck the Teamsters unless I'm ready to risk everything.

Does that make signing that damn featherbedding contract my only alternative?

Tom rolled over and burrowed his head into his pillow, but instead of drifting to sleep, he remembered Gus cornering him today when the meeting broke up.

"Now listen to me." Gus jabbed one finger on Tom's breast, his chin held so high Tom could see Gus's Adam's apple. "Hoffa has singled you out. No! Listen to me, Tom. He knows what a big operator you are. And he knows what an independent cuss you are. Old Man Coffey, he calls you."

Tom walked away again, with Gus running alongside. "Don't you see? Hoffa figures if he can scare Old Man Coffey into signing, all the rest of the little operators will fall in line. Then the Teamsters won't have to sign them up one trucker at a time.

"You gotta sign this contract. It's important. It means a lot to all of us."

Tom groaned and rolled over. *Leave it to Hoffa to sic Gus on me, to try to talk me into doing the Teamsters' work. As if I give a rat's ass about Hoffa's Teamsters problems. Christ!*

Unable to sleep, Tom got out of bed and paced the floor. For a while, he stared out his two-story bedroom window, looking at, but not seeing, the trees in his yard and the humped moon, still waning, casting its angular light on the pavement. *What a class A predicament! Hoffa thinks he's trapped me, but he's got no right to tell me how to run my business. He didn't put any capital into Coffey's Transfer. He never worked long hours for me, day after day, year after year.*

The rest of the night, Tom tossed and turned, trying to decide what to do about that contract. But no matter which way he twisted, Tom couldn't come up with a sane way out of his jam.

A DAMNED DOUBLE VICTORY

By the time Tom appeared at the Cornhusker Hotel meeting room the next day, Jimmy and his entourage had already blown in and swarmed the coffee wagon. Gus handed Tom a cup of brew. Tom blew on it, took a cautious sip, and sat down.

Jimmy scowled and glanced at his watch. Gus, in his usual seat to Tom's left, twisted and asked Jimmy. "Want me to get 'em?"

"Go ahead."

Gus jumped up, rounded the table, and fell into a tête-à-tête with the head of Teamsters Local 608 in Lincoln, Brock Gardner. Brock shuffled a stack of papers he'd pulled from his pocket and plucked out several contracts.

"Whatthehell," Ace muttered, but Tom just shrugged.

Gus cleared his throat. "Shall I give 'em to him?"

Jimmy's tone sounded sharp. "Naw. Here, I'll take the mutherfuckers." He put his scarred hand on the contracts, looked at Tom, and smiled. "Now these here contracts are still CSDC, but I shortened 'em a bit for you. Docked it. Took out that fuckin' special wage scale for peddle drivers."

Tom stiffened, pulled his head back. Ace reached across Tom and snagged a contract, flipped it open, and scanned the lines. Tom opened his old contract; he'd penciled the peddle drivers' section in red. He and Ace compared the sections, and Tom, shocked, looked up at Jimmy. *Why did he do that? Then he remembered Gus saying, "If Hoffa scares you into signing, then the rest of the small truckers will fall in line."*

The altered three-year contract, like the old one, covered all of the Coffey's Transfer drivers in Alma, Holdrege, Lincoln, and Omaha.

"Brock." Jimmy stood up and pulled on his suit jacket. "Take it from here."

Brock nodded and walked around the table toward Tom.

Gus, sitting at the edge of his chair, displayed a victory signal. "You ought to be proud, Old Man Coffey. He hardly ever alters contracts. Maybe never."

Then Gus turned to Brock. "Here. Take my chair." As Gus left, he patted Tom on his shoulder.

Tom watched Hoffa and his entourage leave. "He's going to Alabama," Brock said, spreading the contracts open on the table. "He's got some more southern states to organize down there. Wants to do in the South what he did here in the Midwest with the CSDC."

Brock signed a contract with a sweeping flourish. "Folks say he can't win down south, but I'd put my money on him." He autographed the second contract, pushed both to Tom who looked at Ace. Ace nodded, but Tom hesitated. He knew his name would force his drivers to become Teamsters whether they wanted to or not. Then, with a sigh, he plucked his big striped pen out of his pocket. For a moment, he played with it. Then he signed the contract with handsome reverse *C* on Coffey that he'd learned to pen in school.

So Jimmy and Tom both won. Tom got a special exemption from the Central States contract, and Hoffa got Old Man Coffey's signature on a contract. But it had cost Tom. Three trips to Lincoln, three days work, and 5,518 pounds of butter.

After Dad signed the contract, he didn't whoop and holler when he got home, and he didn't twirl me 'round and 'round. He just sat in the living room, his jaw clenched as he fingered his silver dollar.

TILES CLICKING

"Here, Vera." Dad handed the bulky envelope to his plump secretary.

She opened it and peeped inside. "The contract?"

He nodded. "Put it somewhere safe, somewhere you can get it in an instant—and somewhere where I'll never see the blankety-blank thing."

Vera smiled and looked in the envelope. Then she reached inside with her bejeweled hand and pulled out a handful of Teamster membership cards, blue with an imprint of two horse heads. "Shall I file these too?"

"No." Weary, Dad put a hand against a file cabinet to steady himself. "Those durned dominoes." *That's how his men would fall, the tiles clicking.*

"Dominoes?" Vera stacked the cards in neat piles.

"Just a manner of speaking."

Later, Vera wrote the name of each Coffey's Transfer driver on his card and returned the stack to Dad.

He let them sit on his desk for a few days. He thought of returning them to Vera and asking her to mail them out. He almost did, despite the time and expense of a mailing. But at last, he handed them out himself. He had turned his drivers into Teamsters with the stroke of a pen, and he owed them an explanation. He talked to each driver, man to man.

Vera hid the Teamster contract, but Dad couldn't let go of it. At every cigarette break, he berated himself for signing that paper. Knowing that Jimmy would visit again in 1950 furrowed Dad's brow so often that Mama worried about him.

6 WAITING FOR THE SHOE TO DROP

By 1947, Jimmy Hoffa considered himself pretty hot stuff. He presided over all of Michigan's locals. He negotiated deals for 125,000 drivers at a time. Plus he kept busy organizing those southern trucklines that everyone said he couldn't.

However, Jimmy's home town of Detroit considered him persona non grata. City officials snubbed him; newspapers lambasted the "labor czar" and his "goon squads"; and letters from outraged citizens demanded a crackdown.

Teamsters' leaders, however, ignored Detroit's complaints, focusing instead on Jimmy's skill in building their union. So by the time Jimmy arrived at the August 1947 Teamsters' convention in San Francisco, he had corralled a good-sized number of Teamster votes, especially from Midwesterners who praised his street smarts. Jimmy controlled almost enough votes to go national, but not quite. Not yet.

However, the IBT nominated Jimmy for a national post as trustee. Calling him "our little spark plug from

Detroit," his nominator praised his work in the Southern Conference and expressed sympathy for "what he's going through in the city of Detroit." Jimmy won that trustee election, which assured convention goers that his star would continue to rise.

And it did.

By the early 1950s, he represented almost 650,000 Teamsters.

Santa Claus

Small wonder Jimmy's drivers prized him. As one said, "Jimmy gets us wage hikes, year after year. Some are pretty hefty."

"And no snooty receptionist," another said, "keeps us from the Little Guy." Jimmy's Detroit office door opened directly into the hall. "You got a problem? You march right up and speak one-to-one with him."

For his Teamsters, Jimmy passed out favors, jobs, and gifts. He turned into Santa Claus at Christmas, passing out cash in wads, up to a hundred dollars to those who asked. This way, to the dismay of the local 299 treasurer, Jimmy gave away $48,000 dollars in cash with no accounting for it.

You get cash, if you're lucky.

If you're not, you stand around in the hall, waiting, like eleven guys from Cleveland, Cincinnati, Kansas City, Chicago, and New York, key people that Jimmy planned to see.

But instead of welcoming them, he flung the office door open and walked right over to his whipping boy, Joe Franco, and ignored everyone else. Jimmy stepped right up to long-legged Joe and with one finger pummeled him in the chest, the highest spot that short Jimmy could reach.

"Now get the fuck out of here," he yelled, "you son of a bitch, you cocksucker you, didn't I tell you to go see that fucking guy and tell that motherfucker what I told you to tell him..." On and on he raved.

What the hell's going on? Joe wondered. *There's no guy that I'm supposed to see.*

When Jimmy finished barking at Joe, he looked at the eleven guys. "All right," his voice still rough, "everybody in my office."

After the men filed silently in, Jimmy slammed the door shut.

Joe stood in the hall, wondering what hit him.

His pal, Tommy Burke, slapped his thigh. "Don't you get it, all that crap about what's-his-name and whatchamacallit? He just pumped himself up on you, you asshole. He did a fucking number on you." Tommy laughed. "And that bunch of guys waiting in the hall, Jimmy knew they're thinking, 'Oh, shit man, this son of a bitch is a raving maniac, and this is going to be a tough goddamn meeting.'"

Then in 1950, Jimmy's trajectory to the top of Teamster heaven wobbled. Just a bit.

On February 9, Senator Joe McCarthy, then forty-two, spoke to a women's club in West Virginia. He claimed that the State Department was "infested" with communists. This shot his national profile up like a meteor.

He hired a friend of the family, young Robert Kennedy, to help find possible communists. In this way, Senator McCarthy nurtured Bobby's investigating skills, skills Bobby would use so effectively against Jimmy.

Next, on May 3, the US Senate established a committee to investigate crime in interstate commerce and appointed five men who would be known as the Kefauver Committee. Before the committee dissolved in April 1951, its members held hearings in fourteen cities and listened to six hundred witnesses. During this time, committee members visited Jimmy's Detroit. They examined his growing Michigan empire and its familiarity with mobsters. This scrutiny, although superficial, would inspire later, deeper investigations by other committees, investigations that would weaken the energy of Detroit's "little spark plug."

Not Quite Butter

That awful three-year contract Dad had negotiated with Jimmy in 1947 wasn't due to lapse until June 1, 1950, so a March 1950 phone call from IBT headquarters surprised Dad.

"Hoffa isn't happy," the Teamster official said. "He says we're gaining nothing with your contract." They arranged a series of talks in March.

Dad and his lawyer, Ace Jackson, showed up at the Cornhusker Hotel in Lincoln to find Jimmy Hoffa nowhere in sight.

"Wonder what the Little Guy's up to?" Ace tilted his head to one side.

IBT had sent Karl Keul, the Teamster who looked like Hitler, to be the principal negotiator instead of Jimmy.

Dad, who remembered Keul from the 1947 negotiations, released a deep breath. "Bad as Keul might be," he whispered to Ace, "at least he isn't Jimmy."

The men sat around the same hotel table, Dad and Ace surrounded by Teamsters from Omaha, Lincoln, and Grand Island locals. The coffee wagon arrived at regular intervals.

Dad expected to discuss the 1947 contract, since Jimmy had promised to renegotiate that agreement, but no. They didn't discuss a specific contract. Talks and more talks. March passed, then April and May.

When the June 1 contract deadline lapsed, Jimmy flew in from New York. And he wanted Dad to sign the same old Central States contract just as it had been with that terrible featherbedding clause. The new contract, like the old one, would last three years and would cover all Dad's drivers for his twenty trucks in Omaha, Lincoln, Hastings, Holdrege, and Alma.

Dad protested.

"Sign or strike," Jimmy said.

Dad, still unhappy with his 1947 contract that forced his drivers to become Teamsters, decided to resist. He collected all those union cards that Hoffa's contract had forced him to distribute, returned them to Keul, and hunkered down for a fight.

Each morning Dad drove to his office prepared to see men picketing, a sign that the Teamsters had struck. *It would be a phony strike, of course. The Teamsters weren't attempting to unionize his men. They never bothered to talk to any of his twenty-plus drivers. The Teamsters didn't want members; they were just heaving their clout around, as usual.*

But no pickets materialized. Instead, Dad and Ace kept right on meeting in the Cornhusker Hotel with Keul and his gang. Every now and then, Jimmy flew in from Detroit or New York for a meeting with a lot of high-powered talk that seemed to come to nothing.

Summer of 1950 passed, and still no strike. The meetings dragged on and on. Dad found himself anticipating meetings with Jimmy. Even though they went nowhere, they had a pressure-cooker feeling that Keul's meetings lacked. Keul rambled until his negotiations confused Dad.

By this time, my father suspected that the Teamsters wanted him to operate without a new contract. Keul implied as much. He said, "My primary interest lies in organizing all nonunion truckers in Nebraska. Until I do, I'm inclined to forget the Coffey's Transfer contract."

Eventually, after almost a year, talks ceased. Like thieves in the night, the Teamsters vanished.

Dad stopped looking for pickets.

Soon after, word slid down the grapevine, "Jimmy's too busy to mess with small fry like Coffey's Transfer Company." No wonder! When Jimmy negotiated his last contract, he signed up truckers in twenty-two states.

Dad's heady state of independence from the Teamsters Union would last nearly five years.

FROM CATTLE TO CAMPBELL'S SOUP

My father felt relieved that Jimmy Hoffa was "too busy to mess with small fry." Dad didn't mind being a tadpole in the labor leader's big pond, but in our small pool, Alma, Nebraska, population 1,750, Tom Coffey was the resident bullfrog.

In 1952, Dad owned the biggest business in town. His Coffey's Transfer Company, a fleet of twenty sleek red trucks, serviced customers in more than ninety towns in south central Nebraska and in Kansas. He had survived dozens of competitors as well as flood, drought, blizzards, wrecks, and World War II when he struggled to keep trucks rolling.

Dad congratulated himself on his achievement. Two decades had passed since he'd borrowed a battered old truck, loaded it with cattle, and driven to Omaha over graveled roads. Now forty-five years old, he no longer hauled cattle. Instead, his trucks carried everything from paper, soap, and butter to bridges, airplanes, and elephants, plus huge thermos trucks full of hot chicken broth for Campbell's Soup.

Coffey's Transfer won third place in American Trucking Association's Claim Prevention contest, which truckers considered the "Oscar" of the industry. That made Dad proud. His was the first firm of its size to win the national contest. Judges based prizes on the smallest number of claims compared to business volume. Dad's claim ratio of .009 percent was about half of the national average. Speed of claims settlement counted too. My father settled 97.7 percent of his claims in fewer than thirty days.

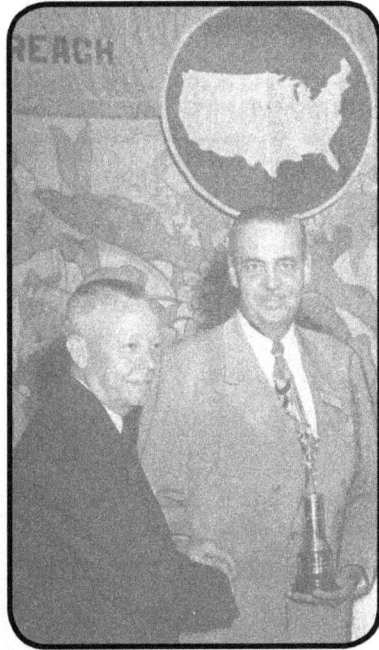

Dad, at right, receiving award from American Trucking Association.

However, Dad sloughed off the importance of being promoted to a Class I motor carrier by the Interstate Commerce Commission. The press described Dad as a trucker of accomplishment, but my dad asked, "What's the point of getting bigger? I'll just be a juicier morsel for the Teamster sharks."

A Few Hog Tales

Then unexpectedly, Republican Governor Val Peterson named Dad to the Nebraska Highway Advisory Committee. Just what my father needed to keep him from thinking about Jimmy Hoffa! So he accepted.

Dad became the gadfly of the eighteen-member committee, which he claimed had donned "a cloak of secrecy." He accused the committee of rubber-stamping. He attacked its report, which recommended sizable increases in taxes to build new roads, calling it "the biggest hoax ever perpetrated on the people of Nebraska."

This made him a bit of a celebrity. Reporters from the *Omaha World-Herald* and other newspapers featured his words. A Sioux City, Iowa–Yankton, South Dakota,

Republican Governor of Nebraska, Val Peterson, 1952.

radio station, WNAX, interviewed him at length. Groups like the Chambers of Commerce and the Kiwanis Clubs solicited his presence.

When he attended the Nebraska Motor Carriers' annual convention, his life changed. There he listened to the governor give the welcome, and he heard the guest speaker, Colonel Jack Major from Kentucky, wax eloquent on "Taxes, Women, and Hogs."

Whoa! Dad's eyes widened. *I could match the governor as a speaker. I could even match the colonel. I've spun tales as good as theirs, and playing poker has taught me how to control my face.* He pushed up his sleeves. *Plus I got a few hog tales of my own to tell: how Uncle Charley put a dead pig in his brother's fancy picnic basket, and how my brothers, those devils, delighted in feeding our three-legged pig malted grain just so they could watch her drunken stagger.*

By morning, Dad knew he would go into politics. Mayor. Then state senator. Maybe even governor. That would keep him too busy to think about that scumbag, Jimmy Hoffa. So he went to work.

Dad had a way with people. At a full-bodied six foot two, he was an imposing man. He could be serious or humorous, depending on the occasion, and he knew how to apply his considerable Irish charm.

He laid his primary groundwork for mayor in Alma by volunteering for nearly every group in town. He served on the school board, helped the Methodist church sort out its finances, joined the Harlan County Shriner lodge, became a member, then president, of the Alma Chamber of Commerce.

In the spring of 1950, he ran for mayor of Alma against a strong, popular candidate, Paul Haeker. The April 4 election, a heavy one, drew more than three hundred voters, 162 for Dad, 148 for Haeker. Dad won just by 14 votes, but he won.

My father was the mayor and I, the mayor's daughter. A few months short of thirteen years old, I soon learned the downside to my new role. I had felt certain my classmates would be so impressed by my new status that they would no longer holler at me, "Teacher's pet! Pthppthppthppth! Teacher's pet!"

I was right, but now they hollered, "You think you're so smart Pthppthppthppth! 'cause your dad's mayor!"

But Dad's being mayor didn't change him much.

One day I ambled in from playing in the yard and caught him asleep in his recliner, flung back, carnivorous mouth slung wide open, lips trembling with the power of his snores.

I gazed at him, wondering what he would do if I dropped something in his mouth. Something that wouldn't hurt him.

I settled on a stalk of celery (more flexible than a ruler), fetched it from the kitchen, and tiptoed to his chair. When I dropped the stalk, Dad chomped down on it like a pit bull, then roared to his feet, hollering.

By that time, I had disappeared out the back door to churn my way up the alley. I stayed out for a long time, long enough to let Dad's indignation die down, long enough for it to transpose into humor. Which it did.

I didn't often get to pull such a good one, and I knew that, in time, he'd give me the credit I deserved.

The Pants Burglar

One evening, Dad slid into his chair at the head of the table and wiggled his eyebrows. "You'll never guess, not in a million years, what happened to me in Omaha." His eyes widened.

"What?" chorused his family.

"Well, Monday, after work, I go to my room in the Castle Hotel, lock the door and click on the chain." He winked. "Can't be too careful in a high-class burg like Omaha."

Dad scooped a spoonful of Mama's ground beef casserole. "I hung up my jacket, dumped my change on the dresser, dropped my pants over the back of a chair, and slept. Like a log." He blew on his spoonful, then ate it. "Woke at daybreak."

"As usual." Mama, a late sleeper, groaned.

Dad ignored her. "I reached to grab my pants off the chair, but they weren't there. I looked all over, but those pants were gone. So was the hundred and ten dollars I had in my pants pocket."

Mama gasped.

"Then I noticed the dresser top where I'd dumped my change. And my lucky silver dollar. Wiped clean." He stirred a bit of casserole on his plate, then stared at his food. "I'd never lost that dollar before."

"Oh, Tom." Mama laid her fork down with a clatter. "You've had that silver dollar since college. I remember you showing it to me. It was the first silver dollar that you earned."

I remembered Dad's dollar, too, its letters worn from all the times he'd flipped it to see who would pay for a cup of coffee.

"Well, I was pretty upset." Tom put down his fork. "My lucky coin was gone, and I felt sure I'd never see it again. When I looked at the door, I could see that someone had pried open the chain, probably came in the room while I slept. So I picked up the phone.

"The operator said, 'Oh, no! Did he force open the door chain?' And when I said he did, she said, 'It's the pants burglar again! Prying off the chain, that's his trademark!'"

Dad scooped up some casserole and ate it. "The bellboy brought me a pair of pants, but its pockets were empty and the legs too short. The Castle Hotel gave me breakfast on the house. I went to the police station and reported the robbery. And a *Triblines* reporter interviewed me. It ran in the next edition of the paper." Dad rummaged in his pockets and pulled out a folded news story. "Here, Pete, read it for us."

Mama read Dad's interview: "I'm heading home where city slickers don't pry the chains off my hotel room and steal my pants and its contents of a hundred and ten smackers.

"And the next time I come to Omaha, I'm going to undress, then have the bellboy take my pants to the hotel office for safe keeping. The government has fixed it so you can't afford to own a two-pant suit, so a fellow can't take any chances of losing his pants."

Dad wrinkled his nose. "I said, 'losing his panties,' but the reporter changed it. Can't trust a reporter."

Mama shook her head. "I don't suppose they'll ever catch the burglar."

"Wrong!" Dad pulled out another news story. "His name is Alvin Konvalin, he's twenty-four years old, and he served time in 1939 for what the reporter called a 'dozen odd-room prowls.' Alvin swore he never touched my pants, but I never saw that hundred and ten smackers again. Then Alvin teared up, confessed that he'd stolen a few coins, and emptied his pockets. Like this."

Dad stood up, reached deep in his pocket, and tossed a handful of coins on the table. The biggest coin of all was his silver dollar. He picked it up and rolled it in his hand. "My lucky buck!"

"Heads I win," I hollered, "tails you lose."

"Oh no, you don't." Dad chuckled, and tossed me a quarter.

Mama rolled her eyes.

MY TWO FRONT TEETH

That first Christmas season when Dad was mayor, the stores on Main Street offered a fantastic raffle. Everything I bought yielded a raffle ticket or two, and the many prizes, scattered among the stores, included choice pieces of merchandise.

After I prowled the aisles of each store to take a close look at every piece of raffle merchandise offered, I decided to put my money on the drugstore. It featured a pitcher set: a big glass pitcher with roses painted on the outside plus eight matching glasses. The perfect gift for Mama. I knew she'd love something so beautiful, but I didn't have enough money to buy it outright.

From that time until raffle day, I bought everything I needed, and some things I didn't need, in the drugstore. Then I put each and every ticket in the box beside the pitcher set.

The day of the drawing turned out splendid for a winter day, the sky bright blue and sun all over the street.

My father the mayor stood on top of a wooden platform with a handful of other people, who gave talks. I waited and waited. Finally my dad had his turn. He announced the many winners for the participating stores. In each case, he'd hold up the item, describe it, and mention the store that had offered it.

I thought he'd never get to the drugstore, but at last he held up the pitcher. It sparkled in the sunlight. I not only crossed my fingers, I crossed my toes, I so hoped to win it.

Then Dad picked up the paper with the winner's name on it. He read it more than once. Then his deep voice rang out into the street: "Folks, I'm a bit embarrassed here. This says my daughter is the winner." People laughed, and so did he, as I ran to the platform. I thought I would burst, from happiness at acquiring Mama's gift, from delight at being seen by so many people, but especially from pride at my handsome father, bending over to reach my hand, which he shook just before he winked at me.

Before we knew it, Christmas season was upon us, and as usual, Dad annoyed me. Whenever I asked him what he wanted for Christmas, he would just grin and burst into song: "All I Want for Christmas Is My Two Front Teeth," that season's favorite.

Dad was the worst person to give a present to. Whenever he wanted anything, he just went to the store and bought it instead of giving us a big hint and waiting. That's why he ended up with such a huge tie collection.

After I heard about those two front teeth a dozen times, I asked Mama to help me. She took me downtown to the dentist's office, and we talked the dentist out of two real front teeth. I wrapped them up in pretty paper and put them under the tree with Dad's name on it.

That night, Margery and I went to bed early. Our beds were in the same room. We lay real still. Then we heard bells ringing, and someone saying, "Ho, ho, ho!" and walking on the roof. Margery squealed and jumped out of bed.

"That's just Daddy," I said. I was thirteen. But Margery wouldn't believe me. Only seven, she tried to open a window and stick her head out to see Santa, but I discouraged her. Anyway, by the time we finished bickering, the bells had stopped ringing.

"It won't be long." I pulled my covers up. "Now keep real still."

For a long time, we heard nothing. Then downstairs, in the room below us, paper rattled. I slipped out of bed, shook Margery awake, and put my fingers to my lips. Silently, we tiptoed across the bedroom to the floor register. We squatted beside it. Below us, we could hear the folks talking and paper rattling. Our gifts! They were wrapping our gifts on the dining room table.

Slowly I took the top of the register off, revealing a hanging metal box. The perforated sides of the box showed the downstairs room. I bent over and leaned way down. Sure enough, I could see Daddy wrapping a big box, maybe a dollhouse. I straightened up and held Margery so she could lean down and see. I don't know what she saw, but it excited her so much she squealed, and Daddy walked over from the table, looked up at us, and said, "What's going on here?" He grinned and turned back to Mama. "They're watching us wrap."

"Oh, no!" Mama cried. She pushed all the boxes to the far end of table so we couldn't see them. Then she came upstairs, pulled Margery out of the register, and made us go to bed.

"I don't want to hear a peep out of you!"

That was easy. Santa had gone and we couldn't spy on the presents, so we just went to sleep.

The sun wasn't even up when Margery woke the folks. They came grumbling out of their beds, pulling on bathrobes. Dad went downstairs and flipped on the Christmas tree bulbs showering light all over the piles of presents on the floor.

Daddy's hair was all tousled, but he was grinning. "Now you each get to pick one present to unwrap while your mother turns on the coffeepot." Soon all of us sat on the floor, pulling out presents and looking at name tags. I kept looking for the little package, green paper with pine cones on it, the package with the two front teeth in it, but I didn't see it for a long time. So small, it just slipped down between the other packages.

When I did find it, I grabbed it and gave it to Dad. "This one's for you."

I watched the perplexed look on his face turn when he saw the teeth. He whooped. Sang "All I Want for Christmas" and whooped again. Later, when we both were standing, he gave me a hug. I watched him put those teeth in his pocket with his silver dollar.

By a Dam Site

Being the mayor's daughter excited me, for Dad became mayor of Alma in 1950 during a remarkable time.

That time stemmed from 1935 when a wall of water up to twelve feet high cascaded down the 500-mile-long Republican River valley, right by Alma. It killed 113 people, gobbled innumerable chickens, and upended bellowing, struggling cattle, killing more than 41,000 head. Their carcasses blocked roads. Churning water destroyed 300 bridges, flooded 340 miles of highway, and submerged 74,500 acres of farmland.

Historians call it Nebraska's deadliest flood, and my father's friend, Carl Curtis, then thirty, saw it. He drove thirty miles from his Minden home to the river, which writhed like a giant serpent, tearing out phone and telegraph lines, uprooting trees like weeds. The water battered farm tractors like tin cans and tore houses and barns from their foundations. Terrified occupants clung to roofs or toppled into the rampaging water.

Curtis vowed he'd do everything possible to prevent such floods in the Republican River valley. And he did. So from the time Curtis set foot in Washington, then a small elegant city whose streetcar tracks ran in front of the White House, he began to scheme about irrigation as well as flood control in Nebraska.

In 1944, in what was considered a stunning success, Representative Curtis managed the passage of the Flood Control Act, a bill that provided irrigation and flood control not just for Nebraska but for a sixth of the United States: the entire Missouri Basin.

In 1950 when Dad became mayor, our small town perched on the edge of a huge US Army Corps of Engineers project, the Harlan County dam and reservoir, thanks to now Senator Curtis. When finished, we would live on the shore of Nebraska's second largest lake.

Dad's two years as mayor coincided with the final stage of this massive undertaking.

Every Sunday, like clockwork, Dad piled us in the car. He drove east along the wanton, lawless, capricious Republican River, and we'd inspect the Harlan County dam area: row after row of army barracks where workers lived in prefab huts, the dam site, and Republican City, population 580. The corps planned to move the entire town to a new, safer site.

I squinted at the familiar buildings. "How can they move something as big as that square old brick town house?" I tugged on Dad's sleeve.

"Oh, piece by piece." Dad's voice boomed inside the car. "Or maybe they won't move it. They won't move all the buildings. Some they'll tear down."

I stared at the town house. In my mind's eye, a big black ball splattered brick.

Not just Republican City would be inundated by the new dam and lake. Farm families also had to leave the rich valley to make room for the twelve-mile-long lake.

Even Alma would be altered. Dad and his city council planned to relocate a whole section of homes, an electric plant, the Burlington railroad depot, and the old water tower.

"I'VE GOT A DOLLAR"

When Dad was mayor and I in my middle teens, he was the parent who disciplined me. Still I thought of him as a chum, even though he could dish out a whopper of a scolding with his foghorn voice. Perhaps he seemed like a chum because he never got mad when I played practical jokes on him. Like the winter day when I happened to notice, during school recess, that Dad had parked his car on the street outside the school. I ambled over, took a look. Sure enough, the keys were inside. So I locked all the car doors. Just to guarantee that he wouldn't get absolutely furious, I made sure the ventilator window tilted open a crack so he could work his way into the car.

Dad continued to teach me "boy" stuff: how to mow around trees with his huge old lawn mower, how to hold a hammer, the difference between a flathead and a Phillips-head screwdriver. One day, after explaining how car engines worked, he gave me a lawn mower engine.

"Same principle as a car," he said. "I've got a dollar that says you can't take it apart."

That was an easy dollar. I soon spread parts over the garage floor.

After he paid me, Dad said, "Now I've got another dollar and this one says you can't put it together."

That was tougher. I got everything together but the pistons. I knew where they went, but I just couldn't make them go there.

"You win," I said.

He examined my almost-built engine. "No, I don't. Takes a special tool to get those pistons in there." He removed the silver clip from his stack of bills, peeled off a dollar, and handed it to me. "Want to help me build a boat?"

This must be another joke, I thought, but no. Looking forward to fishing on the huge lake, Dad started to build a motor boat from plans that he had purchased in a kit. He spent long hours in the garage, often with me by his side, as we worked together on his boat. I started hundreds of screws, and he finished them off.

What good times! I still remember the smell of wood shavings and the sound of his jaunty whistle.

The Glockenspiel

On June 10, 1952, the corps dedicated its $45-million not-yet-finished dam and reservoir.

The all-day celebration drew almost ten thousand people from the Republican River valley. Traffic clogged highways.

A huge parade in Alma kicked off the day-long celebration. A color guard led a march of eleven bands, twenty-eight floats, a drum and bugle corps, ten saddle clubs, a fire department truck, and a line of huge construction trucks used to build the dam.

My sister, Margaret, led the Alma High School band.

My sister, Margaret, led the Alma High School band. I marched with it and carried a heavy glockenspiel, its bulky musical keyboard shaped like a lyre. When I hit its steel keys with a mallet, a bright bell-like tone sliced through the air.

As we neared the end of the hour-long march, I spotted Dad standing in the crowd, his hat and face clearly visible above other heads. Afterward, I scampered to him. "How'd I do?"

"Oh, you were terrific!" A smile played across his face. "Everyone was out of step but you."

In July, we watched gigantic machines eat trees to clear the basin valley.

Then in December, the corps finished the Harlan County dam right on schedule.

Or almost. Engineers still had to plant the last fish in the reservoir. So they did, for a total of more than 150,000 crappie, bass, catfish, bullheads, walleye, perch, drum, and blue gills.

The lake backed up a dozen miles behind the dam, winding in and out of sixty miles of shoreline. Dad could hardly wait to test his just-finished boat.

I was still fifteen that early May 1953 when we launched the big wooden boat. Out across the huge Harlan County reservoir we spun! I took my turn riding on the flat surfboard Dad towed behind his boat. How I loved the speed and the spray!

"Faster, faster," I screamed, and Dad would rev his big engine up, watch me fly across the glimmering water.

Then he cut the engine and grinned as my board slowly submerged, and I fought immersion.

DARK-HORSE CANDIDATE

Daniel Tobin, for forty-five amazing years the stiff-necked, bull-voiced IBT president, had resigned. He nominated as his replacement tall, portly, redheaded Dave Beck, a logical choice. Beck, an organizational genius from

Seattle, already had supplanted President Tobin as the real power in the union.

However, in the wings stood the election's dark-horse candidate: Jimmy Hoffa. He hadn't been strong enough to tip the balance of the 1947 national Teamsters' conference. By 1952, he was.

Jimmy's Midwestern friends pushed him to go for the top. "You've won as much for us as Beck has for his Westerners," they argued.

The Little Guy had longed to capture the Teamsters' presidency by the time he turned forty, and he was now thirty-nine. He had all his Midwestern and Southern delegates to line up against Beck's Western block. However, he hesitated.

"Timing is vital," Jimmy later said, "whether you're in a strike, a fight, or an election, and I didn't think the time was ripe for me to run for the top office." He was powerful, granted, but when he counted his votes, he saw that he was not yet a man who could not be stopped. Why risk defeat?

He decided to avoid a showdown, but he felt bitter. Beck, at fifty-eight, might remain president for the next twenty years, which would mean that time would pass by a Hoffa presidency.

Tobin, who now hinted he might run for the presidency after all, did not need Jimmy's votes. But Beck. That was another matter.

If Jimmy threw his huge block of Midwestern and Southern votes to Beck, the Westerner would be heavily in his debt. Perhaps he would agree to promote Jimmy to a vice-presidency, an especially savory plum Jimmy had been longing to pluck. Best of all, Jimmy could no doubt convince Beck that it would be in his best interests to leave Jimmy alone to run his own business.

Dave Beck, left,
and Jimmy Hoffa.

So the Little Guy emerged from the shadows, ready to help Beck topple Tobin. The two soon reached a truce. Jimmy got Beck's nomination for the vice-presidency, and Beck agreed to keep his hands off Jimmy's business.

A grateful Beck publicly declared he would be happy to step down in favor of Tobin—knowing, of course, that now he would not have to. However, in private, he argued with Tobin. Now, as he had done for years, Beck bent Tobin to his will. He forced Tobin to resign by threatening to strip Tobin of his benefits, including his pension, if he lost. Then Beck promised union funds to jump Tobin's salary, an annual salary for life, from $30,000 to $50,000 ($459,000 in 2017 dollars).

Tobin acquiesced.

For his final humiliation, Tobin endorsed Beck for president, declaring, "There is not the slightest stain on his character. His conscience, I am sure, shines brilliantly in the eyes of God."

The Teamsters elected Beck unanimously. They roared.

"That fat cocksucker," Jimmy told an aide, "he's got no more business being a general president of the Teamsters than a fucking pig."

Jimmy won his vice-presidential election, and at thirty-nine became the youngest man ever elected to the IBT's executive board. That put Jimmy just where he wanted to be. And in good time: the Teamsters had just okayed moving IBT headquarters from Indianapolis, Indiana, to Washington, DC.

Now he could tackle bigger things: how to wrest the presidency from his "good friend" Beck.

However, before Jimmy could do that, he had to mop up one other stubborn Midwestern state that still harbored pockets of unorganized drivers—Nebraska. My father's firm, Coffey's Transfer Company, was one of the Nebraska trucklines in Jimmy's way.

THE ORNERY COFFEY BOYS

At the August 1951 Coffey reunion when I was fourteen, I stood "holding my horses" near the big ice cream churn. Beside me, my father and my wild aunt Mabel talked. Dad stood tall. "I've decided to run for senator." He lifted up on his heels.

Mabel swatted my dad. "Go on! Senator? You fixing to move to Washington, DC?"

"No, no." Dad hooked his thumbs in his belt loops. "Just down to Lincoln. The state legislature."

"Why, Tom!" Mabel squealed. "What do you want to do that for?"

"Well, I've gotten mighty tired of being on the outside looking in. I'm hankering to be on the inside, looking out."

Just then, Uncle Elmer stopped churning and started dipping ice cream, so I paid no more attention to Dad and Mabel.

As usual, the annual Coffey gathering took place on one of the Coffey farms, but the reunion had gotten smaller. Folks had died, and that Denver crowd hadn't come this year. I missed them, especially Uncle Vic, he was such a devil. I remember running to his wife, Rose, hollering, "He's going to put a worm down my neck." Vic, not far away, waved his fist and grinned.

"Come here." Rose grabbed me and held me tight. "I won't let him." She whispered in my ear. "Besides, he doesn't really have a worm. He's just pretending."

But I liked Rose's warm lap, not as bony as Mama's, so I stayed put until Vic went away.

This year's reunion felt strange because my ugly great-aunt Nell wasn't sitting on a chair banging her cane. She had died a couple years ago. Boy, she used to scare the bejeebers out of me. A big old woman, she sat in that chair, and every time she wanted anything, she'd pound her cane and one of my ornery great-uncles would come running.

Might be Charley. If he caught you, he'd tickle you and say, "Gotta keep the sunny side up."

Or Art. He had just one leg, and if you came up to him and asked, "How are you, Art," he'd grin his big grin and say, "I can't kick."

Or George. He could wrap a handkerchief around his hand, put the head of a spike in his palm, grip it with two fingers, and drive it through the side of a barn with a single blow. I tried it. It hurt!

Or Sam. He was just a kid when he fell on a scythe and cut his foot off at the ankle joint. He wore a regular shoe stuffed in the front. One day in school he noticed a girl watching him. He reached down, grabbed the toe of his shoe, turned it round and around. She fainted, he claimed.

All these ornery boys looked after great-aunt Nellie, but I was afraid to look at her: she had very little hair, and what was left she parted in the middle and slicked down on either side. Her voice was big and growly, but the great-uncles waited on her as though she was the queen of Sheba.

"You gotta understand," my father told me, "Nellie had nine brothers, my dad and uncles. She was the only girl. And she spent her life taking care of those ornery Coffey boys. She helped birth their babies, nurse their sick ones, moving from home to home. Their children curled on Nell's lap, she bandaged sore toes, romped with the kids in the yard. She loved to laugh and to tease. So when she fell mortally ill, those ornery Coffey boys left their homes, their businesses, their farms, their jobs to sit up with her."

When Dad finished talking, I went back for seconds on ice cream.

BUFFALO BILL

In that winter of 1952, my dad did file to run for state senator in the Nebraska legislature. Shortly after, he piled Mama, Margery, and me in the car and drove to Lincoln, Nebraska, about 185 miles northeast. Margaret couldn't come. She was enrolled in my folks' old alma mater, Hastings College. I missed her, but all the way Margery and I played car games, the way Margaret and I used to do. We played "how many out-of-state license plates can you spot?"

As we drew closer to Lincoln, we played "who can spot the state capitol first?"

Like Dad, we both loved to win.

Nebraska has a beautiful capitol, tall and lean, its white limestone walls and gold dome sparkling in the sun. I loved watching us move closer and closer until I made out the huge "The Sower" statue, rising high as three tall men above the dome, a statue of a man bending and sewing seed from a bag.

As we entered the capitol, my footsteps echoed across the marble mosaic floor and a hush fell over me. Beside me stretched colorful mosaic murals of Native Americans and pioneers. When we reached the rotunda, light poured down on us from the edges of the celestial dome. But Dad, intent on showing us the legislature in session, didn't want to linger, rubbernecking.

We entered the west chamber. There used to be an east and west chamber, in the old days when Nebraska had a bicameral legislature with a Senate and a legislature like everyone else in the United States. Then our beloved Senator George Norris lobbied for a single house. He wore out two sets of tires driving around the state as he campaigned. He convinced Nebraska voters, so since 1937, Nebraska is the only state with a single house or Unicameral legislature.

We watched the senators, dressed in black business suits. They sat at long rows of boxy wooden desks, shuffling papers or ignoring thick stacks of bound volumes. Some hung about talking to one another in low voices.

When Mama saw Dad talking to a couple of senators, she whisked Margery and me away to the capitol museum where we gazed at a display of bones that had been excavated south of Alma.

I knew about these bones. When plans to build the Harlan County dam became official, university archeologists and paleontologists began scurrying all around areas that would be excavated or that water would cover.

The scholars hoped to find prehistorical bones.

They did find Native American bones. They found bodies in an old Sioux campground where US troops killed Native Americans right before the settlers came. The diggers also found an Indian burial ground. Pawnee, they thought. At least the body had been buried the way the Pawnee usually buried their dead.

That burial ground lay near a massive cottonwood tree, some said the largest tree in Nebraska. The tree measured nearly forty feet around. Spotted Tail, a Sioux, said his ancestors camped under the great tree "many moons" before he was born and had held the tree in reverence. Settlers revered it, too, calling it one of creation's great wonders.

The burial ground and the site of the cottonwood tree weren't far from the cave where my hero, Buffalo Bill, once slept. He wrote all about it, in his Colonel William F. Cody autobiography.

When he was about my age, fifteen, and before he'd killed a gazillion buffalo, he and a friend were fur trapping down by the Republican River, and their ox got killed, and then Bill broke his leg. His friend left for help, but the nearest fort was 125 miles away, and winter was on them. Bill waited in this cave all by himself. He barely made it out with his life!

Down by the Republican River, you could still see Buffalo Bill's cave and the Pawnee burial ground for the price of a hayrack ride through the cottonwoods. I begged and begged to go, but Mama said it cost too much, and besides Buffalo Bill never slept in that cave.

"Oh, Mama, sure enough, he wrote all about it, how he broke his leg and the nearest fort was a hundred and twenty-five miles away."

"The nearest fort. That would have been Fort Kearney, and it's only sixty miles away. That's the way Buffalo Bill exaggerates. Do you see that? The way he blew that up all out of proportion."

"But he couldn't go for help, even if it was only sixty miles. He broke his leg."

"Oh, Marilyn. Just because you read something in a book doesn't mean it's true."

"But the folks with the hayrack say you can still see the cave where he slept."

"Think of it this way, Marilyn. Buffalo Bill and the hayrack people are just like your father. You may love them, but you can't believe everything they say."

And that was that.

I got to see the bones anyway, standing there in the capitol museum. They were sort of dun colored, and one lady skeleton curled up under glass as though she'd just laid down to sleep.

I thought about what Mama said. Maybe the hayride people and Buffalo Bill lied, but I knew for sure I couldn't trust Dad.

I'd learned that when I was about four, the spring he kept talking about catching the Easter bunny. Seemed like every time I turned around, he was rolling his eyes and chanting, "I'm going to get him! I'm going to get him! Going to catch that Easter bunny."

My older sister, Margaret, didn't seem too concerned, so I paid no attention to Dad. I knew that an Easter bunny would come in the night and hide Easter eggs and candy. It did that every year.

But the next morning, Easter morning, I knelt in the dining room looking for eggs hidden under Mama's pretty wooden desk. Then all of a sudden I heard the back door slam and Dad cry out, "I got him! I got him! I got the Easter bunny!"

Dad entered the dining room, dangling a squirming white rabbit by its ears. I burst into tears, got to my feet, walked over to them, and kicked dad in the shins.

Then Margaret, smarter, grabbed the rabbit and plopped it on her lap, where—bang—it defecated, and Mama kept saying, "It's not really the Easter bunny, honey, it's just a rabbit," so I stopped kicking Dad. But I knew I could no longer trust him, even though he built a big rabbit hutch and gave the bunny to Margaret.

The Campaign Trail

When Dad hit the campaign trail, we traipsed along behind him, listening to his speeches.

"I'll do everything in my power to stop wasteful and unnecessary expenditures of public funds," he promised over and over. "I'll hold the line on your taxes."

People applauded, and I felt proud at how distinguished Dad appeared, even with dark bushy eyebrows. He wore a brand new suit: a gray double-breasted business model.

"As your senator," Dad looked potential voters right in their eyes, "you will know where I stand and why."

And he swore that just because he was a trucker he'd never vote against the railroads.

I wanted to believe every word Dad said, but I couldn't, although I couldn't tell which words were true and which not.

The primary election, held on April Fools' Day during ideal weather, chalked up a record number of voters. Dad drew 3,024 votes to Hamilton's 1,456, Ferguson's 834, and Hodge's 517. This meant that, in the general election, Dad would run against the other top vote getter, Frank Hamilton of McCook.

Carl Curtis, the Republican candidate for Congress, also won. In a few more years, he would become Dad's strongest ally in trying to undercut Jimmy Hoffa's power.

The fight ratcheted up as the November election approached. By the end of October, pundits expected a clean sweep for the Republicans in the November 4, 1952, election. They were right. Dwight D. Eisenhower beat Adlai Stevenson, sweeping the nation for Republicans. Dad won, too, with 1,926 votes to Hamilton's 864.

TRUCKLOAD FRICTION

From the opening of the Nebraska legislature's sixty-fifth session in 1953, Dad specialized in roads, as befitted a trucker.

But when radio commentator Stan Matzke, station KRVN, Lexington, Nebraska, broadcast Dad's secret-session vote to kill a bill, Dad fought back. "Matzke's broadcast of our secret votes is a flagrant and deliberate violation of legislative rules."

What a flurry of newspaper editorials Dad's comments caused! They brought the new senator a modicum of notoriety, but nothing to match the amount of fame Senator Joe McCarthy now received. He staged many well-publicized investigations, including his now famous Army-McCarthy hearings. Considered pompous and condescending, McCarthy stood near the peak of his disgrace.

Senator Coffey at his desk in the Unicameral.

That spring, Dad kicked off a debate about truckloads.

A controversial bill, LB 114, sponsored by my father, would boost the required maximum weight of Nebraska truckloads higher than current limits. Large trucks like those Coffey's Transfer used would have even higher limits.

Opposition formed immediately.

State Highway Engineer L. N. Ress placed copies of his letter against LB 114 on the desk of every legislator. It said the increase in truckloads would increase costs. "As truck weight mounts," Ress wrote, "the damage to highways increases in geometric proportion."

Dad took the floor and waved the letter. "That's just so much tommyrot. Nothing but half-truths and almost deliberate lies. If the highway department would spend as much time building roads as they do lobbying, maybe we'd have some decent roads in this state."

The *Omaha World-Herald* jumped into the fight. "Coffey," its editorial noted, "as a chief representative for the trucking industry, shouldn't be fighting for this bill. Everyone had a right to fight for his own business. However, as a senator, when Coffey goes down the line for the trucking industry's program, he can scarcely criticize those who stand up for the public interest."

Dad, in turn, accused the newspaper of trying to "crucify the trucking industry."

"Coffey has grown a little over-excited," the editors replied, "almost hysterical about his legislative program."

Governor Robert B. Crosby vetoed the controversial bill, but on July 12, Dad mustered enough votes to pass the bill over the governor's veto. Then Dad rose. "It's my birthday today, and never have I received a nicer birthday present." This infuriated his opponents.

One snorted, "Tom Coffey's 'birthday present' is going to cost Nebraskans millions of dollars' worth of highway repair."

Despite the hullabaloo, Dad felt restless. Already my father's business had succeeded enough to make him semiretired. He became a rabid golfer and fisherman, heading to the lake in his boat whenever the sun shone.

So why not retire completely? He could sell Coffey's Transfer Company, live off the interest, and throw his hat into the state

Governor Robert B. Crosby of Nebraska.

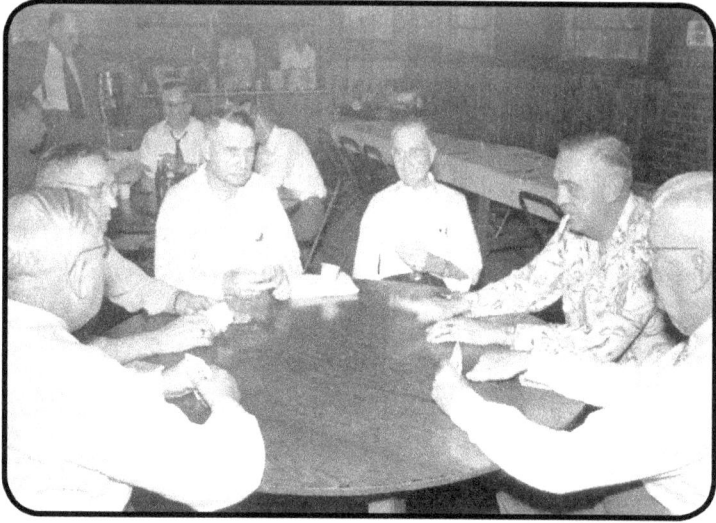

Dad (in print shirt) plays cards with his Senate buddies.

They show their Minnesota lake catch (Dad at right).

ring, run for governor. That way, he would not have to fight another round with that damnable Jimmy Hoffa and his Teamsters.

So he hired Mr. Powell, a Lincoln attorney, to negotiate a sale of the truckline. Dad told Powell not to sell under $100,000. That would provide him with interest enough to see him through the first round. Surely, Coffey's Transfer Company would be worth that.

BACK EAST—McCARTHY

A foul wind blew in from the East Coast in the spring of 1954, and its name was Senator Joseph McCarthy. He arrived with Dad's new television set. We stared at Joe's black hair, his heart-shaped forehead, and his round jowls. We marveled at his audacity in declaring that the US Army was riddled with communists. Hollywood may have crumbled under Joe's charges, but not the army, not with General Eisenhower at the helm.

As we listened, I noticed a slender young guy with thick tousled hair who brought papers to McCarthy's attention. "Who's that?"

"That?" Dad leaned forward and squinted. "Oh, that must be one of Joe's helpers, probably a counsel."

"Counsel?" I wrinkled my nose. "What's that?"

"Like a lawyer, only cheaper." An advertisement filled the screen. "Turn that volume down, will you?"

I walked to the TV and twisted a knob. "That better?"

"That's fine."

I waited, knowing that Dad would want me to twist the volume knob back up as soon as Joe came back on.

Joe McCarthy's counsel was Robert "Bobby" Kennedy, twenty-eight, one of Joe Kennedy Sr.'s boys. While Bobby assisted Joe in the Army/McCarthy hearings, the older, more glamorous Kennedy, thirty-seven, now Senator John Kennedy, railed about communist pressure in Indochina, "the blunt truth," in a speech to the Senate.

The Red Scare raged. Communists popped up everywhere, one under every rug, it seemed. Investigators blacklisted Hollywood stars, accused Democrats, and ratcheted up terror about the gazillion communists overseas. Joe McCarthy alone had held 169 anticommunist hearings during one of the two years Bobby worked for him.

Bobby looked congenial, though some folks said he had a short temper. Others claimed his sincere Roman Catholicism imbued him with high moral standards. Nobody knew yet, of course, that Bobby's investigations would open a path my father would walk to get back at Jimmy Hoffa.

A Bolt of Lightning

In the spring of 1954, Dad filed for reelection to the legislature from the thirty-third district. However, before he could campaign, he staggered under a sharp, stabbing, incapacitating throb on the right side of his face. It struck like a lightning bolt. When it stopped, he felt as though someone had smacked him with a hot poker.

When the pain erupted again, the shocks came in clusters, and the clusters repeated themselves over the course of the day. Soon he realized that any little thing could set off an attack: smiling, talking, kissing, shaving, or combing his hair. Before long, he dreaded even stepping outdoors for fear a gentle breeze might ignite the excruciating pain.

Naturally, Dad consulted his family doctor, William C. Bartlett, MD, who had been doctoring in Alma for fifty years.

"Trigeminal neuralgia," Dr. Bartlett said, "or tic douloureux. Usually caused by pressure on the largest cranial nerve." He prescribed pain medicine.

The medicine modulated Dad's pain a bit, but it didn't stop it. Nor did it stop the attacks. Nothing stopped them but sleep, so Dr. Bartlett recommended that Dad visit the famed Mayo Clinic in Rochester, Minnesota.

Dad went.

"It's odd," the Mayo doctor said, "that you even have tic douloureux. It's an old folks disease. I mostly treat people in their sixties or seventies and usually women, not men under fifty like you."

Dad was forty-nine.

"It's one of the most unbearable nerve disorders known to humans," the doctor said, "certainly more painful than a migraine headache, even more painful than childbirth."

The Mayo doctors recommended the surgery.

"If I don't go under the knife?" Dad asked.

"You can expect the attacks to last for weeks, or even months. And you can expect them to recur, oftener as you age."

The doctors set a date for surgery in a few more days.

Dad returned to his room in the Kahler Hotel, determined to wait until his appointment. However, as he experienced another cluster of attacks, he walked over to the window and looked out, then down. His room was on the top floor. As he stood looking at the street, he thought about jumping.

It wasn't just the tic douloureux, terrible as it was, that drew Dad to the edge. It was the Teamsters. How benign they had seemed in 1929 when Dad started driving his cattle truck to Omaha. Then they seemed pretty much what they claimed to be, a bunch of horse handlers, men who drove teams of horses, men that were just starting to switch over to the newfangled trucks. He heard about them on the Omaha docks. They hardly seemed to be people to make him worry.

But in the late 1930s, he heard about terrible union fights, mostly in Detroit. From what he could tell, these Teamsters, now driving trucks, tried to unionize just about everything on wheels—even the trucks that drove new cars out of Detroit. And it wasn't just working men against employers, it was union men against each other, with baseball bats and knives and even pistols. One driver said he could hardly walk down Detroit's streets without having to step aside from clenched union guys rolling over and over, fighting.

The level of violence chilled Dad. Sometimes men were killed, but then it had seemed far away from Coffey's Transfer.

Not so now. True, Jimmy had not bothered him for several years, but Dad knew the little guy had crept closer and closer to Nebraska. And right along with Jimmy moved his gangsters.

He sent two of those blackguards to Wichita, Kansas, to help organize some resistant taxicab companies. Dad knew one gangster, Richard Kavner, a gun-toting convicted felon who sat in on Dad's 1947 negotiations with Jimmy. Gus

Strickland swore he didn't trust Kavner as far as he "could throw a bull by the tail."

The scuttlebutt said that Kavner teamed up with Jimmy's toughest hoodlum, Robert B. "Barney" Baker. Baker was a twice-convicted 325-pound thug who had been a prizefighter, a strong-arm man on New York docks, a bouncer.

Jimmy considered both Kavner and Baker his personal boys, working together settling the Wichita cab drivers' strike by dynamite bombings and by dumping cabs in the Arkansas River.

Dad knew this pair had been checking out Omaha, hooking up with local mobsters there. How much longer could he hope that he could keep hiding in Alma? This Kavner-Baker duo felt like a noose growing smaller and smaller.

THE ODD EXODUS

Strangely enough—and his doctors agreed—Dad's tic douloureux disappeared as swiftly as it had appeared. He went to sleep, ready to face surgery, but the next day, he woke free of pain. I imagine he rose gingerly, expecting that any untoward movement would raise the ogre. However, nothing did.

He dressed delicately, not wanting to set anything off, and he didn't. The change of air as he moved from his hotel room to the hall, from the hall to the elevator, from the elevator to the hotel dining room did not cause even a twitch. He probably could not believe that he was past it all, that his nerve had somehow mysteriously restored itself.

I suppose he found himself hungry. He liked a big breakfast: two sunny–side up eggs, bacon, toast, hash browns, and coffee. The works. How gently he must have cut his food, bitten and chewed, expecting another cluster of attacks to resume soon. Eventually he must have noticed that he had just spent a longer time pain-free than he had since his attacks began.

He canceled the surgery and drove back to Alma, pain-free all the way.

As the days passed, he probably thought about the pain less and less. However, expecting the tic douloureux to reappear, he asked the secretary of state to remove his name from the general election ballot. His request came four days past the withdrawal deadline so the November ballot listed his name.

Don Thompson, McCook stockman and feeder, Dad's rival in the Senate race, speculated that Dad had pretended to be ill. "Coffey really withdrew because he lost the September primary and knew he would lose the general election," Thompson claimed.

True, the spring primary vote, during Dad's Rochester stay, had come down in Thompson's favor, 2,850 to 2,588. But Dad's illness had been real. Choosing not to campaign, he lost the general election by 3,501 votes with Thompson's 6,072 to Dad's 2,571. My father's career as a senator was over.

Soon something more important was on his mind. The Teamsters had called. Jimmy Hoffa wanted to discuss a contract with him.

7

THE STRIKE

One fine summer morning in 1955, a 325-pound man in a brand new, bright red Cadillac convertible skimmed his way over the long straightaway between Holdrege and Alma, Nebraska.

On the seat beside him lay his shotgun, cleaned, primed, and ready to go. He might have been a hunter, but he wasn't. He was Barney Baker, forty-four, Brooklyn kid turned labor goon.

Barney must have yawned as he drove the last leg of his 250-mile journey from Omaha. His orders from Jimmy Hoffa: to organize Coffey's Transfer Company, headquartered in Alma. *Alma! Crapola! Why hadn't Coffey set up*

Robert "Barney" Baker,
leg breaker and Jimmy's gofer.

shop in Omaha? But no, he had to plunk down his base in a two-bit town perched along a major truck route, a town that watches rigs spin by, hoping to catch a half-dozen drivers for its diner, a dozer for its motel.

Crikey! Barney shifted in his seat and blinked; *this flat land could lull a man to sleep.* He felt the rattle of the railroad crossing as he barreled into town.

Don and Dad cut across Main Street, Don, short, almost chubby, and blond; Dad, tall, well-packed, with bushy black hair.

They noticed a fire-engine–red convertible turn onto Main from the highway across town.

"Who can that be?" Don pushed his glasses up.

Dad shrugged. "Some out-of-towner. Want to bet it isn't?"

"You forgot, Tom. I'm not bettin' you anymore."

As the convertible neared, Dad glimpsed the yellow plate with its black numeral "1" and grinned. *A number one plate definitely belonged to an out-of-towner, probably from Omaha.*

The Cadillac's pointed tail fins flashed by. Dad watched the car park in front of Bud's Cafe. Then he unlocked the door of his modest rectangular brick office building. He and Don went to their desks. The secretary would arrive soon. And a pack of drivers.

"Not on My Time"

Shortly after, Dad heard tires squeal. Glancing through his window, he watched that fire-engine–red convertible pull into the parking space right in front of his office. Out of the car stepped a huge blubbery man with shiny pomaded hair. His clothes hung on him; a wilted shirt collar flapped outside his suit jacket.

By the time the strange fellow sauntered in, Dad waited behind the office counter.

"Barney Baker." He offered Dad a pudgy hand. "Hayadooin?" They shook. "Hey, Boss. Hoffa sent me. I'm the one to organize all the Nebraska lines for him."

Hoffa moving into Nebraska was not good news. "So?"

"Not for nuttin' am I here to tell you that the Teamsters have organized your men. We now represent them."

"Really?" *Twenty-two drivers work for my transfer company, and not one has mentioned the union, not the single driver in Lincoln, the two in Holdrege, the seven in Omaha, or the twelve in Alma.*

"Then prove it." Dad's eyes narrowed. "Bring your pledge cards with a bona fide signature of each man you claim to represent." *They can't or won't do it. Hoffa likes working top down, as he did when we met in '47.*

Barney shifted his weight, mopped his brow with a chubby hand.

Those cauliflower ears of his are impressive.

The organizer looked around the office, then crossed his arms. "Yo, I'm holding a meetin' of yo' guys on yo' dock at ten a.m."

Ten o'clock! Right when we'll be fightin to get out freight orders.

"Not on my time you're not holding any meetings." Dad pushed back his shoulders. "Why don't you just leave."

He stepped from behind the counter and took Barney by the arm. Dad stood six feet two, tall enough to look the organizer in the eye, but he felt stunted alongside the huge Teamster. To Dad's amazement, when he showed Barney the door, he left without a word.

SCUTTLEBUTT

Dad walked over to his office phone, kept on his secretary's desk. He lifted the heavy black receiver and dialed his kid brother Glen, office manager in the Omaha terminal.

Glen, now thirty-six to Dad's forty-eight, answered. "Yes?"

"Are those Teamsters still wooing your drivers?"

"Those fuckers!" Glen's voice wavered. "I can't stand the sight of them, smooth talkers in their flashy new cars."

"But that's all they're doing, just cruising around and talking. Right?"

"Yeah." Glen paused. "Why?"

"Well," Dad spoke in a flat voice. "This guy shows up here, says Hoffa sent him. Wanted to meet with my drivers."

"Did you let him?"

"Hell, no. I showed all four hundred pounds of him to the door."

"Four hundred pounds!" Glen laughed. "Sounds like that bunghole Barney Baker."

"Yeah, that's his name."

"God, Tom, don't you know who that sleaze ball is? Scum of the earth! Stink-bomb tosser, ex-con, bouncer, professional boxer. Christ, Tom, you're lucky he didn't trash your office."

"I believe you. But he didn't bring a gun. If he'd wanted to play rough, he'd of brought a piece with him, wouldn't he?"

"I don't know, Tom. He's so big he could pitch you across the room if he felt like it. Weren't you afraid?"

"The scariest thing Barney said to me was that Hoffa wants him to organize Nebraska's trucklines."

"Christ! I wonder what we're in for." Glen cleared his throat. "Scuttlebutt has it that the Teamsters shifted Barney up here to Omaha after doing Teamster dirty work got too hot for him in Wichita and Kansas City. Barney's working for Hoffa now." Glen's voice dropped. "We got to be careful, Tom."

LIKE AN OPEN SPILLWAY

Six weeks after he'd shown Barney the door, Dad fingered an envelope from the Teamsters, their two-horse logo printed in bright blue. *Damn. Might as well get it over with*, and he slit the envelope open.

Bert Parker's words leaped off the page. The boss of the Omaha local wrote, "Your employees have chosen Omaha Teamsters Local 554 as their collective bargaining agent. We stand ready, willing, and able to meet with you at any reasonable time."

He sounds so rational. What a mask! He's really demanding that I bargain with the Teamsters.

Parker gave Dad three business days to respond. On the morning of third day, Tuesday, August 23, he called local 554. "I'm willing to meet," Dad told Parker. "But you must bring proof that the Teamsters represent the majority of my drivers."

Then he called Glen who sometimes seemed more like a son than a brother. Dad had been the oldest, Glen the youngest of his folks' six kids, all boys. When their parents' deaths left Glen, then eighteen, alone on the farm, Dad took his kid brother under his wing.

"What's Parker like?" Dad asked Glen.

"The bastard's an old-time trucker, like you. Used to make runs to Kansas City or North Platte back when the top-notch roads were gravel. He's pretty old. Come to think of it, the bugger must be as old as you!" Glen's laughter resonated in the receiver.

"How old's that, smarty-pants, 106? 107?"

"Christ, Tom, you should know."

Dad could hear Glen hiccupping.

"That's what I get for hiring a wet-behind-the-ears brother for my manager."

"What's that?"

"Never mind." Dad rubbed the back of his neck. "Is that all you know about Parker?"

"Ya don't need to worry, Tom. Parker's a quiet motherfucka, hardly ever raises his voice. Talks so other people can understand him, not a whole bunch of gobbledygook."

So maybe meeting Parker would be better than watchin' cocky Jimmy Hoffa bound into the room, flashin' his toothy smile, rollin' up his sleeves to show off his big forearm muscles, trying to give me a knuckle-shattering handshake. No way could anybody talk to him. His mouth was like an open spillway, always flowing.

"CHIEF, YOOZE IN THE WAY"

At meeting time, that familiar red Cadillac convertible, top down, pulled in front of Dad's office. Blubbery Barney held the wheel, while an unfamiliar man, probably Parker, occupied the passenger seat, and Gus Strickland, the big wheel of the Teamsters' mid-Nebraska local, held down the backseat. *Tagging along as usual.*

Dad had known Gus for years. Two of Dad's offices lay under Gus's dominion, but Dad's Coffey's Transfer had little to do with Gus's huge local. It ranged from Kansas to South Dakota and cut a hundred-mile swath across central Nebraska.

Dad walked the three union officials through his outer office, which used to be Dad's entire work space until he added two new large private rooms. One held a conference table. Dad led the men there.

Through the room's large interior window, Dad could see Don at his desk in the outer officer, and Don could see him. "Keep your eye on us," Dad'd told Don. "If there's any funny business, call our poor excuse for a sheriff. See what he can do."

Barney started to sit in a chair with arms, then thought better of it. Parker sat at the head of the table, Gus at the foot, so Dad faced Barney.

Parker introduced Barney, making sure Dad knew that Jimmy Hoffa himself had sent Barney to Nebraska.

Dad couldn't resist: "Is it true what they say, that Jimmy's living it up in Washington, DC, now?"

"I wouldn't say living it up." Parker scowled. "But now that he's vice-president, he does have a private office in our Washington, DC, headquarters."

Barney gushed. "In our Marble Palace, that's what folks call it." He leaned toward Dad, his eyes wide. "Hoffa has a private elevator just for him, a splendid view, and somebody buffs his door knobs every night until they gleam." Barney thrust out his big chest.

Parker frowned. "Barney is in charge of organizin' the state. When we're done, nonunion truck drivers won't be able to pick up or deliver any freight in Omaha."

Barney nodded, then tossed two contracts to Dad. "Yo, Big Boss, Hoffa sez sign 'em."

"We negotiated these contracts with the Small Carriers Association." Parker leaned forward. "Know them?"

Dad nodded. "For small truckers like me." *I never joined.*

He looked at the covers. Both contracts took effect last February and would run out January 21, 1961; one was for over-the-road drivers and the other for local dockworkers who also drove. Judging from the contracts he and Jimmy argued about for days in 1947, Dad had a pretty good idea what Barney's contracts covered.

"This is no weasel deal, Boss." Barney shifted on his too-small chair.

"Barney's right." Parker nodded. "Hoffa made special concessions for the Small Carriers Association. When you sign these contracts, you'll have all those concessions too."

"Sure thing," Barney leaned back. "Dollars to donuts."

"They're right, Tom," Gus whispered. "You better listen to them."

High time to change the subject. "Did you bring proof that you represent my men?"

Barney twisted so he could stick his chubby hand into his pants pocket. He pulled out a fistful of signature cards and spun them across the table.

Dad caught the cards and counted them. Seven signed cards requested Teamster representation. Seven of his twenty-two drivers. He recognized every name. Four Omaha dockworkers, one Lincoln dockworker, and two over-the-road-drivers from Alma. *The Alma cards looked fishy; those signatures weren't familiar.* He heard Parker mention "withdrawal cards." *What does that mean?* Dad pocketed the seven cards, and pushed the two contracts back across the table to Barney.

"Breaking the devil's dishes!" Barney let the contracts lie. "Hoffa's not goin' to like this."

"I can't sign these." Dad's nostrils flared. "I have twenty-two drivers, so these seven cards are only a third of them. You know you need signatures from fifty-one percent of my men before you can claim to represent them legally."

Barney shrugged. "Dat don' make no difference."

"Barney's right," Parker gave a crisp nod. "The fact that we signed up only seven men doesn't make a difference. We didn't have the time to sign up more of your men."

"Dat don' matter." Barney shrugged. "Hoffa sez weeze gonna organize yoo from the top down." He drew a line with his forefinger from his forehead to his belly as though he had filleted a trout.

Dad rose. "Let's take a break." He headed out and the Teamsters followed. When they returned to the conference table, Dad had decided not to mention his drivers' signature cards. *Who knew what Parker meant by "withdrawal cards."*

He wouldn't mention the 1947 Taft-Hartley Act, either. He couldn't remember his rights. He knew the act gave him some bargaining powers that unions used to have. That's why Truman—and the unions—called the Taft-Hartley a "slave-labor bill." But Dad had forgotten the details, something about the right of an employer not to bargain with a union, and he had no lawyer present.

So Dad turned the discussion to the two contracts. He explained to Barney how Coffey's Transfer Company operated and why signing the Teamster contracts wouldn't be cost-effective. Their conversation rolled on and on. Sometimes it escalated to argument. They talked for two hours.

"Yo, Hoffa got a Nebraska plan," Barney bragged, "and, Chief, yooze in the way. For all intensive purposes, we gonna organize ev'ry trucker, ev'ry warehouser, and on to storekeepers, includin' ev'ry nail salesman and ev'ry prune peddler."

Dad raised an eyebrow. "By what stretch of the imagination could a prune peddler be called a Teamster?"

"Them little carts has wheels, don' they?" Barney's lip curled. "It's nothin' personal, Boss. You just first on Hoffa's list." He pushed the contract back. "You got a clear choice. Sign up or we'll take you to the cleaners."

Dad's face reddened. "If you push me, I'll demand a consent election with the National Labor Relations Board, let my drivers vote on whether they want the Teamsters to represent them."

Barney whooped. "Chief, we ain't interested in no election."

"I'm going to insist on it." Dad pushed his shoulders back.

Barney smirked, but Parker spoke up instead, his voice calm but firm. "Do that, and we'll stall any election you might insist on until you are bankrupt anyhow."

"Yeah," Barney smirked. "We'll strangulate your operation before you ev'r get an election. We'll throw up some pickets, and you'll be wiped out before anybody votes."

"I'll take my chances." Dad rose, signaling the end of the meeting.

"That Don't Hurt Neither"

As the Alma drivers got off work that night, two of them, Arnold Peterson and Ralph Fischer, stopped by Dad's desk.

"We heard the Teamsters told ya that we'd signed their cards." Arnold leaned forward. "Well, they lied. We'd never signed nothin' for them."

Dad smiled. "I know. I could tell those signatures weren't yours."

"Damn right!" Ralph cracked his knuckles. "Why would we sign when working for you is like being part of a family?"

Arnold, smiling, turned to Ralph. "An' ya know Tom. A pat on the shoulder and he'll say, 'You did a fine job.' That's his trick."

"Come on," Ralph furrowed his brow. "What about the way he hikes our pay ever' time his freight rates go up?"

"That don't hurt neither."

They reached out brawny hands to shake.

Ain't that somethin'! Dad watched them leave. But he wasn't really surprised. He couldn't prove it, but he believed his Alma drivers stood 100 percent behind him. They were independent types like him, most of them neighbors, and some knew he was good for a down payment on a house or an interest-free loan to cover expenses of a baby or an operation.

Dad wished his Lincoln and Omaha drivers would talk to him like Arnold and Ralph. But they had not come forward, leaving him to wonder if the Teamsters had forged some of their cards too.

"Don't Mean Nothin'"

A couple of weeks passed quietly. Then on Friday, September 9, two more Teamsters came to Alma. Dad opened his office door to Barney's best buddy, gangster Richard "Dick" Kavner, and that little snitch, "Pete" Capellupo. Dad knew them both, had known Kavner since '47, when, just a little nobody, he sat in on Dad's negotiations with Hoffa. A convicted felon now, Kavner toted a gun, Dad noted. A tall man, dressed in a fine suit that bulged his buttons a bit. Probably a taste of elegance acquired from his debonair St. Louis boss, Harold Gibbons, known for $200 suits and a lavish lifestyle, all financed by Teamster dollars.

Feisty Capellupo pushed his way through the door first, acting as though he were in charge, although Dad knew him as just an official of Teamsters Local 608 in Lincoln, where he had worked since Teamsters drove horses. Or so Glen said. He also said Hoffa liked Capellupo. Their senses of humor matched. The little Italian acted as a one-way conduit, relaying to Hoffa the lowdown about Midwestern union activities. They burned up a lot of phone wire.

After they sat, Kavner spoke first. "Understand that I'm not just from local number 554 in Omaha." Kavner's voice was steady, low pitched. "I really represent Jimmy Hoffa's International."

"You know me," Capellupo piped up. "From the Lincoln local. But we're both here because Hoffa sent us."

Dad nodded and looked at the two Small Carriers Association contracts Capellupo pushed across the table. "All those concessions are in it." Capellupo furrowed his brow. "Right here."

But Dad decided to talk representation, not contracts. "Are you Teamsters planning to organize all of my drivers or just some of them?"

That set off a lengthy, and often confusing, discussion of how many drivers and what kinds of drivers the Teamsters would want in a unit.

Kavner became evasive, talking sometimes about Omaha and Lincoln drivers, then switching to just Omaha. Then he jumped to over-the-road drivers, those that drove semis from Alma to Omaha, for instance.

Eleven of Dad's thirteen over-the-road drivers drove out of Alma, and for a while, Kavner discussed them. Then he said, "We'll forget the drivers south of Alma," which made no sense; Coffey's Transfer Company had no drivers headquartered there.

What's Kavner up to? Dad couldn't figure it out. Maybe the Teamsters just wanted to make sure his combination of drivers would give the union a majority.

As the meeting ended, Kavner and Capellupo pushed Dad to sign the two Small Carriers Association contracts they'd given to him.

"No," Dad's face tightened. "I can't sign these. You don't have a majority of my drivers."

Kavner stood up, reached over the table, picked up the contracts, and shook them at Dad. "If you don't sign these, we'll hit you with a secondary boycott."

Dad stiffened. The dreaded secondary boycott, or leapfrogging, a Hoffa favorite, chops off revenue by pressuring one truckline to boycott another.

"You can't do that." Dad glared. "Secondary boycotts are illegal."

The felon's laugh sounded menacing. "Try us," Kavner sneered. "Legal, illegal—don't mean nothin' to us."

The News Chilled Him

On September 14, five days after the Teamsters threatened Coffey's Transfer Company with a secondary boycott, Dad got a morning phone call from Glen.

"You'll never guess what that arsehole did!" Glen's voice quivered.

"Converted to Catholicism?"

"This isn't funny, Tom. That weasel talked four of Clark Brothers' drivers to cut out of work and picket the truckline."

Dad stiffened. "You mean Barney struck Clark Brothers?"

"You got it." Glen inhaled deeply.

The news chilled Dad. "I wonder what that Hoffa's up to. He always used to gobble the tiny lines first, then the medium-sized guys. That made easy pickings of the few big truckers left. But Clark's not tiny, and neither am I."

Clark Brothers, a well-known truckline in northeast Nebraska, had a sizable fleet that grossed an annual revenue of $350,000. Dad's twenty-five trucks followed with $200,000 (more than a million dollars in today's figures). So the Teamsters weren't striking the smallest Nebraska carriers; the union had chosen two major lines.

"Do you think that bunghole means to take us down together?" Dad ran his fingers through his thick black hair. "I better call Foy, find out what's up."

Dad's secretary, Vera, rang W. Foy Clark in Norfolk. Dad discovered, not to his surprise, that Teamsters Local 554 had the audacity to begin its campaign against Clark without bothering to represent the line's drivers. The Teamsters hadn't even given Foy trumped-up pledge cards. Looked as though Hoffa planned to organize Clark Brothers from the top down too.

When Foy hung up, Dad stared down at the phone's receiver. The specter of a Coffey's Transfer strike gripped him. When he spoke again, he seemed to talk to himself. "Well, if I've got to join forces with another truckline to battle the Teamsters, I couldn't pick a better ally than Clark Brothers. They're decent folk. Men of their word."

But he thought, *thank God it wasn't me.*

HOFFA CORRALS BARNEY

Dad dropped the Saturday *TV Guide* and scooted into the dining room to reach his ringing wall phone. It was Glen.

"Did you catch this morning's *World-Herald*?" Glen sounded excited.

"Naw. Too busy perusin' the *TV Guide*." Dad shifted the phone's receiver to his better ear.

"What? You got live programming now?"

"No. Still nothing but test patterns."

"Jeez, Tom, we get two channels in Omaha. The new one, KMTV, is mostly news 'n' stuff. But WOW's good. They got this local kid spinning jokes. He's funny. Johnnie somebody-or-other. Carver? Carter? No, Carson. But you won't get him way out there in Alma. That's what you get for livin' in the sticks. Nothing but goddam test patterns."

"All right. Enough already. Give me a minute." Dad let the receiver dangle as he hurried into the living room, then returned with the newspaper. "Here, I've got it."

"Well, crack it open to page three."

Dad did. A photo of Barney Baker, lying on a hospital bed, spread across two columns. "He's in the hospital?" Dad stiffened.

"That's right. But don't send him any get-well cards."

Dad noticed that Barney wore, instead of a hospital gown, a dark suit with an open-collared white shirt, and he held a black phone to his ear. "What the—?"

"It's old Hoffa-Barney routine." Glen laughed. "The heat must be on Barney, 'cause whenever it is, Hoffa puts him in a hospital to keep him out of trouble. Calls it 'weight reducing.' Barney swears he's gonna lose a hundred pounds. But get this, Tom. He's living in an up-to-date hospital room; it's even got air conditioning, a television set, and a direct phone line. He's using that phone to call Omaha Teamsters. Summons them to his room for conferences."

"So he's not out of the action." Dad slumped.

"No way! And the lies he tells those newspaper boys. Listen to this: 'We've never had any rough stuff. If we can't win it clean, we don't want to win it.' Ha! Guess he forgot all about those dynamite bombings in Wichita, the ones that ran him and Kavner out of town. Or how about this one? 'I prefer gentle words.' Makes me want to stick a finger down my throat! That motherfucka couldn't pronounce a gentle word if he knew one."

"Did the *Herald* write up the Clark Brothers strike?"

"Nothing. Not a word. And zippo on the Teamsters threatening you with a secondary boycott." Glen paused. "The *Herald* did call me, some real excited reporter said Barney told him, 'If Coffey isn't here and signed up by Monday morning, we're going to strike.' Asked me to comment, so I did. I told him where that fucking Barney could go. But that reporter didn't use a prickin' thing I said."

"That cussing of yours must of burnt up the newsprint." Dad curbed a laugh.

"Come on, Tom. What fuckin' difference would my swearing make?"

"In the *Omaha World-Herald*? It's a family paper, after all."

WAGIN' A CLEAN FIGHT

Glen arrived late for work Tuesday, September 20, so he could drive his wife, Mary, to the hospital. What a careening route they'd taken, but they arrived before Mary dropped a kid on the car seat. It was their third.

He parked near the terminal and stepped out of his car before he realized that three of his drivers—James Faulhaber, William Henley, and Edward Jansa—just stood around outdoors. Then he saw the banners: "Employees of COFFEY TRANSFER ON STRIKE for union wages and conditions. General Drivers Local No. 554."

He froze. God, that fucking Barney Baker must have put them up to it. But Glen knew better than to throttle the strikers. Instead, he walked into the terminal and called Tom.

Glen, office manager, Coffey's Transfer Omaha terminal and his wife, Mary.

In Omaha early that afternoon, Dad sized up the situation. "Those men sure look legitimate with their banners and all, but they're not. They're illegal," he told Glen. "Why? Because the union doesn't represent my drivers; they just are pretending to. Did they, for instance, give you notice?"

Glen shook his head. "Fuckers just stopped working and started picketing."

"Let's see how fast we can replace them."

Dad knew enough labor law to know that he legally could replace those drivers—permanently. This outraged unions, of course. To them, replacing drivers for keeps seemed unfair; it gave the employer way too much power. Why should a trucker lose his job because he exercised his right to strike? But Congress never bought the union argument. Employers had long had the right to hire permanent replacements.

So Dad worked in the Omaha office, fishing for stand-ins. Every time he hung up the phone, Glen got on it, checking on Mary. About 2 p.m., he hung up and turned around, his face bright as a cherry. "It's a girl! They're fine. Both fine."

"God, Glen, get out of here! Go see them! Stop tying up my phone line."

"You sure you'll be all right?"

"I'm sure." Dad laughed. "Remember, I ran this office when you were in knee pants." Not knee pants in our family. Cutoff overalls. But same idea.

The door slammed behind Glen, and Dad picked up the phone again.

By the time Glen returned later that afternoon, Dad had hired three new drivers—Howard Shurts, Paul

Laughlin, and Duane Graber—on a permanent basis. Dad knew enough not to pay them one cent more than Coffey's Transfer Company had paid the striking drivers. That was illegal as was telling an employee he couldn't join a union or even, for that matter, telling him that he had no business striking. Joining a union and striking were labor's basic rights. And picketing. But not receiving a paycheck.

"Pickets at the Barns"

When Glen stepped into the office later that afternoon, he sputtered, "You will not believe what those fuckin' Teamsters did. I step out of my car to go visit Mary, and I'll be damned but I have to cross a fuckin' picket line to get into the hospital."

"Who's striking the hospital?"

"The Teamsters! The fuckin' Teamsters! Only they're not striking the hospital. All those pickets are waving COFFEY TRANSFER ON STRIKE banners. That goddamn Barney Baker, that fat slob, how dare he throw pickets up against me like that."

"Sit down, Glen. Sit down. Get ahold of yourself before you blow a gasket."

After Glen calmed down a bit, Dad asked, "So how's Mary?"

"Oh, God, Tom, you should have seen her. Big smile like giving birth was nothing. She's such a trooper. And the kid, we'd chosen her name if she was a girl, Patty Sue." Glen choked up, then continued. "Those nurses wrap the babies up so tight I could hardly see anything. But she's got a big round face and your hair."

"Black."

"Black, and a whole bunch of it to boot."

The phone rang. Dad picked it up. The one-sided conversation kept Dad listening. When he hung up, he turned back to Glen. "That was Parker. Says there are pickets at the barns. Meaning at our terminal, and the hospital, but also at the Clark Brothers' barns. I better check my other terminals." He turned back to the phone, but no one was on strike in Lincoln, Holdrege, or Alma, only Omaha. It would stay that way. The fight would play out mostly in the Omaha area.

"Nothing anywhere but here," he told Glen, "but the Teamsters are claiming they have an imaginary picket line around all my operations. A bunch of poets, those guys."

Friday, Glen arrived at work to find his usual parking space occupied. A car also blocked the Coffey's Transfer driveway, and a half-dozen parked cars rimmed the terminal.

Glen whistled. *Oh, God, Barney's imported a herd of goons.* The men in the cars did look like a bunch of hoodlums, but more alarming, they leisurely cleaned shotguns in full view of the passing traffic. They would clean shotguns—among other activities—for five long months.

"What are you doing?" Glen asked.

"It's hunting season," one answered. "We're getting ready to do some shooting."

Glen called Dad who again drove to Omaha. When he arrived and saw Barney's hired thugs, his resistance to the Teamsters hardened. *Obviously,* he thought, *Barney intends to frighten me into signing those contracts. But he doesn't know me. I'm not an easy man to scare.*

However, after the "hunters" showed up at the Coffey's Transfer terminal, Glen pocketed his pistol and rode with his drivers to Omaha terminals to pick up or receive freight.

AWE, JEEZ! MORE BUTTER

Teamster violence continued, both day and night, from late September through most of February 1956. Sometimes it flared up at a customer's dock where warehouse workers loaded a parked Coffey's Transfer truck. Other times it broke out around the Coffey terminal.

Glen no longer parked his trucks in an open lot, not with the Teamsters strong-arm squad in operation. Instead, his drivers put Coffey rigs inside Capital Garage, a public parking space in Omaha. Even that wasn't safe. The Teamsters raided a truckload of butter located inside the garage and scattered its contents, leaving it to melt on the garage floor.

Day after day, week after week, month after month, carloads of gun-cleaning men showed up. Sometimes six cars, sometimes eight. Sometimes they didn't block the driveway, so Glen could manage to get a truck pulled away from the terminal.

However, every time he did get a truck on the road, a Teamsters' car would follow it. If the Coffey truck stopped to load or unload freight, the thugs would get out of their cars, display their COFFEY TRANSFER ON STRIKE banners and picket the terminal.

After a while, the fight escalated to violence. As weeks passed, and Dad still hadn't given in, Teamsters slashed Coffey's Transfer truck tires. They yanked wiring out of truck motors. They pulled kingpins so the truck's trailer would drop. They cut the air hoses on trucks or stuffed the hoses with wadded paper so the brakes would fail. They threw bricks through the office window, poured sugar into gas tanks to gum the motors, and dynamited equipment.

Glen protected the trucks as best he could by locking the hoods, padlocking gas tanks shut, hiring guards, and following Coffey's Transfer trucks to the edge of town.

Barney, now out of the hospital, organized the strike from a Blackstone Hotel suite. His spending and eating habits became legendary. He ate gargantuan meals, paying $15 to $30 each. And drove that brand new, bright red Cadillac loaned to him by a gracious employer who'd signed a Teamsters contract.

One night Arnold Peterson, one of Dad's favorite drivers, left Omaha on his return run home to Alma. On his way, a speeding car shot past him and heaved a railroad spike at his truck. It struck the cab. Arnold stopped, walked back, and retrieved the spike. In Alma, he showed it to Dad.

Together they examined the cab. The hurtling spike had struck the cab with force enough to scar the sheet steel. Arnold pointed at the imprint. "If that spike had hit the windshield, who knows what would have happened?"

Dad knew only too well. It troubled him that Arnold had taken a personal chance to drive for Coffey's Transfer—indeed, that all of his men now took that risk.

After more time passed, the Teamsters threatened drivers and made intimidating phone calls to nearly every one of the Omaha drivers' wives. A wife would pick up the phone to hear an anonymous male voice say something like, "If you want your Johnny to get home safely after Washington Elementary lets out at three-thirty today, you better tell your old man to stop driving for Coffey." Enough men quit so that Coffey's Transfer began to work shorthanded.

Drivers' wives weren't the only ones to receive phone calls. Knowing that trucking is a twenty-four-hour business, Dad kept a phone on the nightstand beside his bed. Midnight calls from drivers stuck on the road hadn't bothered him, but the ones he got now did. The phone would ring. He'd answer, but no one replied. He heard no dial tone, so he knew someone was on the line, and he'd hang up. He'd lie awake after these calls, staring at the dark room and wondering about his future. Zelma had read articles to him about Teamster fires and dynamite in Texas, about a Tennessee trucker shot at twenty times, about $4,000 worth of truck tires slashed in an Ohio terminal.

A well-known investigative reporter, Clark R. Mollenhoff, came to town on assignment for *Look Magazine*. Mollenhoff, reputed to be a reporter as tenacious as a bulldog, specialized in exposing corrupt labor practices. He interviewed W. Foy Clark and Tom Coffey. Inch by inch, and pound by pound, Mollenhoff was a match for my father in size, and he questioned Dad in a deep booming voice.

"The Clark and Coffey officials," the reporter noted, "were frantic. The violence that plagued their operations, they said, started when the huge pistol-packing waterfront hoodlum, Barney Baker, came in to organize them."

Alarmed by so much violence, Dad had sent protest telegrams to Nebraska's governor Victor E. "Vic" Anderson and Omaha's mayor John R. "Johnny" Rosenblatt, demanding protection. Neither official replied. Dad received only a couple of snippets of sympathy in a few paragraphs in the *Omaha World-Herald*.

Omaha Mayor Johnny Rosenblatt at his desk.

Nebraska Governor Victor "Vic" Anderson.

Law enforcement felt helpless. Since most crimes were local, officials couldn't call the FBI for help. A police official stopped Dad in Omaha one day to say, "What the Teamsters are doing to you, they could do to any business in Nebraska, and we couldn't stop them."

BACK EAST—JIMMY AND "DIO"

"That fat cocksucker." Jimmy Hoffa rubbed the back of his neck. "Dave Beck's got no more business being general president of the Teamsters than a fucking pig."

"Don't wear well, huh?" Jimmy's buddy, Giovanni "Johnny Dio" Dioguardi, raised one black eyebrow.

"Damn right!" Jimmy flinched at his memory of helping Beck win the presidency in 1952. "I'm ready to topple His Majesty the Wheel off his throne—but I need a little help."

"Doing what?"

"Creating locals. They say you're damned proficient at it."

Creating phony union locals was not the only way Johnny Dio excelled. By 1955, he had become a famously corrupt Teamster leader and one of New York's most notorious gangsters. He had come into the profession honestly, following his father (executed by mobsters), his

Giovanni "Johnny Dio" Dioguardi, Jimmy's partner in crime.

uncle, and a brother into not one but two New York crime families: the Genoveses and the Luccheses.

"So you need votes." Dio twirled his chair around and returned with a large map of the New York/New Jersey area labeled New York City Teamsters, Joint Council 16. The powerful council claimed 125,000 members; it would swing plenty of weight in the upcoming 1957 Teamster election for president.

Dio spread the map on his desk. "See those red dots? Each dot is a Teamsters' local. So we could create maybe a dozen more, maybe even fifteen." He punched the map in places where the red dots lay far apart.

Jimmy beamed.

It took them the better part of a month to complete the task, but when they were done, they had created fifteen new Teamsters' locals in the Joint Council 16 area.

Dio gave each local a number, a location, and a convicted felon to lead it. Dio's gangsters included labor racketeers, bootleggers, armed robbers, black market operators, bookmakers, narcotics peddlers, gamblers, and extortionists.

And union members?

None.

These locals didn't need members. Their headmen would cast votes for Jimmy's man. In the case of Joint Council 16, that man would be John J. O'Rourke, who hoped to wrest the council chair away from its current Beck supporter, Martin T. Lacey. If O'Rourke won the election and headed the large, powerful Joint Council 16, other important councils and locals would likely join a Jimmy bandwagon, and, together, they'd topple Beck.

Nothing remained but to charter the new Teamster locals so their headmen could legally vote.

O'Rourke fought to have the "Dio locals" admitted to the Joint Council, and a major political battle broke out in the Teamsters Union over whether to admit the new locals. So Hoffa leaned on Beck, and, at last, Beck agreed to accept the new locals.

O'Rourke won the 1957 election.

Then Lacey sued, and a court decided in Lacey's favor.

After all of that, Lacey withdrew, leaving O'Rourke and Hoffa forces to take over New York.

The irony: O'Rourke would have won without a single phony local voting for him. Even worse for Jimmy, all the hullaballoo about those phony locals would open him up to charges of ties to organized crime.

Jimmy's friendship with Dio would prove to be the beginning of the Little Guy's downward course, even though he would win court battles and attain the presidency.

LEAPFROGGING

Dad flinched when he read a September *Omaha World-Herald* interview with Barney. "We Teamsters got a $36 million strike fund," Barney told reporters, "but don't you get me wrong. We're wagin' a clean fight."

However, a clean fight it was not. Besides tires punctured, kingpins pulled, air hoses cut, and spikes hurled, the Teamsters utilized Hoffa's favorite organizing tool. Hoffa called it "leapfrogging." Congress called it "secondary boycott" and outlawed it.

Leapfrogging is a tool designed to bring a truckline owner to his knees by chopping off his income. The Teamsters never smacked the owner directly; instead, the union leaped right over the owner and forced a secondary truckline to do the union's dirty work.

Truckers routinely paid other trucklines to ship goods to remote destinations. In the usual order of shipping, Clark or Coffey brought freight to secondary trucklines in Omaha to be shipped to out-of-state terminals. The Teamsters chose these secondary Omaha trucklines to boycott Clark or Coffey.

If a truckline refused to boycott Clark or Coffey, the Teamsters picketed and threatened strike, or actually did strike. But few refused. They didn't want to bring the wrath of the Teamsters down on their businesses.

Before using boycotts, Hoffa dealt with truckers like Clark and Coffey by applying direct pressure. Siccing the Mob on them. Bombing its trucks, say. The sort of thing Barney and Kavner did in Wichita when they pitched a taxicab into the river or dynamited reluctant firms.

Glen, with his pistol in his pocket, discovered the first boycott of Coffey's Transfer. When he and driver Howard Shurts stopped at the Santa Fe Trail Transportation Company to pick up freight, three employees shrugged. "Nothing today."

"This smells fishy," Glen told Howard, so they entered the office of Mr. Thomas, the terminal manager. There Howard signed freight bills as he usually did.

Thomas didn't speak. When Howard finished signing the bills, Thomas scooped them up. "Follow me."

The three walked to the Santa Fe Trail dock, where Thomas handed the bills to an employee. He pulled away, refusing to touch them. "Don't give those to me!"

"Why not?"

"Coffey's on strike."

A second worker shook his head. "The union is trying to organize Coffey's Transfer."

A third employee reached for the bills, then hesitated, and pulled away. "Look, I'd like to take them, but I don't dare."

"Why not?"

"I don't want to get in trouble with the union."

Thomas shrugged and handed the bills to Glen.

When Glen and another driver, Emil Severyn, stopped at C. A. Swanson and Sons later that day, its employees accepted Coffey's Transfer freight bills. That was a relief. Glen waited while Emil loaded their truck with help from the Swanson employees.

Then Barney Baker clomped down the dock and threw around his weight, still considerable despite his hospital stay. "Stop loading that friggin' truck!"

All work halted.

"You can't do that!" Glen shook his fist at Barney. "Secondary boycott is illegal!"

Barney laughed. "That's too damn bad. Wars start illegally too. My orders are you're to sign a contract."

"Go to hell." Glen turned and helped Emil load the Coffey truck.

COMPLAINING TO THE NLRB

Dad remembered Dick Kavner's threat to invoke just such a boycott if Dad didn't sign the contracts Kavner and Pete Capellupo waved in his face. And he knew that when the Teamsters had struck Clark Brothers on September 14, Foy Clark wasted little time in fighting back.

On Friday September 16, Clark Brothers filed a complaint against the Teamsters with the National Labor Relations Board (NLRB), a federal agency that oversees unfair labor practices. Foy blamed Omaha's local 554 for using boycotts to force him to bargain, even though the local didn't represent Clark's employees.

So on September 20, Dad joined Foy Clark and filed a similar charge with the NLRB. Dad used the same lawyer as Clark had used: Edson Smith of Swarr, May, Royce, Smith and Story.

Dad and Foy became a team, their lawyer, Smith, working together for both of them.

Since secondary boycotts violated the federal 1947 Taft-Hartley Act, Smith sued the national Teamsters as well as local 554.

The NLRB investigators agreed that the Teamsters hoped the work stoppage would make Coffey or Clark bargain with local 554 as though it represented their drivers, which, of course, it did not. The NLRB then joined with Smith and filed secondary boycott charges against the Teamsters, asking the US District Court to issue an injunction to stop the boycotts.

Thanks to all this action, Dad felt well-protected.

Glen and his driver, Duane Graber, showed up at the Bos Freight Lines to ship freight. As soon as Malcolm Foley, the warehouse worker and a local 554 member, saw them, he phoned the union hall and asked for Parker.

"Can their freight be handled?" Foley paused. "I'm a union man. All I want to know is what do I do? Do I or don't I?"

After another pause, Foley reached into a cubbyhole and pulled out a Teamster contract. Glen watched Foley read the contract's "hot cargo" clause. The warehouse worker then refused the Coffey's Transfer shipment.

Jimmy Hoffa himself had invented the "hot cargo" clause to use in Teamster contracts. He created it to sidestep the 1947 Taft-Hartley law against secondary boycotts. Using the clause, Teamsters could legally refuse to handle "unfair goods"—that is, goods from a firm clashing with the Teamsters.

Any old Teamster could activate a "hot cargo" clause. Sometimes Parker okayed them; at other times Barney or one of several local 554 officers did; but even a Teamster warehouse worker could.

Most trucklines that did business with either Coffey or Clark had these "hot cargo" clauses. Indeed, almost all Teamster contracts contained the clause. In this way, Hoffa authorized boycotting.

MEAT HOOKS

Glen kept right on trying to find customers for his freight. He walked down dock after dock of trucklines that once considered Coffey's Transfer Company a regular customer. Or pulled up to a warehouse, expecting to pick up a load that Coffey's Transfer Company could deliver, but finding nothing. He talked to terminal manager after terminal manager, hoping that one would accept Coffey's Transfer freight.

Glen never knew what kind of reception he'd meet. Sometimes men in charge would sign for the freight, and the Coffey driver would unload it and set it on the dock. At other times, managers would say, "No, we can't handle it."

Pickets standing in front of a customer's terminal to prevent Glen and his driver from pulling up to the dock really angered Glen. Sometimes he could arrange to meet that customer's truck a block or two away. To protect himself, he and his driver carried meat hooks. If some of Barney's boys came after them, Glen and his driver would step into the street and shout, "Come ahead," as they brandished their hooks.

"Quick, the Lights"

Dad called me, yesterday, and all but begged me to come home from Kearney State Teachers College. It was October 21, 1955. I didn't want to.

At Kearney, I had become my own person, not Tom Coffey's daughter, daughter of the mayor, the state senator, owner of the biggest business in town. I loved my new freedom.

On the other hand, Dad rarely asked me for anything. So I plunked down my $1.82 fare for the Slowpoke Special and rode the bus sixty miles home.

While I lived at college, my mother and I corresponded daily, so I knew all about Teamster goons polishing their shotguns.

"This fight is taking its toll on your dad," she wrote. "Don't expect him to look the same. He's lost some weight."

But Mama's letters didn't prepare me for the scarecrow that rose gaunt from his recliner to hug me. His clothes hung on him like a drape.

"Gee, Dad," I mumbled into his shoulder. "How much have you lost?"

"Twenty-five pounds. Since I saw you last."

I stepped back and looked at him. His cheeks caved inward, and flaps of skin hung from his lower jaw. And his gorgeous head of hair, raven black, had turned snow white.

I patted Dad's cardigan. Sure enough, I felt, under his sweater, the outline of his pill box in his shirt pocket where he habitually carried it. It contained nitroglycerin pills.

When he showed me the pills a couple of years ago, he pounded his fist against his chest. "If I have another heart attack, I'll take one of these little pills and stick it under my tongue."

"That will stop the attack?"

"Should. But you better not punch my pillbox. Nitroglycerin is the same stuff you find in dynamite. You wouldn't want me to explode."

"Go on," I said. I rarely knew whether he was serious or joshing. Later I found out that, since the 1860s, manufacturers had used nitroglycerin as the active ingredient in making explosives, including dynamite. But Dad's tiny pills had been diluted with some inert material, so punching him wouldn't set off anything but his temper.

I gulped and hugged Dad, tight, my stomach hard as a rock. I knew he'd been under terrible pressure, of course, but I hadn't expected this. Dread filled me. My calves shook. I couldn't speak. For the first time I thought it might be possible for the Teamsters to kill him, if they didn't let up.

The Strike Seemed Far Away

We gathered that autumn evening in my family's recently redecorated living room to watch TV. My dad, not yet snoring, stretched in his recliner, eyes closed, while Mama perched on her favorite armchair, crocheting. My sister Margery, thirteen, and I, eighteen, draped ourselves along the overstuffed couch, our knees butting the glass-topped coffee table.

The transformed room, with its soft roses and greens, soothed me. My classy mother had designed it herself. The couch matched the rose draperies, while the chairs echoed the pale green carpet; leafy patterns spattered the walls. I couldn't imagine a more harmonious place.

None of us had much to say. The awful Teamsters' strike at Dad's Omaha office had escalated that week from picketing to guys smashing the tops of Coffey's Transfer Company trucks with rocks dropped off viaducts. Jimmy Hoffa and Dad had been fighting, off and on, since 1946. No one knew what Hoffa's Teamsters might do next. In other places, the union had fought with baseball bats, knives, guns—even bombs.

But Dad's strike seemed far away to me that evening. After all, Omaha lay four hours from our home in a vast rural area in south central Nebraska, so far south we almost lived in Kansas.

We settled in to watch some programs, Dad's choice, of course. It was his TV, although it had lost the splendor that exalted it last year, 1954. Then it was the first set ever seen in our tiny town of Alma. Dad had been so proud of it; he raced home from work every night to watch the only program then playing: test patterns.

When the long-awaited programs materialized, our family rarely viewed them together. In our house, the folks watched prime time, my sister the late-night movies, and I ignored the fabulous machine, preferring books. However, this Saturday evening we watched together because Dad had summoned me home for the weekend from Kearney State Teachers College. To disappear to my upstairs room with a novel, as I often had, would be rude.

IKE OUT OF HIS OXYGEN TENT

That evening we worked our way through the usual Saturday night assortment of shows, laughing at Jimmy Durante's gigantic schnozzola, the crazy antics on *The Life of Riley*, and the low life depicted in the *Damon Runyon Theater*. Watching Dad laugh felt good. I hadn't seen much of that this weekend.

At 10 p.m., we switched to the news to catch the latest about Ike, whose recent heart seizure had landed him in the Denver hospital. Things were looking up. The doctors hadn't let the president watch the World Series, but he was no longer in the oxygen tent and could even sign his full name.

Then, without a smidgen of warning, we heard a sharp crack. *A rock hitting the front porch,* I thought, but Dad slammed out of his recliner and barked, "Quick, the lights." I glanced at him, startled to see fear etch his face.

In an instant, the room was dark, and Dad was hustling us, like a sheepdog herding a flock of ewes, to the back of the house. Silent, we watched him flip on the backyard lights and peer out the kitchen window. Nothing. We listened as he made his way to the front of the house. I heard the snap of the porch light switch and listened to the front door creak open. *He's so brave,* I thought. *What if it's a bomb?*

His footsteps echoed on the wooden front porch while, in the kitchen, we held our breaths. The night lay around us so quiet, I flinched when the refrigerator motor kicked on.

Then we heard his call, "All's clear," and saw the living room lights go on. We rushed to see him.

"It was nothing," he said. He crumpled into his chair; his chin dropped to his chest.

"Nothing?" I still felt frightened. "It had to be something: it was so loud and sounded so close. What could it have been?"

"I don't know." He gave me a blank look. "Maybe a car backfiring. Or some kids being funny."

Later, Dad shuffled off to the kitchen with Mama to unplug the perpetual electric coffee pot and grab a late-night snack. I heard Mama say, "You're sure jumpy tonight, Tom."

"I know," he replied as they disappeared around the corner. "And I feel like such a fool."

I headed toward the sanctuary of my bedroom. To get there, I stepped over Margery's body sprawled on the living room rug, already hooked into a late-night show.

Halfway up the staircase, I stopped and glanced back down at the peaceful living room. It seemed smaller, somehow.

How vulnerable we are, I thought. *Events miles away have touched our lives.*

I didn't know it then, of course, but Dad's war with Hoffa's Teamsters would not just touch our lives. It would transform them, beyond recall.

SPINNING THE SILVER DOLLAR

Each time Glen reported to Dad that another truckline had boycotted Coffey's Transfer, Dad's eyes would turn flinty and he'd cuss. "Oh, well," he'd grip his chair, "we can get along without that truckline."

But when Glen returned from Des Moines Transportation Company that autumn, he dared not look Dad in the eye.

"All right, all right." Dad frowned. "So what happened?"

"Well, Paul Laughlin and I went to Des Moines." Glen walked over and looked out the window. "We pulled into the dock as usual. But the dockworker said, 'Don't unload your freight; we can't handle it for you.'" Glen turned, glanced at Dad, then turned back. "And I asked, 'What do you mean?' And he said, 'Due to your trouble, we can only handle government bills of lading.'"

"So they took nothing." Dad snapped.

"Nothing." Glen turned. He thought Dad might cry, he was gripping the chair's arms so tightly that his knuckles had turned white.

"God, Glen." Dad's voice cracked. "What are we going to do?"

Glen forced a smile. "Why don't you ship me to Detroit, let me shoot Hoffa."

Dad looked up, saw Glen's grin, and released his grip.

They both knew what the Des Moines boycott meant. Coffey's Transfer shipped more freight with Des Moines than any other line. A lot more. About 80 percent of Dad's outgoing freight went through Des Moines, and Coffey's Transfer received about 60 percent of its incoming interstate freight from them.

Dad rose and paced. "But I'll not take this sitting down. There must be something I can do."

"Why don't you call Des Moines, and some of the others? You've known most of those guys for years."

Dad rubbed his chin. "Most of them I count as my friends, old friends. And you're right. I've done business with some of them for twenty years. I could make it a personal appeal."

The chair scraped the floor as Dad pulled it close to the phone. Before he sat down, he reached in his pocket, pulled out his silver dollar, and spun it on the desk.

Glen didn't have to ask what Dad was doing.

Despite Glen's daily efforts to find customers, Dad's out-of-state shipments dropped down and down. About 50 percent of his total business depended on these interstate shipments, most of them out of Omaha. He shipped freight with about ten Omaha trucklines, including Santa Fe Trail, Iowa-Nebraska Transportation, Merchants Motor Freight, Darling Transfer, and Bos Freight Lines, but especially with Des Moines Transportation.

Dad believed the owners of these lines to be old friends. But when he called them, they all expressed the same thing: "Sorry, Tom. I don't dare go along with you. You know how it is; the Teamsters'll strike me in Chicago or Kansas City if I interline with you."

Dad knew they were right in assessing how hot the Teamsters might make it for outfits loyal to him, but the rejection pinched just the same.

However, one of these truckers, Ralph Darling of Darling Transfer, a close business friend, declared, "Oh, don't worry, Tom. You can count on me. I'll keep on giving Coffey's Transfer my business."

At least that brought a little relief.

Settlement Notices

On December 8, 1955, at long last, a leg up for Dad!

The NLRB, in a significant step forward, arranged for Coffey's Transfer and Teamsters Local 554 to sign what the board called a Settlement Agreement. The agreement stated that the union would encourage their members to start doing business with Coffey's Transfer.

To motivate this, the NLRB created a notice to be posted for sixty days in Teamster offices and in suitable trucklines. It announced that the Teamsters had stopped its illegal activities. No strikes, no refusals to handle goods, no forcing folks to stop doing business with Coffey's Transfer.

If the Teamsters agreed, then the NLRB would withdraw its secondary boycott charges against the union. Bert Parker, head of local 554, and David D. Weinberg, its lawyer, signed the notice.

Glen leaped into action. By Saturday, December 10, he had hauled settlement notices to fifteen Omaha trucklines. He asked each to post notices where their employees could read them. He also asked the trucklines to handle Coffey's Transfer freight again.

Most carriers posted the notice. Even Parker placed his notice conspicuously—near a window where members walked up to pay dues. He seemed to participate in the agreement, but he did not. After he'd posted his notice, he refused to answer questions about it, not from warehouse employees who dropped by or from many phone calls from members asking what the notice meant. He simply would not discuss the matter.

Local 554 officers, supposed to tell employees that orders not to handle Coffey's Transfer freight were no longer in effect, did not. Instead, they deliberately confused members like Mr. Terrano, a Burlington Trucklines checker, who called Parker to "find out what's the score?"

"Should I receive Coffey's freight?" he huffed as he asked Parker. "I need to know where I stand, because I am the man in the middle. I would take it from both ends. I want to be certain what I do. I don't know which way to stand, whether to refuse the freight or take the freight."

He didn't find out from Parker.

Most local 554 members, uncertain of Teamster intent and, like Terrano, afraid of union retaliation, generally refused to handle Dad's freight. By this method, the Teamsters resumed their prior secondary boycott.

Nevertheless, the Omaha trucklines improved their business relationship with Coffey's Transfer, and Glen delivered and picked up freight from many of them—for almost a week.

OH, NO! NOT BUTTER

On Thursday morning, December 15, Glen rode with his driver to Iowa-Nebraska Transportation Company. His truck, half full, carried more than 12,000 pounds of butter. Given the December 8 Settlement Agreement, he expected to deliver the butter to be shipped to New York City.

When Glen and his driver arrived, they checked with the terminal manager and dispatcher, Dick Brandt. Brandt, in turn, told Jim Frohm, a dockworker and union member, to load the butter onto an Iowa-Nebraska trailer.

Frohm refused. "I don't have to handle it."

Brandt's eyes narrowed. "Why not?"

"It's my constitutional right to refuse to handle merchandise." Frohm cocked his head. "Besides which, there's a picket line around Coffey's place."

Brandt frowned. "But there's no picket line around his truck."

Frohm shrugged. "Say what you like, I just ain't gonna accept it."

Brandt tried to locate some other dock worker to handle the butter, but they all refused. That didn't surprise Glen. He'd heard from his drivers that sometimes they could deliver freight, but increasingly not. The Teamsters' actions endangered the NLRB agreement.

FORCED TO SIGN

Emil J. Severyn, who'd driven for Coffey's Transfer for six years, went to Union Freightways in late December to deliver freight.

Union Freightways had an odd specialty: it shipped live hogs from Omaha to Barstow, California. Here's how. It loaded a semi with hogs, dropped the temperature into the midthirties, and then drove like hell, nonstop, to California and unloaded hogs at a local slaughterhouse.

But Emil had more than hogs in mind. The Settlement Agreement with the Teamsters had loosened shipping up a bit, so he expected to send some goods to Chicago.

Uncertain what he'd find, Emil glanced around the dock looking for Teamster organizers, Parker or Barney or any of local 554's officers, but he saw none.

As he entered, a boy sang out, "Coffey's Transfer is here."

Emil spotted a Freightways employee and former Teamster representative, Sweeney, walking ahead of him. Emil heard two dockworkers call out to Sweeney, "Coffey's Transfer is here." But the checker kept walking.

That doesn't mean a thing. Emil knit his brows. *Handling freight isn't Sweeney's job.*

So Emil handed his freight bill to Cliff, the man in charge of the dock. Cliff took the bill, peered at it, then walked to a guy running a lift truck. They spoke, and the man on the lift truck shook his head.

Cliff returned. "Come on. I'll find out about it."

The two walked together until Cliff stopped. "You stay here. I'll find out."

He disappeared into an office. When he returned, Cliff handed Emil the bill and walked away.

"Are you going to handle it?" Emil stiffened.

"No."

"Why not?"

"See them in there." Cliff pointed to a small office on the dock where Emil often stopped to pick up merchandise. "Morehouse's office," Emil called it.

Inside, Merle Morehouse, wearing a suit as usual, looked at Emil. "Bud, as far as I am concerned, you are not in business."

Emil decided to give his shipment one more shot. He walked back to the office of Bob Robbins, another dispatcher. Robbins didn't normally handle interline freight, but Emil had known the dispatcher for five years. He was a Teamsters' steward, a loyal union man, so Emil felt he could talk candidly to Robbins about the situation.

The two talked a bit. Then Emil asked about the settlement notice posted on the Union Freightways dock.

"Oh, that's nothing." Robbins chuckled. "The union was forced to sign them."

"So you or the boys won't handle the freight?"

"You'll have to talk to them." Robbins turned back to his work. "But I won't."

That did it.

On December 21, Smith, Dad's attorney, notified the NLRB that the union had violated the Settlement Agreement.

A Short-Lived Breakthrough

The Settlement Agreement, although temporary, did boost all of Dad's shipments.

Take the case of the important Des Moines Transportation Company.

In October and November, after the September strikes on Coffey and Clark, Des Moines gave no freight nor received any. However, after the December 8 agreement, business returned to normal.

During that time, Des Moines delivered to Dad, as usual, about 60 percent of its available incoming merchandise. Coffey's Transfer Company, in turn, delivered about 80 percent of its outgoing state freight to Des Moines.

Then on January 10, 1956, the Teamsters—with no warning—struck the Des Moines company's terminal in Minneapolis. Newspapers and television covered the strike. Work stopped from 5 p.m. to 8:30 the next morning. Then the Teamster pickets disappeared.

They disappeared because Des Moines, unable to function, agreed to stop shipping freight with Coffey's Transfer Company and Clark Brothers. After that, Des Moines no longer accepted any freight from or to Dad's truckline.

This pattern held true for other Omaha lines who normally shipped freight for Clark or Coffey, with one exception: Ralph Darling's truckline. All during both strikes, from September into January, Ralph Darling's truckline regularly shipped a substantial amount of freight for both Coffey and Clark.

Of course Darling's small operation couldn't make up for the amount of freight lost when Des Moines Transfer and the others stopped shipping, but Foy Clark and Dad knew they could count on Ralph.

"Goin' to Close You Up"

That Friday morning, January 13, 1956, a Clark Brothers truck pulled into Ralph Darling's Omaha terminal to transfer freight. In the terminal waited a big Darling Transfer truck. It had cruised in from Oakland, California, carrying a load of Clorox, not the watered-down bleach produced by rivals, but Clorox full strength, able to disinfect wounds and purify water.

The two trucks parked back to back in the street while drivers and dockworkers unloaded boxes full of amber bottles from the Darling truck and put them into the Clark truck to be delivered to its customer.

Across the street, Barney Baker's buddy, Leslie Morganson, vice-president of local 554, watched the unloading and reloading from his car. It took more than an hour.

When the Clark Brothers truck pulled out, Morganson headed back to union headquarters on South 90th Street. There he placed a call to Teamsters Local 41 in Kansas City.

In Kansas City that afternoon, a band of Teamsters—a vice-president and two business reps—from local 41 materialized on the Darling Transfer dock.

The dockworkers looked up. They recognized Teamster business rep Clouse. He oversaw Darling's local contract. When Clouse had the dockworkers' attention, he ordered, "Time to take a vacation. We are calling you boys out."

One worker piped up. "What for?"

"Trouble in Omaha," Clouse replied.

Soon the employees punched out and evaporated.

Clouse and Kappleman, a vice-president, then met with Darling's terminal manager.

"I've got bad news for you," Clouse told Weaver, the manager. "I'm going to close you up."

"Why?" Weaver asked.

Clouse shrugged, but Kappleman stated, "It's due to trouble on the north end, interlining with nonunion carriers. It's nothing down here at this end. You are all right here."

The dockworkers had disappeared, but Darling's drivers waited in the street.

"Better call those drivers in," Clouse told Weaver. He did.

After the drivers punched out, nothing moved at Darling's Kansas City dock.

"I Hate Like Hell to Do This"

Ralph Darling, in Omaha, received news of the strike from several of his Kansas City employees. Then Kappleman called with a telephone number. "This number will hook you right up with the Detroit Teamsters. All you have to do is promise to ship nothing with Clark Brothers or with Coffey's Transfer."

Ralph winced. He hated to stop interlining with those two, especially Coffey. They'd become close business friends. But if the Teamsters had closed Darling Transfer down, Ralph couldn't ship anything for anybody.

He called Detroit.

After a couple of holds, a jovial Jimmy Hoffa came on the line. "So, Ralph. You going to keep truckin' with those two prickheads?"

Ralph reluctantly agreed to stop shipping with Clark Brothers or Coffey's Transfer. Then before offices closed at 5 p.m., Ralph called Foy Clark. Telling Foy felt bad enough, but then he had to call Dad's Omaha office.

"I don't know how to tell you this," Ralph declared, "but I can't interline with you no more."

"Can't interline anymore? What's the problem?"

"Oh, Tom, I hate like hell to do this to you, but they've got me by the short hair. They've shut down my Kansas City terminal."

The Election Squabble

What a day that Tuesday had been! The Teamsters' strike first thing in the morning September 20, the long drive to

Omaha, pickets at Dad's terminal, pickets at the hospital where Mary gave birth, trying to calm Glen, replacing drivers, making sure the Teamsters' "imaginary picket line" didn't swallow up his offices in Lincoln, Holdrege, or Alma.

But before he jumped back into his Olds for the trip home, Dad called one of his Lincoln lawyers, Ralph W. Slocum. "We've gone under the muzzle," Dad told Slocum, "but I've kept the trucks rolling. Do you think you can get me an election with the NLRB?"

"Sure. I'll file a petition right away."

Slocum and Dad knew the importance of that petition. It had the power to curtail the Teamsters' strike. If Dad won a National Labor Relations Board election, he could prove that the Teamsters didn't, in fact, represent his drivers, which the union pretended to do.

Dad remembered the August day Barney Baker had whooped, "We'll stall any election. You'll be broke before a single vote is counted."

"I expect the NLRB's big enough to help," Dad told Slocum. "After all, it's government. Big as Hoffa is, he isn't bigger than Uncle Sam."

THE TEAMSTERS' ATTACK DOG

The NLRB operated a network of regional offices, including an office in Kansas City that covered Omaha. So Slocum's petition made its way to Michael Lucero, NLRB's field examiner in the Kansas City office.

Lucero called Dad on Tuesday, September 27. They set a date, October 10, for an election among the twenty-two drivers of Coffey's Transfer Company.

Immediately the Teamsters' attack-dog lawyer, David D. Weinberg, rushed to the union's defense. His specialty: stalling. Weinberg and Parker called Lucero.

"Twenty-two drivers? Impossible," Parker grumbled. "Local 554 covers only Coffey's Omaha drivers, maybe five of them."

Weinberg also argued, "How can you consider an election? You haven't even held a hearing to find out if Coffey's Transfer Company qualifies for one."

Dad, alarmed by Weinberg's argument, wrote a letter detailing Dad's fitness for an NLRB election. He sent that letter on.

Lucero, caught off guard, agreed to the hearing the Teamsters wanted. He set an October 12 date for it. No sooner had he set the date than Weinberg couldn't make it; he would be in court.

Lucero reset the hearing to October 20, but Weinberg overturned that too.

The NLRB finally held its hearing October 25, more than two weeks after the original election date with no election now in sight. And with the Teamsters boycotting Coffey's Transfer freight since September 20.

Dad, after bickering with Weinberg, won the argument about where the hearing would be held: Omaha or Alma. The NLRB hearing officer, Margaret L. Fassig, held the meeting in the Alma courthouse, a short drive for Dad but not for Weinberg.

Fassig opened the investigation at 10 a.m. October 25, 1955, and swore in the only witness, Tom Coffey. Slocum and Weinberg took turns questioning Dad until the hearing closed at 1:30.

To be eligible for an NLRB election, Dad had to show that Coffey's Transfer shipped freight between states. Dad felt sure he'd pass that test. The Interstate Commerce Commission had classified Coffey's Transfer Company as a Class I motor carrier.

His truckline also had to earn more than $100,000 annually in between-state shipments. Out of his last year total revenue, he'd earned $102,756.64 from those shipments, so that, too, made the cut.

But Weinberg's questioning ranged widely. It covered every aspect of Dad's operation, from the total amount of money he made, to the bank where he kept his payroll and the way he dispersed his drivers in an ordinary day. Dad described every meeting he'd ever had with the Teamsters, including the early meetings in 1946, 1947, and 1950.

"Did your three striking drivers quit," Weinberg asked Dad, "or did you fire them?" A significant question: Fired drivers could vote.

"They simply failed to show up for work," Dad said. "We haven't spoken since."

He defended his belief that voting in the election should be companywide and listened to Weinberg argue for an election of local drivers in Omaha and Lincoln.

Dad's lawyer, Slocum, asked Weinberg if the International Brotherhood of Teamsters was sponsoring a strike on Coffey's Transfer Company, but Weinberg couldn't answer. Probably because the strike wasn't "official" since technically Dad's drivers had not struck.

"Mr. Coffey received no notice of a strike," Slocum said. "In fact, he did not know that a strike had actually been called on his employees until Mr. Weinberg just now said so."

"All he had to do," Weinberg said, "was read the pickets. They picketed with signs 'On Strike.' What more do you want?"

More Time

After the hearing ended, Weinberg wangled for more time to file his required brief. The NLRB gave him an extension to November 15, but he wanted ten more days.

Dad, infuriated, shot off Western Union wires to two NLRB executives in Washington, DC: "Teamsters have men out on strike. Important that matter be expedited without any delay whatsoever. No additional time should be given for filings. No good reason exists for extension of time. This case should be given attention. Please no delays."

The NLRB did extend Weinberg's deadline, but by only two more days. Weinberg filed his brief "on time" November 17. He argued that Coffey's Transfer Company didn't meet NLRB standards for an election because his revenue of $102,756.64 was too close to the $100,000 requirement. "A difference of 10 percent could place the firm outside NLRB coverage."

The NLRB disagreed. It accepted Dad's figure and cleared him for an election. But it did accept Weinberg's argument that the election would be held only in Omaha where Coffey's Transfer's former drivers were on strike.

By this time, the Teamsters had held up Dad's freight for almost two months.

On December 12, the NLRB decided to hold the Coffey's Transfer election on December 29, now ten weeks after the original date. It also decided that only current Omaha drivers could vote.

Weinberg, of course, protested. "Those three picketing drivers should vote. Glen deprived them of their legitimate rights."

But Glen disagreed. "When we replaced those picketing men, that made them ineligible to vote."

"We'll meet December 28 in Omaha for a preelection conference to discuss these differences," Lucero decided.

Preparations for the election began. Lucero ordered fifteen ballots and sent out election notices. Acting as the examiner, Lucero would hold the election in the Omaha office.

However, all this was moot.

Two days after Christmas, Dad received a telegram from Lucero stating that the NLRB had postponed the preelection conference, set for the next day, as well as the election.

Why? Well, as Dad feared, Weinberg had delayed again.

He had filed unfair labor practices charges against the NLRB and Dad. The NLRB canceled the election to investigate Weinberg's charges. The three men who picketed Dad's terminal—Faulhaber, Henley, and Jansa— were among those suing. Weinberg wanted these three men to be eligible to vote.

Lucero's telegram chagrined Dad. Everything was ready for the December 29 election. Glen had hung in "conspicuous places" the official Notice of Election with its sample ballot. The Teamsters and Dad had selected election observers to help conduct the balloting. The board-ordered tally of ballots was waiting to be filled, and the Certification on Conduct of Election just needed Dad's signature, and Parker's, to set the election in motion.

On January 18, 1956, after a flurry of memos and phone calls, the NLRB board set Tuesday, January 24, as the date for the long-awaited election. The flurry was in part because of disagreement over whether to set the date so soon; the NLRB had yet to rule on Weinberg's charge of unfair labor practices. But shortly after, it dismissed his charge.

Of course, Weinberg appealed the decision. In it, he argued that the NLRB couldn't hold an election during the time he had to file a union appeal.

Next, he protested holding the election at the Coffey's Transfer Omaha office. "That would force strikers to cross the established picket line," he reasoned.

These actions of Weinberg did not prevent the board from holding the election, but they did stop it from issuing a final vote count. Under its regulations, the NLRB could not complete an election if a complaint was pending. In this fashion, the Teamsters, unable to halt the election, stalled the results.

The union's chance of winning was exceedingly slim. Coffey drivers outnumbered Teamsters four to three, so the union stood to gain by stalling.

"We Teamsters don't much care who wins," a union official told Dad. "Besides, even if you win, you'll still have a secondary boycott on your hands."

That, of course, was true. Indeed, it was the whole point.

At Last, the Election!

Despite all the legal maneuvering, on Tuesday, January 24, 1956, the NLRB did hold an election from 8 to 8:30 a.m. in Coffey's Omaha office. Finally! More than four months had passed since Slocum requested an NLRB election for Dad.

On that wintry morning, seven drivers crossed the picket lines to cast their votes.

Harold L. Hudson had replaced Lucero. Dad gave Hudson the Coffey payroll list with the names of his four eligible drivers: Howard Shurts, Emil J. Severyn, Duane Graber, and Carvin Moreland. These four men made up Coffey's entire Omaha staff of truck drivers. Drivers James Faulhaber, William Henley, and Ed Jansa, who stopped working for Coffey's Transfer Company to picket for the Teamsters, also voted.

After the seven voted, the NLRB tallied results, refusing to count the three Teamster votes. None of the four Coffey drivers voted for the union, so Dad won the election.

But that was not the end of matters.

Hudson gave a copy of NLRB's tally of ballots to both parties to sign, but Weinberg refused. He also refused to sign the Certification on Conduct of Election. He was not about to certify that the NLRB had conducted the balloting fairly.

Then Hudson told Weinberg how to file objections, which he did. He knew that procedure would take weeks, at least.

In fact, nearly four months passed before the NLRB could legally announce Dad's victory. As usual, Weinberg posed every challenge he could to give the union more time to support the Teamsters' highly effective secondary boycott, an illegal leapfrogging that daily drained the lifeblood out of Dad's business.

The Peevish Judge

On February 2, 1956, the NLRB in Kansas City filed suit against the Teamsters in Omaha's Federal District Court. The suit zeroed in on the Teamsters' illegal use of the secondary boycott in its strike against Coffey's Transfer.

Four days later, Weinberg answered the charges. "The Teamsters are not guilty of unfair labor practices; Tom Coffey is." The lawyer argued that local 554 struck Coffey's Transfer because Dad interfered with his drivers' right to join that local.

"As for the Settlement Agreement," Weinberg insisted, "Local No. 554 didn't breach it. On the contrary, the local complied with it."

Weinberg wanted the court to dismiss the NLRB petition. However, the court did not. Instead, it held a hearing to determine whether the Teamsters had violated the Settlement Agreement.

A lot rested on this case. If Weinberg won, the district court wouldn't prohibit the Teamsters' strike and illegal boycott.

Dad and his lawyer made sure they arrived in the Omaha court promptly Monday morning, February 13, 1956.

There a highly regarded but peevish judge presided. The Honorable James A. Donohoe, seventy-eight, was the Omaha court's chief judge. A balding man who amply filled out his black robe, Donohoe had been a federal judge since 1933. He showed no sign of retiring. Indeed, he had vowed, "I'm going to die in the harness."

Not in a good mood that day, the judge often became exasperated with the lawyers, in particular with Joseph I. Nachman, the NLRB attorney who ran the hearing. For instance, when Nachman asked Donohoe to reconsider a ruling, the judge pontificated, "The Court has ruled. I never change my ruling, unless it is clearly wrong." Later,

The Honorable James A. Donohoe.

Donohoe told Nachman, "If you will listen to me, you will understand better."

"A STRANGE NOTION"

Nachman had seven witnesses ready to testify, among them Albert "Bert" Parker, head of the Omaha's local. Nachman struggled to make Parker admit that he had undermined the Settlement Agreement and/or overseen illegal secondary boycotts.

Presented with a newspaper clipping, Parker identified a photo of Barney Baker and conceded that the 325-pound thug had been in Omaha at the time of the Coffey's Transfer strike. But when Nachman asked Parker to describe his discussion with Baker about the Coffey strike, Weinberg called that testimony "incompetent, irrelevant, and immaterial."

Donohoe corrected Weinberg. "It is hearsay."

"Hearsay," Weinberg repeated.

"That is what is the matter with it," the judge said.

Parker interpreted the Settlement Agreement narrowly. "I executed the Settlement Agreement when I posted the notice conspicuously on the glass partition near the union hall entrance. You can see it. It's still there."

Parker shifted in his chair. "I knew that we shouldn't encourage members to turn down Coffey freight."

"Did you tell your members to stop?" Nachman asked. "No."

Weinberg began in his turn to question Parker, but Nachman objected to the cross-examination.

"You have a strange notion about conducting proceedings of this kind," the irascible Donohoe told Nachman. "You called the witness. Weinberg didn't put Parker on the stand. Weinberg has a right to cross-examine a witness you call on any matters you have gone into."

Under Weinberg's questioning, Parker agreed that the Settlement Agreement notice said he should not encourage employees of trucklines to refuse to handle Coffey freight, and he claimed he hadn't.

Parker again said that when he answered phone calls from truckline employees asking about the notice, he answered that he couldn't discuss the matter. He never told any caller that he was now free to handle Coffey's goods.

As Parker put it, "I don't believe I would have any jurisdiction over anyone except my members."

Parker's testimony took up more than half the workday and did little to establish that the Teamsters had broken the December 8 Settlement Agreement. Neither did the testimony of W. Foy Clark of Clark Brothers, who testified after Parker.

"Not Running a School"

Later, Glen Coffey described taking Settlement Agreement notices around December 10 to his regular terminals. Glen asked his customers to post them conspicuously, and, in most cases, they did. But Nachman's questioning hit a barrier when he asked Glen, "Were you able to do business after that with these carriers?"

Irrelevant, Weinberg countered, and Donohoe sustained the objection.

"May I make an offer of proof on that?" Nachman asked, hoping to explain to the judge how his proposed line of questioning would be relevant to the case.

"Yes, you may make it," Donohoe quipped. "Don't make it as long as your last."

Glen then testified about two attempts to deliver his freight, the first to Iowa-Nebraska Transportation Company and the second to Des Moines Transfer. Glen's testimony finally established that Teamsters had blocked Coffey's Transfer freight, making the Settlement Agreement unsuccessful.

During the day, the judge became increasingly testy. He seemed to enjoy badgering Nachman. When Nachman asked Glen whether he knew if there was a strike at Des Moines Transportation Company on or about January 10, Weinberg objected to Nachman's lack of preparation for the question.

"Let's get the foundation," Donohoe instructed.

"I would be very glad to do it," Nachman said, "but I don't understand what Your Honor thinks I have left out."

The petulant judge said, "You are the lawyer who is trying the case."

"Yes sir," Nachman said. "I thought I had all the factors in there."

But Donohoe just needled. "I'm not running a school of evidence."

While Weinberg and Nachman quarreled about whether the Des Moines Transportation strike was admissible as evidence, Donohoe told the lawyers, "Let's move on. I am about to quit." And quit they did, truncating Glen's testimony. Glen had no time to explain that the refusal of Coffey freight by Des Moines Transportation was due to a Teamster strike at its Minneapolis terminal, a strike that ended when Des Moines agreed to stop interlining with Coffey's Transfer.

A Log Jam

As they adjourned for the day, Donohoe addressed the lawyers: "Even to this day I did not understand there was going to be any such hearing as we have had here.

"When you came out to my home, I gave you an order to show cause, and I assumed naturally it would be filed and you gentlemen would get together after the answer was filed and agree upon a time when I could arrange my other business and give you the right-of-way.

"Instead of that, you march in on me this morning without any notice or warning, or anything else, with a courtroom filled with witnesses, and so I made such arrangements as I could and gave you today.

"Now then, the day is ended. How much more time do you expect to take in this matter?"

Weinberg said he had three or four witnesses; Nachman had three witnesses left and some depositions to offer.

"Coming in here without notice, it is an interference and a log jam," Donohoe said. "That is what I have to keep away from."

The judge offered them two hours the following morning, but Weinberg thought that, with his witnesses coming after Nachman's, he probably couldn't finish in that time.

"If you find you can get through by tomorrow noon by conferring with each other, I will take your word for it," said the judge, "but when you get through and I cut you off, I don't expect you to complain."

The lawyers decided not to continue the following morning but at a time that the judge would set, so the court held the hearing over until time became available on Judge Donohoe's calendar.

But no one set that date. Before it could arrive, Donohoe complained of feeling ill after an evening meal. His wife called a doctor who sent the judge to a hospital. The illness Donohoe felt was a heart attack; he died the following morning.

On Wednesday, February 29, the day of Judge Donohoe's funeral, the federal court closed in his honor. A US district judge since 1933, the plainspoken man attained his desire of dying "in the harness." His family and friends considered him a kindly man, but the lawyers who argued in his court called him cantankerous.

The death of Judge Donohoe was a mixed blessing for the NLRB. On the positive side was the possibility that the new judge, John W. Delehant, might be more receptive to its argument. On the negative side was the fact that Donohoe's death had delayed the whole process of getting an injunction to halt the Teamsters' illegal activities.

WHOMPED!

Judge Donohoe's death blindsided Dad. It eroded one of his two legal strategies, both designed to halt the Teamsters' ability to gut his business.

Dad's first strategy had been to win the election and prove that the Teamsters did not represent his Omaha drivers. That would render its strike illegal.

When he'd talked with Michael Lucero on September 27 and set a date for the election, he thought the NLRB would hold that election in a couple of weeks, but nearly four months passed before the January 24 vote. Now February was advancing, and the NLRB still had not finalized those seven ballots, thanks to that Teamster lawyer Weinberg.

Weinberg's plans for stalling seemed endless. The lawyer demanded an unnecessary hearing. He postponed dates repeatedly. By the December 29 balloting date, Weinberg had delayed voting by eighty-six irreplaceable days. Still he blocked. He trumped up charges of unfair labor practices against Dad. They didn't fly, but the hearings shelved the election for twenty-six more vital days.

As soon as Coffey drivers voted, Weinberg blocked again. He ran to the federal district courts in Nebraska and Washington, DC, claiming the National Labor Relations Act was unconstitutional. Both judges granted orders restraining the NLRB from acting on the Coffey vote. Thirty more days obstructed.

By February 23, 1956, when Weinberg appealed to have the NLRB report on Coffey's election overturned, he already had managed to hold up the election for 134 irretrievable days, and the final resolution of the prized election was not in sight. How much longer would it be?

Not only did Weinberg stall the election, but the NLRB—and fate—ensnarled Dad's second strategy, to halt the Teamsters' illegal secondary boycott. The NLRB, although slow, had backed Dad all the way. Believing that the charges Dad filed against the Teamsters were true, the national board had arranged the December 8 Settlement Agreement between local 554 and Coffey's Transfer Company. That board action had eaten up seven weeks and two days.

For a while, Dad could see that the agreement worked as it should; he shipped and received freight from interline trucklines once more. However, not even two weeks passed before trucklines, pressured by the Teamsters, began denying his goods again. On December 21, Dad notified the NLRB about the Teamsters' violation of the agreement.

Again, when the NLRB investigated, it found "reason to believe" Dad's claim and sued the union in the US District Court in Omaha on February 3, six weeks and two days later. Had that suit been successful, the court would have stopped the Teamsters' strike and its secondary boycott. Instead of a victory, fate stepped in, placing on the bench a judge who refused to retire, a judge who dropped dead instead of ruling on the matter. Who knew when the court would call a new hearing?

In a matter of months, the Teamsters were destroying the truckline that took Dad twenty-seven years to build.

Since the September strike, Coffey's gross revenue had plummeted. The Teamsters' boycott decimated half of his annual revenue, the portion that Dad's interline shipments with Des Moines Transportation and other trucklines normally provided.

At the same time, his expenses multiplied. The outlay for his own labor had snowballed now that he routinely spent long, hard days driving the 242 miles between Omaha and Alma. When he wasn't behind the wheel or overseeing truck troubles in one of his shops, he was in court. Consequently, his legal expenditures spiraled. His lawyers' fees now ran between $500 and $700 a month, which would translate into $4,000 to $6,000 a month in today's dollars. But no matter how hard his lawyers, Ralph Slocum and Edson Smith, fought, they seemed to get nowhere.

"Give Up the Business"

Near the end of February, Dad drove his accountant, Don Cary, from Alma to Omaha to meet with Glen and the two lawyers. They told him that the Teamsters might well stall for another couple of months. The accountant, Don, told Dad that his truckline would never last that long. Dad was well aware of that. He knew he was facing a problem typical of small operators like himself; he had nothing in reserve. Small operators manage on a little margin. They do fine as long as business is reasonably brisk. However, hit a slow period, a drought, they quickly fall into the red.

By the end of February, Dad was desperate. His cash was gone, and the bank had halved his credit. Even worse, the strike and the uncertain deliveries created so much bitterness, he feared that his customers would be permanently lost. How could he possibly confront the prolonged court battle he surely faced without sliding into bankruptcy?

"Give up the business," his lawyers said. "You can make a living."

But how? Now forty-nine years old, Dad had spent his whole life in trucking.

If only he'd been able to deal with that Jimmy Hoffa and his Teamsters! He might have dealt with the men in local 554, if only Jimmy would let them alone. But no. He had to send his number one labor goon, that 325-pound thug Barney Baker, out to Omaha to supervise the local folks.

And who could talk to Barney? The big blubbery guy had Dad's brother so blind mad and fuming that Glen rode around with a shotgun on the front seat and a pistol in his glove compartment. That mix of Barney and Glen was volatile. Dad knew that his brother was trailing Coffey's Transfer trucks out of town at night.

"If I catch those Teamsters at something," Glen swore, "I'll shoot."

Dad knew his hotheaded little brother well enough to know he meant it.

Expenses up, revenue down, customers mad, endless court cases, bankruptcy in sight, a brother ready to kill. Maybe Dad's lawyers were right. Maybe he shouldn't keep fighting.

Finally, when it came right down to the instant of deciding, Dad realized he'd rather lose a truckline than a beloved brother. So he decided to quit.

Hoffa Rose like a Specter

Tom Coffey had never experienced such silence as the silence that enveloped him when he walked into his main office Monday morning, February 27, 1956. His whole Alma, Nebraska, crew of fifteen drivers lounged about the room, sitting on desks or standing quietly, shifting from one foot to the other. All wore their work clothes, as though ready to head out on their usual runs, to Omaha or Colby, Kansas, or one of the ninety-four towns that Coffey's Transfer Company serviced. Not one man spoke.

Dad wished that his assistant manager, Don Cary, stood beside him. Don's presence, he knew, would ground him. After all, they had worked hand-in-glove for seventeen years, ever since Dad talked Don out of becoming a mortician.

However, Don lay in the local hospital. Dad had taken him there the moment the two men returned the previous night from Omaha after they met with Dad's hotheaded brother and the lawyers. As Dad listened to Don, the figures man, detail the company's past and expected losses, Dad knew he could not last much longer. He had to meet his weekly payroll for thirty-five employees, and he was due to license twenty-five trucks for the current year.

By the end of that painful meeting, Dad decided to take the action he now felt loathe to execute.

"I'm so tired, Tom," Don kept saying during the three-and-a-half-hour drive back to Alma, Don often asleep at Dad's side. And finally, "I've never been this tired in my life."

Hemorrhaging ulcers, the doctor said.

As soon as Dad heard, he understood what caused them. Stress. Tension from dealing with that damnable illegal Teamsters' strike, that contemptible, vicious strike in his Omaha office, that interminable strike that had run for twenty-three weeks now and for no good reason.

His men did not want to be Teamsters. Oh, maybe one or two, but not these men sitting in this room about to hear what they already knew they did not want to know. Goddamn that Jimmy Hoffa! He had taught Don the meaning of stress, and Dad too. He no longer slept much, waiting for the inevitable middle-of-the-night threatening phone call or worrying about his confrontational brother praying for a chance to clobber a Teamster with meat hooks.

Tom Coffey, my dad, must have taken a deep steadying breath as he stood to face the small audience, mostly men, who depended on him for their weekly paychecks. They waited so quietly that when the furnace kicked on, it sounded like a semi ignition. Dad knew they sensed what he was about to say.

Then his voice shattered the silence.

As he spoke, Hoffa no doubt rose like a specter beside him, looking the way Dad had seen him last, a solid little guy, his dark hair in a short brush cut, and a "big, beautiful, butter-eating smile and beautiful front teeth" splitting his baby face in two.

Afterward, Dad could not remember exactly what he told the men, but he knew he conveyed the essentials: that he had decided to sell out. As of Wednesday, he would close all his offices (Alma, Holdrege, Hastings, Lincoln, Omaha). Then liquidation of his equipment would begin.

Dad watched his drivers' expectant faces crumble. Some faces he had known for decades. Some men lived nearby or, like him, attended the Methodist church or served on the school board. "I'll see to it that you all get jobs." His words tasted like ash in his mouth. He hoped he could keep that promise.

When Dad lost Coffey's Transfer Company, he not only lost his business, but he also lost his dream of becoming Nebraska's governor. He had tasted political success, first as mayor of Alma, next as a senator in the state's Unicameral legislature. His primary obstacle was money. If he could get enough money for living expenses, then he could plunge into statewide politics. In 1953, he had put Coffey's Transfer Company up for sale. He hoped for a $100,000 offer, which would provide enough interest to live on, but the only offer, $80,000, was too small, so he decided to build up the value of his business. Surely, in a few more years, he could command a $100,000 sale. But not now. Not with a company that had gone belly up.

Hoffa had seen to that. He destroyed not only Dad's business but also his future.

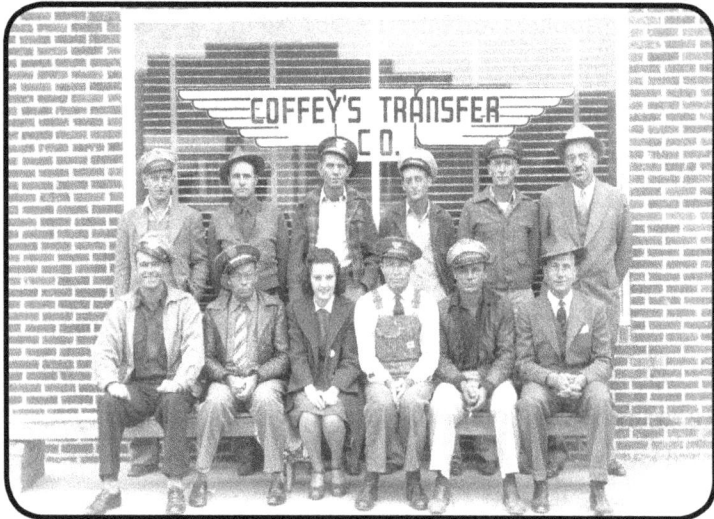

Tom Coffey, back row, right, and his secretary and drivers.
Don Cary, front row, right.

Now Dad would no longer head Coffey's Transfer Company nor would he pitch his hat into the ring to run for governor. Now he must do exactly what his drivers would do, look for a job. After twenty-seven years of being his own boss, Dad would have to take orders from someone else.

However, one thing he knew. He would not sit still for this. No matter what it took, he would get back at that punk Jimmy Hoffa.

8 REVENGE

That February 1956, I checked my mailbox the instant I loped into Kearney State's Case Hall. A letter from Mama. Unable to wait, I tore the envelope open and read as I headed upstairs, one hand on the banister to steady myself.

When I saw what Mama had written, I sat right down on a step and reread her words one at a time: Dad had decided to sell out. I hunched over and clutched the letter to my chest. *What would this mean? Would I have to drop out of college and get a job waiting tables in Bud's Cafe?*

I swallowed hard, got up, and headed to my room.

By the time I arrived, I realized that, bad as Dad's selling out was for me, it was bound to be worse for him. I had to put him first. When I entered my room, with its still unmade bed, my eyes narrowed. My portable Smith-Corona typewriter, out of its carrying case as usual, waited on my desk. A present from Dad. *Oh, how could I comfort him?*

Then words rose in my mind. At first a trickling and then a geyser. I had to catch it fast!

I dumped my books on the bed, wound a blank piece of paper around the platen, and wrote, among other things, "You are the backbone of our family. I saw you this weekend, really worried, and for the first time I realized that THIS fight might be a losing one, that perhaps Daddy couldn't fix and, like Mama's dress she threw away because of the zipper that split down the middle, you might have to throw away a lifetime's work because of one bad spot."

Like all good writers, I exaggerated a bit to make the letter interesting, and I polished and polished and polished it, typing it over and over again. When satisfied, I went back downstairs and put my letter in the outgoing mailbox. I hoped it might cheer Dad up a bit. Little did I think that what I'd written would become my first national publication.

PIECE BY PIECE

Getting rid of Coffey's Transfer Company took almost as much work as running it. First, Dad prepared and made a public announcement that he had closed down his company.

When that news reached the Kearney State's campus that February, I became something of a celebrity. Most people, particularly my teachers, were warm and sympathetic about the news, but one young man I had dated chose to treat me like a fallen social creature. I felt astonished at the pleasure Charlie took in my misfortune. Needless to say, we stopped dating, even though he eventually asked me out a few weeks later when I had won a state championship in oratory and become something of a celebrity again, this time in my own right.

Next Dad suspended his operations in Alma, Holdrege, Hastings, Lincoln, and Omaha. That, to his discomfort, put some thirty-five employees out of work.

Then he contacted Mr. Powell, a Lincoln attorney. Dad had listed his business for sale with Powell since 1953, hoping to get $100,000 for it and retire, but he no longer had a thriving company to sell.

"I've been forced out of business," he told Powell, "so sell Coffey's Transfer for any price you can get, even if you have to sell it piecemeal."

Using those terms, Powell soon found a buyer, and Dad sold his operating license and his equipment to Burlington Trucklines for $30,000 cash. That was a far cry from the $100,000 he'd hoped to reap or even from the $80,000 he'd been offered in 1953, and turned down.

A 1956 Burlington truck.

THE ELECTION WIN

Dad was no longer in the trucking business, but the National Labor Relations Board—and Weinberg, the lawyer for the Teamsters—marched right on with hearing after hearing, most issues old.

First, they dealt with the Coffey's Transfer election. Harold L. Hudson, field examiner for NLRB, notified my dad that ballots would be counted in Lincoln on March 28, and invited Dad to witness it.

Dad groaned at the prospect of watching ballots counted for a nonexistent business. Maybe his friend, Ray Osborn, would represent him.

"Why don't you just not go?" My finger held my place in the controversial novel, *Peyton Place.*

"If I win that election, it will prove that the Teamster strike was illegal, and I could sue them for running me out of business."

"Is that what you're planning to do?"

"Maybe. The odds are a bit stiff. The Teamsters have never settled with anyone, Smith says. But I might try."

So Ray Osborn watched ballots for Dad. A good choice. Osborn was the only person daffier about Ford trucks than Dad. Osborn customized them and drove all over the country showing his creations off. And he lived only fifty miles from Lincoln.

On the morning of March 28, Osborn saw the NLRB field examiner open and count the four legal ballots deposited by the four Coffey's Transfer drivers in Omaha. All four voted against the union. The three illegal Teamster votes weren't counted. In the NLRB's formal language, "A majority of four valid votes has not been cast for the union."

"How do you like that?" Dad's eyes widened. "We beat the hell out of the Teamsters, and I've only been out of business for a month."

Still the election wasn't over. The NLRB's regional director had to prepare a revised tally of ballots, including a count of challenged ballots, and serve them on the union and Dad.

Dad received his notice on April Fool's Day. "Good timing," he observed.

BACK EAST–CORROSIVE ACID

Jimmy and gangster Dio agreed, something had to be done about this journalist, Victor Riesel, who just couldn't keep his nose out of union business. They'd sent him a handful of death threats, but that hadn't stopped the peppery, short man. He just went right on to publish his *New York Daily Mirror* labor column saying that trucking unions were controlled by criminal elements. He even used Johnny Dio's new locals as an example. This had to stop.

"We could off him," Dio said.

"Yeah, but that's too fuckin' easy. He wouldn't live to know what he'd done wrong."

So Jimmy and Dio threw around possibilities until they came up with a particularly vicious one. Dio got right on it.

That Thursday, April 5, 1956, from midnight until 2 a.m., Victor Riesel broadcast from a New York radio station, as usual. He'd decided to ignore the death threats he'd received. He'd be damned if he'd stop announcing what he found when he investigated labor racketeering.

The program over, he and his twenty-three-year-old secretary, Betty Nevins, walked to Lindy's, a Manhattan favorite, to unwind and talk. At forty-one, he needed a secretary. He syndicated his column in 193 newspapers and ran a popular talk-radio show besides. Betty stood tall with shoulder-length blond hair.

About 3 a.m., they left. Victor, by habit, smoothed back his dark hair, took off his glasses, and tucked them in his shirt pocket. That increased his confidence. They headed toward his secretary's car.

Then Abraham Telvi, a slender, black-haired man wearing a blue and white jacket, stepped out of the shadows and threw a vial of sulfuric acid into Victor's eyes.

The acid hit like a deluge, covering his forehead, eyes, and cheeks.

"My gosh!" Victor shouted. He staggered. "My gosh!"

He let himself be dragged back into Lindy's where Betty flushed Victor's face with water.

Outside, Telvi sauntered away trying to wipe a splash of acid off his face. "I should'a got more than five hundred bucks," he groused.

St. Clare's Hospital doctors struggled to save Victor's sight. His unbearable pain was "beyond imagining," Victor said. His "eyes and face felt like they were on fire." Four weeks later, the doctors announced that Victor's vision had been completely lost. Permanent scars, from the acid, marked his forehead, eyebrows, cheek, and jowls.

"Fiendish Attack"

News of the "fiendish attack" on Victor circulated quickly. Overnight his case became a cause célèbre. Soon radio studios, journalists, and labor unions—supported by the *New York Times*—raised $41,000 to help find the vicious acid-tossing villain.

Victor, in a dramatic appearance on *Meet the Press* television, wore dark glasses and charged that labor mobsters had ordered the attack. Bandages wrapped his burned hands, but he raised a clenched fist and called on Congress to form a permanent committee to fight criminals in organized labor.

Vice-President Richard Nixon sent a letter of support. Even President Eisenhower, who had watched *Meet the Press*, warned he'd take action against the labor criminals. Congress became eager to act.

Dad called me. "Did you hear about that blinding of Victor Riesel?"

I winced. "They're saying Hoffa did it."

"Oh, that's disgusting. The man has no morals."

The Federal Bureau of Investigation fingered one Abraham Telvi as the hitman, but they could not arrest him. He was dead, murdered by the mobsters who had hired him. He'd had the guts to demand $50,000 more for a job well done.

The bureau tried three mobsters who helped Dio find a hitman. All three pled or were found guilty.

The FBI linked Jimmy and Dio to the attack and tried Dapper Mr. D, as they called him. But Dio went unpunished. The two mobster witnesses against Dio were struck with sudden cases of amnesia. They couldn't remember a thing that had happened

So Dio—and Jimmy—got off scot-free.

"Just the First Step"

Even after the election case closed, the NLRB kept right on working. Now that it had figured out who won the election, it had to decide whether to find the Teamsters guilty of secondary boycott.

The Teamsters, however, took another tack. When Burlington began to operate its new business in Alma on April 26, Weinberg decided to challenge Dad's sale to Burlington Truck Lines. This set off a whole new round of hearings.

Before Burlington Truck Lines could legally take over Dad's company, the Interstate Commerce Commission (ICC) and the State Railway Commission had to approve the sale.

So Dad found himself in Omaha again, in a courtroom, testifying before an NLRB trial examiner, detailing the fine points of his sale to Burlington including the annual rental he would receive and the fact that he'd promised not to return to trucking for five years.

I didn't get it. "What's in it for the Teamsters?"

"Honey, they don't want me to be able to prove that they ran me out of business. So they're trying to keep me in business by destroying my Burlington sale."

"That's just dumb."

Dad laughed. "But if I can prove they ran me out of business, then I can sue them." He showed me the detailed exhibit he'd prepared. It showed his interline shipping, company by company, from before the Teamsters struck him and then how the amount declined week after week.

Each time Dad mentioned suing, he sounded more certain.

Lincoln, the Big City

In addition to settling the sale of Coffey's Transfer, Dad, like his drivers, had been job hunting. On May 8, 1956, he accepted a position in Lincoln, Nebraska, as state purchasing agent. Dad gave me an option: continue studying at Kearney State or move to Lincoln and attend the University of Nebraska.

At first I resisted the idea of moving to a much bigger school, but the more I thought about it, the more a move to Lincoln seemed like a good idea.

My first year of college had been a resounding success; everything I touched seemed to turn to gold. My grades were excellent, and, in addition to winning the state oratory prize, I had won first prize in a contest for my short story. But my teachers pressured me to major in education— Kearney was, after all, a teachers' college—and I was far from certain I wanted to teach. The university would give me a wider range.

But the turning point proved to be my social life. Life in Case Hall had become uncomfortable after I was accused—anonymously, of course—of being a lesbian. The accusation rested on a party a few of us had thrown, an innocent enough party that got slightly boisterous and spilled out into the hallway. A few of us were wearing nothing but underpants and French berets. Word flashed around the dormitory that we were queer.

The irony of the accusation wasn't lost on me. At that time, I couldn't dodge a boyfriend who had become too possessive. I had decided to break up with Doug at about the same time he decided that he couldn't—and wouldn't—

live without me. He used to hang around the dormitory entrance, waiting for me to leave for class, so he could pursue me down the sidewalk, arguing with me. I feared Doug. Primarily, I was afraid that he wouldn't let go and that I'd have to face the fall semester in Kearney with the unwanted ex-boyfriend in tow. So I chose Lincoln.

I was right about Doug's tenacity, for after we moved to Lincoln, he found out where I lived, somehow, and one day showed up on my doorstep. In an unprecedented move, I appealed to my father to intervene. Generously, he did.

Through the living room window, I watched Dad and Doug standing on the front lawn near the street. They talked and talked, about what I couldn't imagine. I never knew what my dad said to the young man, but it worked. I never saw Doug again.

Suing Hoffa's Pants Off

The Teamsters wouldn't leave Dad alone. When the NLRB argued that Dad's recent testimony about Burlington wasn't pertinent, Weinberg insisted that it was. Judge J. W. Delehant ruled in the union's favor May 8.

And that hoodlum, Barney Baker, didn't disappear either. Reports came to Glen's ears, and then to ours, of Barney's wild swoops into Chicago, Omaha, Kansas City, Minneapolis, and Des Moines, spending money recklessly, money from the dues of rank-and-file Teamsters.

Back in Kansas City, the NLRB couldn't figure out what to focus on first. Should it grant a temporary injunction on the Teamsters strike of a business that no longer existed? Should it ask the court to prohibit that strike altogether and stop the Teamsters' secondary boycott? Or should the NLRB wait until it could act on the Teamsters' breaking of the December 8 Settlement Agreement?

Dad shook his head. "Too much, too late." Nothing that the NLRB had done had helped him in time.

Leaving Alma to relocate in Lincoln felt like moving away from home all over again. Dad chose for us a modest place, smaller than our Alma house. Located not too far away was the governor's residence Dad once had hoped to occupy. Mama gave me a room of my own, a small room in back that needed painting.

"I'll paint it," I bargained, "if you let me choose the colors."

I chose a vivid pink with a baby blue trim. I thought it would be gorgeous, but it was garish, and I spent as little time in it as possible.

Instead, I borrowed Mama's car, a bright red Chevy convertible. Dad had given it to her a few years ago, but she hated it. "You won't see me driving such a conspicuous car." So the convertible became, for all practical purposes, mine. I'd fold down the top and buzz off, ranging around the university campus, zooming out past the penitentiary and beyond the flat motels that clung to the city's rims.

I loved to drive. Dad taught me how. After he taught me "everything he knew," he had me sign up for driver's ed.

"Just in case I forgot something." His slow grin let me know he didn't mean what he said.

I struggled to drive as well as Dad did, but no matter how hard I practiced, I never could get the knack of topping a hill at just the right speed to make my stomach fall below my knees at the crest. Of course, Lincoln's flat streets presented no challenge.

But no matter how I roamed in my new community, I always got home in time for supper. Grabbing an evening meal at home became good sport, with Dad spinning tales about life in the state capitol.

"This guy dropped by to see me this afternoon, sez he knows Jimmy Hoffa." Dad spread his napkin on his lap, smoothed it on his knees. "Says Jimmy's the kind of guy doesn't know when to stop." Dad grinned. "He says that Jimmy's gonna keep climbing until he gets to the 102nd floor." Dad snorted. "And then, not knowing he's at the top, he'll step off and that will be the end of him." When my father whooped, I knew that in his imagination, he had just given Jimmy a little push.

Later, over meatloaf, I heard that smarty-pants Weinberg had lost his big case. He'd been arguing that the NLRB should drop all claims against the Teamsters since Dad was no longer in business. But the latest judge didn't buy Weinberg's argument.

So, in August, trial examiner Louis Libbin of NLRB in Washington recommended that Teamsters Local 554 be ordered to stop alleged unfair labor practices—that is, secondary boycotts, which affected both Clark Brothers and Coffey's Transfer Company.

That's all it took.

As soon as Dad heard, he shot over to Omaha to meet with W. Foy Clark of Clark Brothers and Edson Smith, their common lawyer. The three agreed to sue Jimmy Hoffa's pants off, and Smith prepared the necessary papers.

"Just the first step," Dad's eyes sparkled that night at supper, "in getting back at that punk Jimmy Hoffa."

Out West—Bobby and Beck

Clark R. Mollenhoff, that muckraking journalist who had reported that my dad felt "frantic" about 1955 Teamsters' violence in Omaha, had investigated that union since 1953. Mollenhoff didn't like what he'd found, so he browbeat Bobby Kennedy into investigating the Teamsters—not Hoffa, but Dave Beck, president of the nation's largest and richest union.

From the outside, Beck looked respectable. He belonged to a university board, chaired international union conferences, and knew many Republican politicians, including President Eisenhower. Beck saw himself as a "labor statesman," but some Teamsters irreverently called him "His Majesty, the Wheel."

So Bobby and his assistants went on a fact-finding journey: Chicago, Los Angeles, and Seattle, Beck's home base, where they found Beck better known than the mayor.

After Bobby's assistant, Carmine Bellino, a high-level investigator and a financial whiz, examined the available data, he deduced that Beck was a crook. And not a petty one. He had misused hundreds of thousands of dollars of Teamsters' money. On himself and his family alone, Beck had spent tens of thousands of dollars on personal items: golf clubs, outboard motors, a freezer, chairs, love seats, twenty-one pairs of nylon stockings. Teamsters' headquarters paid $163,000 for Beck's large, brick ranch home and several smaller houses occupied by his mother, a bodyguard, and others. Beck lived in the big house rent-free—for life.

Bobby came back to Washington, DC, with fifty-two examples of Beck's misuse of power and money. He firmly believed that Dave Beck, Jimmy's boss, needed to be toppled. Nothing, of course, would make Jimmy happier.

Back East—Indian Wrestling

Dapper Eddie Cheyfitz wanted, in the worst way, to put Jimmy Hoffa, forty-four, and Bobby Kennedy, thirty-one, together. *They have so much in common, those two*, Eddie thought. *Both pugnacious go-getters, spunky bantamweights, habitual workaholics, and physical fitness nuts. Maybe they'd even hit it off.*

Besides, a Washington lawyer-fixer-PR man, Eddie knew both men.

He and Jimmy were close. Jimmy had hired the PR guy to clean up Dio's image, a formidable task.

Redheaded Eddie had known Bobby only a year, but they got on, although Eddie didn't know that Bobby already had an FBI report on Jimmy. However, Eddie did know that Senator McClellan had named Bobby chief counsel of a new Senate Rackets Committee out to investigate labor. And Eddie knew Bobby was all geared up to go after Teamsters' President Dave Beck.

So the dandy little lawyer set to work on Bobby. First, he toured Bobby through the Teamsters' nearly new, flamboyant $5 million headquarters, the shimmering Marble Palace, as it's called.

"I see the union's picked a strategic location." Bobby nodded toward the nearby Capitol where he worked. "A hop, skip, and a jump puts you in a senator's lap."

Eddie laughed and led Bobby inside for a prearranged tour of President Beck's sumptuous burled walnut and glass office. Bobby scrutinized Beck's palatial desk, his book cases and his photographs, and his wastebasket, empty. Then Bobby and Eddie looked out Beck's massive window at the groomed expanse of grass between them and the Capitol.

"Jimmy's a changed man." Eddie licked his lips and smiled. "You know, he could be a real force for good within the Teamsters."

"You wouldn't me ribbing me, would you, Eddie?" Bobby turned and eyed the dapper little man. "Sounds as though you're saying that after a wild and reckless youth during which he had perhaps committed some evil deeds, Jimmy has transformed."

Eddie's voice bubbled. "Let me arrange a visit, and you can see for yourself."

As they left the palace, Bobby delivered a light punch to Eddie's shoulder. "I got to hand it to you. You've got me curious about that tough little Teamster." And he agreed to the visit.

Next Eddie had to convince Jimmy, a task that made him feel nervous, even a bit embarrassed.

"Jimmy," he blurted, "Bobby Kennedy wants to have a private meeting with you."

"Jeez, about what?" Jimmy flicked his eyes toward the ceiling. "Complaining about the damn late-night lights in Teamster headquarters?" Jimmy pursed his lips. "Bobby said he came out of the Capitol one evening, all geared to go home until he saw that our lights were still on. Figured we were still working so he turned around and went back to work." Jimmy tugged at his tie, already askew. "So I gave an order: leave our fuckin' lights on all night."

Eddie shook his head. "You devil." They both laughed.

Jimmy's eyes flicked over to his lawyer. "You know I got nothing to talk to that cocksucker about."

"I really don't know what he wants," Eddie confessed, "but if it's okay with you, we could have dinner at my place."

Jimmy didn't hesitate. "Okay, go ahead, set up the fuckin' meeting."

Eddie's eyes bulged.

"Ah, Eddie, you should know my theory by now. I open the door to my sleaze-ball enemies, because I know all about my frigging friends." Jimmy chortled.

Eddie set the meeting for Tuesday evening, February 19.

By Monday morning, Bobby had a bad case of cold feet. He stood in J. Edgar Hoover's office. Hoover, a formidable figure, had directed the FBI for twenty-two years. He and Bobby worked together.

"I should never have agreed to meet Hoffa." Bobby rubbed the back of his neck. "I don't know what got into me. Curiosity, I suppose." He glanced at Hoover's phone. "But it isn't too late to call and cancel." Bobby stopped and looked at Hoover whose sharp, white shirt collar almost swallowed his short, thick neck.

"I wouldn't advise that, Bobby." Hoover's dark brows drew closer. His face tightened. "It might look peculiar. Hoffa's flying in from Detroit just for this meeting."

WIMPY HANDSHAKE AND WHITE SOCKS

Outside Eddie's white brick house in Chevy Chase, Maryland, snow fell steady and straight, dusting his bushes and sidewalk, and fogging his window glass. Jimmy arrived first. White pellets of snow splattered his black overcoat. Eddie brushed the flakes off as cool winter air swirled around their ankles. Soon Bobby arrived, too, bringing his Boston accent with him.

Bobby's handshake felt wimpy, Jimmy said later. Bobby couldn't believe how short Jimmy was or that he wore his suit pants cuffed over white socks.

"Drinks?" Eddie offered, but both his guests said no. Jimmy never drank.

They sat at Eddie's dining room table where he served them a roast beef dinner and conversation. He talked about everything but Jimmy meeting Bobby, about the weather, and about Dave Beck, the Teamsters' president, and his thirty-seven-year-old son and only child, Dave Beck Jr.

"Beck has ruined Junior. He won't let his son make a decision. He chooses his friends. He even orders his meals." Eddie passed the mashed potatoes. "Can't Dave see he's turning his boy into a jellyfish?"

"Well, Junior looks well-fed enough." Bobby had noticed Junior's fleshy round head. "But I agree. Beck's attitude toward his boy is the worst."

Jimmy jumped into the silence that followed and talked, as usual, about how tough he was, about the dozens of picket-line fights he'd had with cops, and how he'd won. "It's true that I've got a crap long record of violence, but I beat nearly all of them motherfuckers. Smartass employers try to cross me, I'd destroy them."

"Gentlemen." Eddie stood. "Let's adjourn to the living room."

Bobby stood too. "Eddie, I'd like to talk to Jimmy alone." With that Boston accent, Bobby sounded as though he spoke to a butler. And like a butler, Eddie picked up some dishes and retreated to the kitchen, out of sight, but not out of earshot.

Jimmy slouched on the couch, while Bobby stood, his back to the fireplace.

"I came here, Jimmy, so I could set a few things straight in my mind."

Jimmy shrugged. "Okay by me."

"How much money do the Teamsters pay you?"

Jimmy stiffened. "Frankly, I don't think that's any of your goddamned business."

Bobby's face reddened. "Look here, Jimmy. Let's keep this friendly."

"Okay." Jimmy grinned. "Somewhat friendly anyway."

"How come you never went to college?"

"What the fuck! Don't get me started." But Jimmy did start up, telling Bobby of his fatherless childhood, his poverty-ridden mother, the Depression. "The Hoffa family had no silk sheets."

But questions kept coming, as though Bobby already were the DA he would become—questions about the Teamsters, racketeers, the underworld. Jimmy denied any connection.

"How about those paper locals that gangster helped you with?"

"Geez, you mean Dio?"

Bobby nodded.

"That wasn't Dio's doing, that was my own fuckin' doing. As for Dio, he's a friend of mine. I'm entitled to my own goddamned friends, aren't I?"

In the silence that followed, Bobby smiled and leaned back against the fireplace. "I'm told you're one pretty tough fellow."

Jimmy struggled to keep his face straight. "Now who in damnation could have told you that?"

"But not so tough I couldn't beat you at Indian hand wrestling."

"What?" Jimmy whooped.

"I said I can best you in Indian hand wrestling."

"Are you nuts? We came here to talk, not to play kid games."

But Bobby stood up and loosened his necktie. "You afraid?"

"Forget it, Bobby. I don't want to hand wrestle you."

But Bobby took off his jacket and rolled up his sleeves. "You not chicken, are you?"

"Ah, hell. Man you are really something else."

"Come on, Jimmy. You got cold feet?"

So Jimmy stood up, pulled his jacket off, but left his shirt sleeves unrolled. Together they pulled chairs up to a table and sat down. They positioned their elbows on the table, grasped hands.

"I'm ready whenever the fuck you are."

When Bobby moved, Jimmy held both hands upright for a couple of seconds and boom! he toppled Bobby's arm and cracked his knuckles flat to the tabletop.

"Whoa!" Bobby shook his arm. "You're just lucky. Let's try again."

This time, both arms remained upright. The tendons on Bobby's neck stood out; he grabbed the edge of the table and pushed hard, but again, Jimmy slammed Bobby's arm to the table. And grinned.

Bobby said nothing. He just rose, his face so red it looked on fire, grabbed his jacket and his overcoat and burst out into the snowstorm. He didn't even say "good-night" to Eddie.

BACK EAST—$1,000 UP FRONT

In the meantime, Jimmy had been busy. Six days before the dinner, he'd met in Detroit with a New York lawyer, John Cheasty, who had traveled from Washington posing as Eddie Smith. They met in the Teamsters' office late at night. Jimmy wanted Cheasty, a short smiling man with thinning gray hair, to get a job on that new Rackets Committee and spy on its investigators.

Dave Beck, Jimmy's boss and IBT president, needed to be toppled, and the Rackets Committee might have enough dirt on Beck to do so. Its initial charge of tax evasion sent Beck fleeing to Europe to avoid the committee's subpoenas. Jimmy could use some shrewd Rackets Committee figures to oust Beck and replace him as Teamsters' president.

Jimmy reached into a drawer, handed $1,000 in cash to Cheasty, and offered him a retainer of $2,000 a month for nine months. Cheasty accepted.

Senator John McClellan, head of Rackets Committee.

Back in Washington, Cheasty, his voice shrill, called Bobby Kennedy. "I have some information that will make your hair stand on end."

After Cheasty told Bobby, they hurried to recount the story to Senator McClellan, the committee chair, who called in FBI Director J. Edgar Hoover.

"Here's the deal." Hoover scowled. "We could set a trap for Hoffa if you, Cheasty, are willing to be the bait."

Cheasty hemmed and hawed. He murmured about his heart condition. But at last he decided to "play along."

He called Hoffa, and they agreed to meet March 12, 1957, at Dupont Circle in Washington to receive Cheasty's first report. When they met, hidden FBI cameras rolled and captured pictures of Cheasty giving Hoffa a committee memo about Dave Beck.

"It's enough to cook Beck's goose," Cheasty piped.

Jimmy slipped Cheasty $2,000 cash, not knowing that the goose the Rackets Committee intended to cook would be Jimmy's.

AT THE DUPONT PLAZA HOTEL

Jimmy found out the next day at the Dupont Plaza Hotel, when he crossed the lobby to the elevator, headed for his room. Five guys, wearing identical gray suits and wide-brimmed hats, approached him.

"FBI," said one.

Jimmy's face tightened. "Big fucking deal. Why are you stopping me?"

"You're under arrest." A few men fanned out behind Jimmy.

"For what?" He shoved his hands in his pockets.

"Just come with us."

Jimmy's nostrils flared. "Like hell I will." He punched the elevator button. "First I'm goin' to my friggin' room, make a phone call. Then I'll come."

The five men surrounded Jimmy. He threw both hands up. "Goddammit, don't bug me. You want trouble, you can have it. These people in the lobby, most of them are my guys. So go ahead, make a fuckin' fuss, and we're gonna have one hell of a fight."

The agents pulled back. Jimmy called Edward Bennett Williams, his lawyer, then went with the FBI to precinct headquarters. At the station house, Bobby Kennedy waited along with a gang of newspaper guys.

What a victory this was for Bobby, who'd come to the courthouse just to see Hoffa arraigned! Oddly enough, while the two waited, they chewed the fat, ending in a good-natured debate over who could do the most push-ups.

After the FBI photographed Hoffa, fingerprinted him, and booked him on bribery and conspiracy charges, Kennedy said, "We finally got you, Hoffa."

Jimmy scowled. "You ain't got one fuckin' goddamn thing."

But Jimmy's bribery case—Cheasty's testimony plus the FBI photos—looked airtight. So airtight that Bobby, bragging to reporters about the case, quipped: "If Hoffa is acquitted, I'll jump off the Capitol dome."

He thought he spoke off the record, but someone printed his boast.

Squirming on the Witness Chair

Two weeks later, the Rackets Committee called Dave Beck to testify again. He had already returned from Europe to sit once in front of the investigators. The first time Bobby Kennedy had questioned Beck, he refused sixty-five times to answer questions. He refused to testify on the grounds that he might incriminate himself—that is, he took the

Fifth. The next time, he took it 117 times, as Bobby plied Beck with questions about his misuse of Teamsters' power and money.

Thanks to television, more than a million Americans watched Beck squirming on the witness chair as Bobby tried, in vain, to show the Teamsters' president's support to racketeers and organized crime.

Few doubted Beck's guilt. The Rackets Committee still had Bobby's fifty-two examples of the president's misuse of power and money.

Shortly after ducking Bobby's many questions, Dave Beck announced that he would not seek reelection to the general presidency of the Teamsters in October. Music to Jimmy's heart!

Then one May night, Dad told us that chubby Carl Curtis had dropped by his state purchasing agent office again.

Dad drummed his feet on the floor. "And guess what?" His words piled all over each other. "Joe McCarthy's dead, so McClellan named cream puff Curtis to serve on the Rackets Committee instead. He says they're gonna call Jimmy in to testify. Gonna take a look at secondary boycotts. Boy, does Curtis hate them! Almost as much as I do."

Dad cut a piece of meatloaf, popped it in his mouth, chewed, swallowed, patted his lips dry. "I treated Carl to coffee, and he said, 'Just between the two of us, that Bobby Kennedy sure is a spoiled brat. Doesn't have the patience to build a solid legal case against the men he's questioning. So he just engages in shouting matches.'"

Dad swirled a piece of meatloaf into its juices. His voice softened. "And guess what. Carl wanted to know if I'd be willing to come to Washington, DC, and testify against Hoffa before this committee."

Dad whooped. "I nearly broke his arm off, I pumped it so hard."

Just like that. A second chance to get back at that punk Jimmy Hoffa!

Joe's Comeback

In the meantime, Jimmy's bribery trial opened that June 24 in Washington, DC, with eight African Americans sitting in the jury box, to no one's surprise. African Americans made up more than half of Washington's population.

And who should jump in to take advantage of that but Barney Baker, at one time an organizer for a Teamsters' local—full of blacks—in Washington. When Jimmy's trial started, Baker sped to the city to cultivate his old friends. They led him to black former heavyweight boxing champion Joe Louis.

Bobby Kennedy, of course, still felt the case looked easy. He expected it to be Jimmy's "knockout blow." Its timing seemed perfect. Instead of Jimmy ascending to the Teamsters' presidency in October, as expected, the FBI would lead him to jail for bribery. Bobby listened, with satisfaction, as Cheasty testified, not fully registering that Jimmy's adroit lawyer chewed apart much of Cheasty's three and a half days of testimony.

Then, on July 15, just before the final afternoon session, who should make a surprise appearance in the courtroom but the great Joe Louis. Onlookers inhaled.

Jimmy jumped up when he spotted Joe, greeted the former heavyweight boxing champion as one old friend greets another. Jimmy clapped his hand on Louis's shoulder, and Joe put his hand on Jimmy's arm and grinned at the onlookers.

"I've come to wish Hoffa well. He's an old friend of mine," he lied. The two men did know each other, but only slightly. Joe may have felt closer to Barney who paid for Joe's travel, his hotel—and his appearance.

After the "not guilty" verdict came in, Edward Bennett Williams, Jimmy's lawyer, hollered across the room to Bobby, "Shall I send you a parachute?"

Bobby scowled.

Joe, still in the courtroom, mingled with the jubilant crowd. The courtroom became a carnival. Barney showed up, bringing a cake in the shape of the United States Capitol. The Capitol was topped by a figurine Robert Kennedy jumping from the dome with a parachute.

"Cake, Bobby?" Jimmy hollered.

But Bobby, pushing his way out the door, didn't respond.

"Like Little Boys in a School Yard"

"Look, Mama, look!" I bellowed into the kitchen one afternoon later that August.

"Oh what is it now, Marilyn?" Mama came into the living room, wiping her hands on a dish towel.

I pointed to the TV. She stepped forward, squinted. "Why it looks like Jimmy Hoffa."

"It is, Mama." The image shifted. "And those are the Kennedy brothers. That's Robert. And the one in the middle, talking, that's Senator John."

Mama slid down on the edge of Dad's recliner, the better to see. The camera flashed back and forth. In one direction, it showed Bobby Kennedy, the official questioner for the Rackets Committee, between his brother John and another senator who said, "All right, with that record straightened out now, we may proceed." The men sat almost shoulder to shoulder.

Then Bobby spoke: "Mr. Hoffa, did you know Mr. Joseph Holtzman?" and the camera swung to Jimmy, sitting all by himself, his chest pulled up high, his dark hair gleaming under the lights.

"You'd think he could afford a decent haircut," Mama muttered, and we heard Jimmy answer, "Yes, I did."

Bobby: He was a close friend of yours, was he?

Jimmy: I knew Joe Holtzman.

Bobby: He was a close friend of yours?

Jimmy: I knew Joe Holtzman.

Bobby sounded annoyed: He was a close friend of yours?

So did Hoffa: I knew Joe Holtzman.

Bobby barked: He was a close friend of yours?

Jimmy: Just a moment. I knew Joe Holtzman (Jimmy jabbed his finger at Bobby), and he wasn't any particular friend of mine.

Bobby seethed: Just answer the question.

"I better call your father." Mama stood and headed out back where Dad tinkered in the garage. And I watched Jimmy in fascination. He never took the Fifth, but he never revealed anything either.

Holtzman was a helpful friend of Hoffa's and a labor consultant in Detroit who was adroit at negotiating on Hoffa's behalf. Negotiating Teamsters' style in the sense that Holtzman would go into a business first and shake them down. Then Hoffa would come in and collect.

Sometimes Senator John Kennedy took the floor, shaking his finger at Jimmy, and reading him the riot act. I didn't know it of course, and maybe John didn't either, but the more the Kennedy boys tried to make Jimmy fess up in remorse, the bigger they made him seem. Historians later said that the Kennedys made a name for themselves with their questioning, but they also made a name for Jimmy. From that broadcast on, Jimmy Hoffa became a national figure.

I listened until Bobby, furious, said, "Mr. Hoffa, you have not answered any questions for the last twenty-five minutes."

Jimmy hiked his shoulders and replied, "That isn't true!"

And he hadn't even climbed to the presidency of the Teamsters Union yet.

And he wouldn't. Not if Bobby could help it.

UNFIT TO LEAD THE TEAMSTERS

It's August 24, 1957, and Jimmy's running for president of the Teamsters. He ran in style, publishing a platform with nine points. One point promised more area-wide contracts, of course—that's his specialty. In another point, he tried to make cozy with the AFL-CIO, an organization on the brink of throwing the Teamsters out.

But when Bobby heard the next point, that Hoffa supported the Fifth Amendment, the chief counsel erupted: "Hoffa never takes the Fifth. He doesn't have to. His testimony is a curious and practically unfathomable mixture of ambiguity, verbosity, audacity, and mendacity.

That protects him, but he needs the Fifth to keep others from incriminating him."

Bobby immersed himself and his whole staff into scrutinizing Jimmy. Only five weeks and two days remained until the Teamsters' convention started in Miami September 30. With any luck, Bobby and his boys could create a rebellious Teamster membership that would reject Jimmy's presidential bid.

On Tuesday, September 24, Jimmy went to Miami to get ready for the convention when Bobby opened the Rackets Committee hearings. Typically, these hearings ran from 10:00 a.m. to noon, but Bobby set them early in the morning and ran them as late as 9:30 p.m.

Senator McClellan, the chair, charged Jimmy with thirty-three "improper" activities (all discarded later) and said he was unfit to lead the Teamsters. McClellan scheduled Jimmy to take the stand on Saturday, two days before the week-long Teamsters' convention opened.

Jimmy sent a flurry of lawyers to the Senate; they postponed this meeting until after the convention. But newspaper headlines all over the nation announced Jimmy's thirty-three improper activities, and the Secretary of Labor cautioned Teamster delegates to "consider carefully" those charges.

Then a New York grand jury charged Jimmy with perjury, an old wiretapping indictment the court would set aside later.

And thirteen "dissident" Teamsters, aided by Kennedy's staff, asked a federal court in Washington to halt the election. "The delegate selection's been rigged," they claimed.

The court granted the Teamsters' request but set it aside the next day, after the newspapers had reported it.

Yet Kennedy continued to believe that those delegates weren't qualified, and McClellan wired Teamsters' officers in Miami that the union "might not" have chosen delegates legally.

"Thinking they had Jimmy down, they piled on like little boys in a school yard," writes Jim Clay, Jimmy's biographer.

Until the last day of the Teamsters' convention, the election outcome seemed uncertain, primarily because some stormy convention delegates didn't want a hot-button president like Jimmy. But at last, the Teamsters chose Jimmy for president by a whopping 72 percent vote.

Bobby reeled when he learned that Hoffa had won. "I find it hard to believe."

"I don't wonder the fucker was amazed," Hoffa said, "in view of what he did to defeat me."

DIRTY BACK-ALLEY POLITICS

But problems kept dropping around Jimmy "like confetti at a country fair," said his lawyer.

Or perhaps like snowflakes.

Snow covered the world-famous boardwalk at Atlantic City, New Jersey, as the convention of American Federation of Labor and Congress of Industrial Organizations (AFL-CIO) opened December 5, 1957.

Many Teamsters took their places in this large group of unions. The Teamsters held significant power in the AFL-CIO. The organization could count on at least $750,000 a year from the union, but this Thursday, its powerful place was threatened, some said by Jimmy winning the presidency, others said by Bobby Kennedy.

AFL-CIO president and founder George Meany, known for his long flat cheeks, opened the meeting. Meany made it clear that he had nothing against the Teamsters' rank and file, only against its new leader.

Then he turned and shook his fist at a picture of Jimmy. "I won't drum the Teamsters Union out of the AFL-CIO if it removes its new president." He backed away from the picture with a shudder. "Jimmy Hoffa's corruption disgusts me!" Then he returned to the podium and demanded that Jimmy, who was not there, respond.

Jimmy, in New York on trial for wiretapping a grand jury, a trial that would end in a hung jury, sent his reply through the press: "We'll see."

What to do about the Teamsters became the talk of the convention. When the roll call came, the delegates voted nearly 5 to 1 to drum out the Teamsters.

When Jimmy heard, he exploded. "This makes me really red-assed. Because I know that fuckin' Bobby whispered in a lot of ears at the top." Then he laughed. "Those ears were scared as hell they'd be investigated by the Rackets Committee if they crossed Kennedy." He flinched. "It's all nothing but dirty back-alley politics by that little bastard."

Getting Ready to Get Hoffa

I'd nearly forgotten about the Rackets Committee when Dad came home in December 1957 with a list in his fist of people summoned to Washington, DC, to testify before that Senate committee. He led the list of eight, but Glen was also on it, and W. Foy Clark of Clark Brothers and Albert Parker from Omaha's Teamsters Local 554.

The big day was almost a year away, but Dad spent evening after evening preparing his notes or pouring over a Washington tour guide he'd picked up somewhere.

By November 1958, Dad decided that the Rackets Committee occasion was historic enough to warrant taking the entire family; we'd leave a day early so we could see a few of the sights.

"I guess you'll have to skip school so you can come along." Dad grinned.

I hastened to obey. My professors excused me from classes, and a journalism professor assigned me to write about the hearings themselves, so I went to Washington, notebook in hand, resolved to be a first-class reporter.

The trip to Washington gave me my first glimpse of the East, that mythological region that faced the sea.

In retrospect, I remember best the great turnpikes— Pennsylvania's turnpike in particular—and the awe they created in me. I'd never seen turnpikes; interstate highways had yet to penetrate the Great Plains. These great streaming masses of concrete implied the staggering population of the eastern states. For not only were these highways huge, they were as often as not full: hundreds of automobiles streamed in both directions. Sometimes, along the great divided highways, you couldn't see automobiles in the opposite lane at all. And back East, no one got stuck behind a slow-moving tractor: these highways had more than one lane.

Nothing prepared me for Washington, the way government went on and on and on here. *The Mecca of the United States*, I called it. Its monumental statues and white buildings included the Marble Palace, home of the Teamsters.

"Let's go in and take a look." I flattened my nose against the car window.

But Dad drove on. "I've seen about as much of the Teamsters as I want to see." He paused. "Anyway, I feel as though I've been inside. Jimmy used to brag about it so often in negotiations."

"Does he have an office there?"

Dad snorted. "You bet he does! With a private elevator and brass door knobs that get buffed every night until they gleam. Or so he claimed."

I carried my notebook with me everywhere. "This morning," I wrote, "we viewed Lincoln's death pillow in the house where he died. It was almost morbid the way details of his death have been preserved. Lincoln, because of his height, lay diagonally across the bed."

From Lincoln's death bed, we visited Arlington Cemetery to see the changing of the guard at the Tomb of the Unknown Soldier. The pomp reminded me of England, of Christopher and Alice viewing the guard change at Buckingham Palace in the children's book Mama had read to us.

At the cemetery, we watched a military burial, then the marine memorial of the soldiers raising the flag at Iwo Jima plus Mt. Vernon and Alexandria.

But none of it was as fascinating as the hearings.

Big Barney's Show

Over supper that night at the hotel dining room, Glen filled us in on the Rackets Committee antics that we'd missed.

"Big Barney was in the hot seat when I got there. I recognized him right away, but he pretended not to know me." Glen laughed. "I sat as close as I could to him, close enough to hear his lawyer whispering, 'Take the Fifth. Take the Fifth.'

"But Barney shrugged his lawyer off, squirmed in the red leather chair, big enough to hold him. What a showman he is! Senator Curtis said he cut up like this yesterday, too, cracking up the audience, including Jimmy."

"Jimmy was there?" Dad stopped sawing his mushroom-covered steak.

"You bet! So Tom, you missed your chance to punch him in the nose."

"More likely spit in his eye!" Dad popped his steak in his mouth.

"So Bobby Kennedy asked Barney, 'Did you know Cockeyed Dunne?'

"Old Barney grinned at the audience. 'I didn't know him as Cockeyed Dunne. I knew him as John Dunne.'

"But Bobby didn't laugh. He asked, 'Where is he now?'

"Barney rolled his eyes heavenward. 'He has met his maker.'

"Bobby ignored the tittering. 'How did he do that?'

"'I believe through electrocution in the city of New York of the state of New York.'

"Jimmy roared, but Bobby pushed right on, asking about every hoodlum I'd ever heard of and plenty that I hadn't but Barney knew them all.

"'Everywhere you go there has been violence.' Kennedy's voice sounded solemn. 'The people you associate with are the scum of the United States, and you are a part of them.'

"But you know what?" Glen slapped his knee. "Barney didn't seem one bit remorseful."

Dad's Turn

The next morning, November 20, dawned sunny and chilly, still freezing cold as we bundled up and headed to the Capitol. The huge building stood all cream colored in the sunlight.

My sister, Margery, sixteen, headed for the monumental stairs, a hundred steps, I thought.

"Beat you to the top," she moved toward them.

"We can't do that." I jerked her elbow and whispered, "Remember, Dad's heart."

But Margery, that imp, skittered up the steps.

About halfway up, she stopped, turned, and looked down at us—me, Mama, Dad—watching her. She grinned. Dad whistled, gestured, and we turned toward an alternate entrance. After a while, Margery joined us.

My little sister Margery, age sixteen.

In the corridor outside the Senate hearing room, standing on the marble stairs, I met that famous man, Robert Kennedy, counsel for the committee. His shock of hair looked unruly, out of place for a man in his position! His handshake felt polite but not his necktie. Gold rimmed the wide horizontal stripes of his bold silk tie.

In the hearing room itself, which seemed carved

out of a single piece of wood, sat the committee, including Senator John L. McClellan, chairman, and Senator Carl Curtis. From where we sat, I could see Kennedy and Albert Parker, business agent for Teamsters Local 554, Omaha. Parker testified before Dad did. Or "didn't testify" is more like it. Unlike Barney, Parker took the Fifth Amendment forty-six times. I counted them.

We also heard testimony from Texas; it made me realize how lucky we had been in the Nebraska fight. Oh, one of their stories rang familiar: rocks and bottles hurled at the windshields of oncoming trucks. But Teamsters there beat men, shot them, overturned trucks, bombed warehouses, destroyed property, blocked highways, set trucks on fire, dynamited terminals, and planned murder. However, young Buck Owens, a Teamsters' organizer from Texas, bragged that he drew the line at murder or hurting women and children.

Then my dad testified. He read from his notes in a clear, steady voice, detailing the now-familiar story. His meetings with Barney and Kavner, those gangsters, who represented Jimmy Hoffa of the Teamsters. The strike with its pickets. Tires slashed, punctured with ice picks, the wiring torn out of trucks, and kingpins pulled. Threatening phone calls. The truckload of butter dumped on a public garage floor.

When Dad mentioned the Teamsters' secondary boycott, he submitted the exhibit he'd made, showing his losses of tonnage week by week. He mentioned some trucking firms who refused to turn freight over to him, and he singled out Darling Transfer who did business with him "until the Teamsters struck Darling in Kansas City. The union used the same tactic with Des Moines Transfer, striking its Minneapolis terminal until it agreed to stop doing business with me."

Bobby Kennedy and Dad then went over his history blow by blow, detail by detail, all the way to Judge Donohoe's untimely death. Their back-and-forth questions and answers sounded like cross-examination in a trial.

When Dad described the NLRB election that lasted longer than the strike, committee members protested. "Why did the NLRB delay so long? Take three months to count seven votes?"

"Legal delaying tactics," an NLRB representative replied. "One man's red tape is another man's due process."

"This inaction is inexcusable." Senator Curtis's face turned red. "That election should have been disposed of by the middle of October. It would have ended the secondary boycott right then instead of dragging on all those months."

"That's correct," Dad said.

"But instead, you had to continue paying all the expenses of Coffey's Transfer, of course. Equipment and licensing and taxes and insurance?"

"Yes, sir. And we were still operating our intrastate freight services. We didn't cease operation until March 1."

Then Senator McClellan, the chairman of the committee, spoke: "It is ridiculous that seven votes couldn't be counted in fifteen minutes and certified one way or the other. Even if every vote were challenged, it ought not to take over three days for one man to go down there and get the information as to the qualifications and eligibility of the seven who voted, and make a finding on it."

Next Senator Ervin, with his puffy red nose, rose and spoke in his thick North Carolina accent. "I have heard the poet report that wretches hang so that jurors may dine. You just starved to death while justice was traveling on leaded feet, despite the fact that you had a just cause that ought to have been adjudicated by any man with the intelligence of the grade of a moron in not over thirty minutes. That is the tragic commentary on the way justice is administered in the industrial field in the United States."

"Mr. Coffey," Senator Curtis spoke up, "if you don't mind, do you have an idea of what your loss was on your truckline by being forced out of business?"

"Two-thirds of the value of my franchise and my physical property."

"And that says nothing," Senator Curtis said, "of your loss of future business and the earnings in this activity, does it not?"

Dad nodded. "That is correct."

They talked about the secondary boycott and how, by the time the federal court found the Teamsters guilty, Dad was out of business.

Mr. Kennedy asked, "So you won everything, but lost your business?"

And Dad said, "That is right. I never lost a case before a federal court or before the NLRB, but I lost my business."

MEN LOVE DARKNESS

Then McClellan swore in Glen, now working for Ford Van Lines in Omaha. He described how, during the strike, he actually went out on the trucks and made or attempted to make deliveries and pickups.

"In one case, I had thirty-seven letters asking our company to pick up goods from the Omaha Cold Storage Company in Omaha. I took those letters to Omaha Cold and gave them to its manager, David Saunders, so that he would get them ready for me the next day.

"He told me that he couldn't handle my orders; that he had been put on a Teamster blacklist. 'As long as I do business with you, no other truckline will do business with me,' he said."

Glen and the committee focused on these blacklist letters, including samples Glen had, until Chairman McClellan asked, "You do solemnly swear that the evidence, given before this Senate select committee shall be the truth, the whole truth, and nothing but the truth, so help you God?" Glen swore and stepped down.

Next came W. Foy Clark, still a copartner in Clark Brothers Transfer Company in Omaha. It hadn't gone out of business. When I heard his side of the story, it sounded a lot like Dad's—a strike, secondary boycott, attempted election, and court case—but Clark experienced even more damage.

"We had a fire," Clark said, "which burned almost completely one truck, and two others were damaged extensively, and our terminal at Omaha was burned considerably. Arson."

Senator Ervin popped up. "There is something in the scriptures which says that men love darkness rather than light because it conceals evil. We run into that at times when violence involves injury of property."

Senator Curtis shifted to another topic. "How effective was the boycott against you?"

"We were fortunate," Clark said, "inasmuch as we did a great share of our business in intrastate and local business, which the Teamsters didn't so tightly control, and probably our business was cut in two, about the middle, and we were able to continue operation at half-mast."

"That's the only reason you were able to keep going?" Senator Curtis wanted to know.

"Yes. It saved our lives."

"And the boycott?" Senator Curtis asked. "Is it still going on?"

Clark nodded. "We still have a one-man picket line at our Omaha office, and we still can't do business with many of the interline carriers in Omaha."

Then it was over, for that day at least. I stretched and headed out with the family.

"You were terrific," I told Dad.

"Right!" he pulled his earlobe. "And now I'm going to take you to eat supper in a restaurant you'll never forget." And he did.

THE UNFORGETTABLE MEAL

Dad took us to a nearby row house, skinny, and we waited for a little elevator to take us to the third floor, which opened into a big, classy dining room. The bustling waiters and the maître d' wore snazzy red jackets. Margery mock-flirted with our waiter who responded in kind until we cracked up with laughter.

The restaurant's kitchen sat right in the middle of the dining room. We sat close enough so I could see the cooks grilling meat. The food tasted delicious; my steak melted in my mouth.

Then the dessert menu arrived.

"Cherries jubilee. What's that?" Margery wrinkled her nose.

"It's a cherry and ice cream dessert that's set on fire before you eat it," Mama looked at Margery. "But don't you dare order it. Look at how expensive it is, the priciest on the menu."

However, when the waiter took our orders, Margery requested cherries jubilee.

"But it has brandy in it." Teetotaling Mama looked horrified until Dad patted her hand. "Don't worry, honey. The alcohol will all burn off in the fire."

Cherries jubilee was worth every penny. The waiter put on quite a show. The room lights dimmed as he lit the dessert with a whoosh, and orange flames leaped into the air turning blue as they subsided.

After we ate, I leaned toward Margery. "So how was it?"

"Pretty good. Especially the brandy." She patted her lips with the cloth napkin. "I think I'll order another."

We all laughed, but I wouldn't have put it past her. She's the prettiest and the youngest in our family, so she gets away with everything.

The Landrum-Griffin Act

Jimmy Hoffa and his Teamsters Union not only drove my father out of business but, in doing so, unwittingly drove our family into life on a stage larger than we had known before. First relocating to Lincoln, then the trip to Washington enlarged our vista.

Listening to men testify at the Rackets Committee, I understood that what had happened to my father was not simply a local matter, not just a squabble between a union and a manager. It was a matter of national import. To my relief, I also understood that we were not alone in what had been to us a disaster.

Time proved me right.

Before a year had passed, Senator John Kennedy had piloted a labor reform bill through the Senate, and Congress had voted the bill into law. Folks called the law, informally, the Landrum-Griffin Act after its sponsors.

The act, based on more than 1,500 sworn witnesses over two and a half years of racketeering hearings, became law September 9, 1959. A labor reform measure, it regulated internal union affairs.

More to Dad's pleasure, it closed loopholes in laws governing secondary boycotts, outlawing boycotts such as the one that drove my father out of business. Many authorities in the labor management field believe that the conflict between my dad and Jimmy Hoffa "directly led" to the congressional passage of the secondary boycott features in the Landrum-Griffin bill.

To us, this felt like a major payback to that punk Jimmy Hoffa.

BUSLOADS FOR BOYCOTTS

Four buses dispatched loads of people, men mostly, in work clothes. I clutched my reporter notebook and looked them over. Who were they? To find out, I climbed in an empty private bus before the driver left and asked.

"Teamsters," the driver said. "Every one of them."

Before he could close the door on me, I jumped back and found myself surrounded by Teamsters.

"Yeah, we're from Omaha," one grinned. His dusty gray hair failed to cover a bald spot. "We're here on holiday."

"Holiday?" That made no sense to me.

"Labor holiday. No work today."

"And the transportation to Lincoln was free."

We hightailed it to the capitol as another bus unloaded behind us. That made five buses.

As I looked at the Teamsters, I noticed I had double vision. Half saw them as my father must, the enemy. But the other half looked at them the way my English professor would. He'd introduced me to the *Wobblies*.

I shook my head and scooted inside the state capitol. The place was jammed with Teamsters; they clogged the rotunda and stood in the hallways and squatted on balcony window ledges. I raced by them to the east Senate chamber. When I found it, the door was closed. I cracked it open.

"I'm with Tom Coffey," I said, and the door swung aside to let me in. Behind me, someone hissed.

EXHIBIT A

We were all there March 4, 1959, for a hearing about a legislative bill, LB 560, to outlaw secondary boycotts in Nebraska. I considered it my dad's bill, drummed up by his many friends in the legislature when Dad's business went south in 1956. His senator buddies hoped to halt Jimmy Hoffa's intent to unionize everything on wheels in Nebraska.

I spotted the empty seat up front that Dad had saved for me and worked my way to it. Before I sat down, I turned and looked at the full room. I worked on assignment for the student newspaper, *Daily Nebraskan,* so I used the method I'd been taught to count a room: I thought I'd counted 600, mostly Teamsters, caps still on their heads, jammed in elbow to elbow, but I couldn't believe my statistics. The next day, though, professional reporters listed the crowd at 700 or 750, the biggest group that year.

When Senator Ray Simmons of Fremont, chief sponsor of the bill, stepped to the microphone, the crowd erupted in boos.

The committee chairman, Senator Peter Claussen, stood and called the crowd to order. "Now let's have a little decorum here," Claussen gripped the microphone. "Let's give everybody a fair chance to be heard."

When the crowd quieted, Senator Simmons continued. "Now if you came here thinking you'd see Jimmy Hoffa, you won't. We invited him to come because he was involved in some union contracts signed here in Nebraska, but he's not coming."

Too many other irons in the fire, I thought, *court dates and the like.*

"And don't think this bill," Senator Simmons looked the crowd over, "is aimed against labor's bargaining rights or pickets or other labor rights. It's not. It's simply a bill designed to stop secondary boycotts. That's all."

Dad spoke next. He stood tall but relaxed, his suit jacket open and dangling. One hand grasped the mic, the other held a rolled-up batch of notes.

"I am exhibit A of the secondary boycott." His voice rolled clearly across the crowd. "I am the former owner and operator of the Coffey's Transfer Company. I was forced out of business by secondary boycotts."

The crowd booed, but quieted when Senator Claussen stood.

"No," Dad said, "being forced out of business was quite deliberate. Barney Baker, a Teamster official, told me, 'Sign up or we'll put you out of business.' That's how they do it.

The organizer goes to the owner and tells him to sign a union contract. The owner says, 'Go organize the men.' But that's not done. Instead, the union invokes secondary boycotts by pressuring Teamster lines to quit doing business with nonunion lines. That's how they put me on my knees. I sold to Burlington when my lawyers said I couldn't fight a prolonged court battle without going bankrupt.

"Now Jimmy Hoffa himself told me his program in Nebraska. He plans to organize all the truckers, and then the wholesale houses and retail outlets until he's organized every big outlet. And Barney Baker told me the Teamsters plan to organize 'every prune peddler and nail salesman' in the state.

"I asked Barney, 'How can you justify that?'

"'Grocery carts have wheels, don't they?' Baker said.

"And I believe the Teamsters could take over Nebraska. Baker bragged about the size of the union—one million, four hundred thousand men strong—and the amount of money the union had set aside to organize Nebraska: thirty-six million dollars. They are strong and determined. So I am more afraid of the secondary boycott and of Jimmy Hoffa than I am of Russia."

The crowd broke into whistles, boos, hisses, and jeers.

Dad glanced at them and sat down.

"VICIOUS ANTILABOR LEGISLATION"

The crowd rustled and chattered until the next speaker rose: Gordon Preble, the state president of the AFL-CIO, looking smart in a bow tie and a wisp of a mustache riding on his lip like an upside-down V. Applause broke out when Preble stepped to the microphone.

"No demonstrations!" cried Senator Claussen.

"Folks," Preble said, "don't think Senator Claussen's picking on you. The Unicameral has a 'nonapplause' rule for all its hearings." He shuffled some papers and continued. "Now as for this LB 560, it's vicious antilabor legislation. It's one-sided. This legislation is biased. What we need in Nebraska is a state law

Gordon Preble,
AFL-CIO state president.

that would protect both employer and employee. This bill is a one-way street. Under it, employers could create a boycott situation just to charge unions with violating the law."

Preble paused and glanced around the packed room. "If Nebraska had a labor relations act like other states do, then it wouldn't need LB 560. We haven't grown great in America by passing legislation of this type."

Applause, largely from the busloads of Teamsters, rang out in defiance of the "no applause" rule. Preble stepped down.

I felt so confused. How could the same bill mean such different things to Dad and Preble? And to the hundreds of Teamsters in the room?

Testimony continued to ring out from people I'd never heard of, although I did get to see Dave Weinberg, the Teamsters' attack-dog lawyer whose ability to delay had almost jettisoned Dad's election. Dave looked younger than Dad, with a chiseled face and thick black hair, kind of good-looking, I thought.

Dave didn't speak long, but he managed to declare LB 560 unconstitutional at least a half-dozen times. "It's a dictatorship bill!" Color rose in his cheeks.

Three and a half hours of heated discussion had passed when the hearing broke up.

The senators in the Labor and Public Welfare Committee went into executive session to consider the bill. I hung around with the regular news reporters; we waited until chairman Senator Peter Claussen announced that the committee had advanced LB 560 to the floor of the Nebraska legislature by a vote of four to two.

Four to two! So even the senators hadn't agreed on the merits of the bill. How puzzling!

Pie in the Sky When You Die

That night I holed up in my garish bedroom and tried to sort the matter out. I wouldn't be puzzled, if it hadn't been for my creative writing professor, Wilbur Gaffney, his girth so big we'd called him "The Walrus." He was the craziest teacher ever! He'd amble into class, pass papers back, and ask if we had any questions. If we didn't, he'd pull out a rumpled copy of Lewis Carroll's *Alice's Adventures in Wonderland* and read to us, his voice different for each character.

Gaffney had called me into his office to discuss my paper about Dad's strike. He gave me an A, but he asked, "Are you just against labor because your dad is?"

What a jolt! "Of course." I stiffened. "Isn't everybody against labor but the Teamsters?"

He smiled. "Not quite." And he scribbled the word Wobblies on my paper. "Look it up and let me know what you think."

I returned armed. "Wobblies are just like the Teamsters," I shook my research papers at him, "only their symbol is red and round, not horses' heads. And they like lumberjacks, not truckers. But they both say the same things: 'The working class and the employing class have nothing in common.' About the only way they're different is the Wobblies like to sing."

"Do they!" Gaffney inhaled and belted out a tune.

He's singing that old hymn, "In the Sweet By and By," I thought. *But his words twisted and came out, "You'll get pie in the sky when you die."*

We just looked at each other. Then I said, "Where'd you learn that?"

"Oh, about thirty years ago when I was riding the rails." Gaffney snitched my paper and wrote "Ludlow Massacre" on one corner in his red pen. "Take a look at that." I grabbed my paper and hightailed it to the library to see what Gaffney meant.

Oh, it was a terrible tale, taking place in a tent city of Wobblies with John D. Rockefeller's soldiers shooting and killing striking coal miners, his militia turning a machine gun on their camp, murdering men, women, and children. And then that night the militia set the tent city on fire. It went up in flames full of screams and groans as the strikers and their women and children struggled to escape, some asphyxiated and burned to death.

I couldn't believe what Rockefeller had ordered. My dad would never do anything like that.

I didn't know what to think, so I didn't drop by Gaffney's office for at least a month, and when I did, neither of us mentioned the Ludlow Massacre.

So much friction! Not only in that Wobbly tent city, but also in the Unicameral. Must have been 700 people thought my dad wrong and Mr. Preble right. I shook my head. It made no sense. I couldn't even think straight.

OUT OF A JOB—AGAIN

On January 1, Dad's job as state purchasing agent ended. The Democrats had won—so rare in Nebraska—leaving Dad, a Republican in a Republican administration. So that was that.

Fortunately, Dad knew he didn't want to spend the rest of his working life as a purchasing agent. He'd spent time figuring out what he'd like to do, what he could do well. After he researched the matter and consulted with friends, he opted for a career as a city manager.

When Sidney, Nebraska, advertised, he applied and was chosen from forty applicants, so off the folks went to this flat town in southwest Nebraska that bordered farms to the east and ranches to the west. A small town, but nearly five times larger than Alma, Sidney's population pushed what would be its high of 8,004 people in 1960.

Dad was in Sidney May 7, 1959, when the news broke: LB 560, that antisecondary boycott legislation, had become law.

His phone rang. First the reporter for the *Omaha World-Herald* called and then the *Sidney Sun-Telegraph*.

Dad, of course, praised the senators for passing an "extremely important piece of legislation," one that will "prove to be one of the most important pieces of legislation to come out of the sixty-ninth session."

This law, he explained, will protect the small businessman and the legitimate laboring man "from labor gangsters in the East such as Hoffa."

He added, almost as an afterthought, words that would become headlines: "It's a good law—because it has teeth in it."

"Hot damn," he said to me when we spoke by phone. "That's twice—national and Nebraska—I got that punk Jimmy Hoffa."

Dad didn't mention it to me, but I still lived in Lincoln and read the local papers, so I knew that Governor Victor Anderson had not signed LB 560 into law. He didn't veto it, but he didn't sign it either. It "passed into law without the governor's signature."

"What does that mean?" I asked my favorite journalism prof, Neale Copple.

"You know how to research," he said. "Go take a look at the state *Legislative Journal.*"

So I did.

Turned out Governor Anderson couldn't make up his mind. He couldn't sign the bill because, like Dave Weinberg, the Teamsters' lawyer, Anderson worried about the bill's constitutionality. On the other hand, he couldn't veto it because so many people believed "that it can do that which it cannot do." So Anderson decided to permit LB 560 to pass into law so its proponents could prove "that the law is not a snare and a delusion."

Goodness, I thought. The governor sounds as mixed up as I am.

STUNNED

That June, I got my BA from the University of Nebraska. Dr. William E. Hall, head of the journalism department, gave me an Outstanding Senior Woman Journalist award. The university had already published my senior research paper, "Executive Sessions in the Nebraska Legislature." So nothing remained to do but get a job. In Denver, probably. Certainly I didn't intend to stay in Nebraska.

I went to see Dr. Hall, strange looking for a man, a mop of black curly hair and a soft round face.

"A job?" He shuffled some papers on his desk. "I'm sure we can arrange something for you. You want to stay in Lincoln?"

"No. Out of state. Denver, I'm thinking."

He pursed his lips. "Denver? Can't help you there."

"But you could write a letter of recommendation that I could take with me."

He stiffened and shook his head. "Can't do that. You only get a letter of recommendation from me if your first job after graduation is in Nebraska."

I must have looked dumbfounded as Dr. Hall explained his reasoning. It went something like this, "The state legislators provide money to run the department, and they're concerned about the number of students leaving Nebraska after graduation. So I make sure my students stay here, for their first jobs. I keep track of my student placements so I can show the senators that a high percentage of my journalism students stay here, much higher than other departments. And the senators reward me monetarily."

We sat silent for a moment. Dr. Hall shuffled some papers, looked up and barked. "So what will it be? Lincoln? Omaha? Hastings? Scottsbluff?"

Stunned, I rose to leave. "I'm going to Denver," I said at the door.

I caught the Zephyr to Denver and applied to every publication in the town. Only one, a liquor publication, offered me a job. I took it. The job consisted of rewriting the liquor ads so they read like editorials; that lowered the publication's postage. This job hardly met my idea of journalism. But it paid the rent, so I stayed, until Martha, an older woman there, counseled me on how to keep my job.

"When he asks you to come home with him" ("he" being the baggy-suited gray-haired boss), "go." Martha laughed. "I know it works, because I said yes and I'm still here."

I took the next Zephyr back to Lincoln. Dr. Hall smiled and arranged an immediate job for me on the *Lincoln Evening Journal*'s copy desk and, shortly after, a better paying job as general news reporter on the *Hastings Daily Tribune* in Hastings, Nebraska.

I was in Lincoln when Dad called to crow. The Chicago Employers Association had written him up. Indeed, they'd put together a whole booklet telling his story. "It's not that big, only fourteen pages."

"Who wrote it? Hemingway?" I tittered.

Dad ignored my giggle. "A. M. Pennington. Ever hear of him?"

"Or her. No. I'll bet he's anti-Teamster if he's writing for employers."

"Well, here's what the title page says," and Dad read: "Coffey was an American whose business was broken and whose security of self and family was smashed because he refused to do business according to the dictates of The International Brotherhood of Teamsters and to compel his employees to belong and pay dues to that organization for the right to work. This is his story—a story of boycott, of conspiracy, of persecution, of ponderous and ineffective law—and of final defeat."

"That's pretty neat, Dad. Can you spare a booklet?"

"Sure. They should have plenty. They printed off a quarter of a million copies."

"Oh, that's great." I chuckled. "Going to send one to Jimmy?"

"No point in doing that. He doesn't know how to read anything but contracts."

SHUT YOUR CHOPS

Bobby Kennedy's Rackets Committee ground to a halt, and Bobby kept busy writing his book, *The Enemy Within,* about his experiences as counsel on the committee. By the end of the year, he had become campaign manager for Jack's run for the presidency.

However, the government still hounded Jimmy.

The departments of Justice and Labor hoped to topple Jimmy from his presidency. In addition, some dozen grand juries inspected Jimmy's Teamsters' leaders for legalities. Already major Jimmy backers, including Barney Baker, faced more than twenty-five indictments for extortion or misuse of Teamsters' funds.

The new Landrum-Griffin Act added another kick. Under the act, Teamsters who'd carried out a major crime couldn't hold a union office for five years, so Jimmy had to check to see if anyone on payroll fit that definition. Five did. Instead of firing them, he gave them leaves of absences.

"I spend so much time in this fuckin' courtroom or that," Jimmy said, "I could hang out a shingle as a lawyer myself." He liked to eyeball legal cases that law school professors and lawyers sent to him. A battery of at least a hundred lawyers worked for him, and Jimmy often questioned them and made suggestions. Those who knew him well said Jimmy's powers of retention were superb, as was his knowledge of details, his analytical ability, and, of course, his persuasiveness.

In November 1959, Jimmy met top Teamsters' officials from across the country in the Teamsters' Marble Palace in Washington. Jimmy pulled the drapes shut across the room's picture window. Then he lectured his audience: "Don't ever discuss Teamster affairs if somebody can overhear you." His listeners knew he was being persecuted by the government, but to them he sounded overly cautious, maybe even paranoid.

About forty-five minutes into the meeting, Jimmy, looking smug, pulled the drapes open. Two men, in the distance, waved at him.

"Take a damned good look at those guys." Jimmy turned from the window. "And remember what I told you."

"Who are they?" someone asked.

"Luckily, they're our boys. They'll be here in a couple minutes with a surprise for you."

The surprise was a small recorder the two men displayed.

"Play the fuckin' tape," Jimmy said.

The Teamsters' officials looked aghast as they heard their very own words played back.

"I put a little wireless broadcasting device in my inside coat pocket," Jimmy said. "It fuckin' broadcast to the recorder 350 yards away."

The officials murmured in amazement.

"You get my point. In our position today, the best thing we can do is keep our mouths zippered."

CHIANTI AND A CANDLE

Reporting at the *Hastings Daily Tribune* had its moments. I scooped the radio station reporter on a news story only to discover that the same outfit owned both the newspaper and the station. I put my foot in that one. Then I covered a murder trial that lasted for days. Each day I'd write up the breaking story at three different deadlines—for the radio station. And the police chief offered to show me his considerable pornography collection, all seized legitimately from men who should know better, he chuckled.

I said nothing. I was a member of the Silent Generation, and silent many of us were. We inherited a past of nuclear mushroom clouds, of skin sliding off bones, of more than 100,000 dead in a matter of days, our present cluttered by Joe McCarthy and the Korean War. Speechless. A strange condition for a woman who aspired to be a writer.

That I still lived in Nebraska made me feel distraught. The state, at that time, seemed sterile to me. Behind the habitual Midwestern smile lurked a judgment as harsh as that of the Bible-belt Jehovah on which it was based. Living seemed largely a question of minding your p's and q's, something I was not particularly adept at. Something I resented.

Then chance or fate or serendipity dropped Jack Kerouac's *On the Road* into my hands, introducing me to beatniks and travel. The words of his novel poured into my veins as fast as they must have flowed out of his fingers: nonstop onto an unbroken roll of United Press teletype paper. Kerouac's words shot through me—boom, boom, boom—like a fusillade. I was undone, a changed person.

I bought a straw-covered bottle of Chianti, a candle, and a pad of paper. Then, slightly inebriated, I began to write by candlelight, scribbling words onto paper as fast as my hand could compose, following instinctively Kerouac's model of spontaneous prose. He obviously felt free to wing it; why shouldn't I? For I, in those blissfully naïve prefeminist days, felt the equal of any man.

I knew I had to get out of Nebraska. "I'm quitting," I told my boss.

He stood tall and lanky looking down at me. His voice quavered. "What's the matter with you kids today?" His nostrils flared. "My son can't hold a decent job and now you."

I tried to speak, but he cut me off. "Go on. Get out of here." He twirled and strode out of the room.

Denver, New Orleans, California

My Iowa friend, Pat, met me in the Denver Greyhound station. We gazed at a gigantic United States map. So many opportunities. Where should we go?

Pat closed her eyes, I twirled her around, and she pointed her finger. In no time we were New Orleans bound.

We traveled on our savings. When they ran low, we signed up with a temporary agency and worked until we saved enough to move on. When San Francisco proved too cold for the clothes we owned, we headed south. San Diego's temperature felt okay, so we found work. I typed and Pat sorted mail in a tuna factory.

One day, I answered a knock on our motel room door to see a policeman. "You Marilyn Coffey?"

I nodded.

"Your dad says for you to call home, pronto!"

I closed the door. "Would you believe that, Pat? How in the world did Dad know where I was?"

"You haven't called him?"

"I was going to, but I never got around to it."

Long-distance calls cost a lot. I waited until evening when the rates went down and dialed from a phone booth, hoping that something wasn't wrong with Mama. Or Dad. Or my sisters. Or even with Butchy, Mama's Pekinese, although I didn't think Dad would spend money on a long-distance call about a dog.

I smiled when I heard Dad's voice. At least he was okay.

"I've been trying to find you. Those tests you took in Hastings before you left? Well, one came back indicating the possibility of syphilis."

"Syphilis!" My face turned scarlet. What must he think of me?

"Probably a false-positive, the doctor says, but you need to take a test there in San Diego to finds out if it's true. I wouldn't worry about it."

Just before I hung up, I asked how he found me. He laughed. "Well, I'm city manager now. And that means managing Sidney's police force."

"Yeah, but how did they know I was in San Diego."

Dad snorted. "They must of hired Rex the Wonder Dog."

I ran out of quarters, so I didn't find out. And the San Diego test, thank goodness, showed no sign of syphilis.

The Portland Strike

Pat and I headed toward Portland, Oregon. She wanted to settle there so I thought I'd find a newspaper job and settle down too. When I called, the *Oregon Journal* sounded interested in hiring me, so I walked to the newspaper building to apply.

Lines of men and women circled the building. Pickets. If I were Dad, I thought, I'd cross that picket line, walk into the building, and quite possibly ace a job. If.

Instead, I'd talked to some pickets, who looked more like colleagues than union types—no Barney Baker bumping people into line. Before they struck, their job had been to cast the metal cylinders that produced the paper used in the giant printing presses. This costly process took four workers. The paper owner, Sam Newhouse, wanted to import German machines that required only one operator.

The bitter, violent strike, one said, was in its second year, with no end in sight despite brawls on the picket line, dynamiting newspaper delivery vans, and a rival union newspaper, *The Portland Reporter*. Maybe I'd like to write for them?

I couldn't bring myself to cross that picket line for a job on the *Oregon Journal*. Nor could I apply to work on a union-controlled paper.

So I counted my money. Enough to train home to Nebraska where I borrowed $200 from my sister Margery and boarded the train to New York City.

New York! I knew that's where I wanted to live, where Gaffney, my creative writing teacher, had lived most of his life. "You want to write?" he said. "You should live there. That's where all the big publishers are."

So Time Hurtled By

"Hush." Tom Henshaw, my drinking buddy, tapped my hand. "They're about to start." I zipped my lip and scooted my bar stool to get a better look at the New York City bar's television set.

A half-dozen feature writers seated around us worked, like Tom, for the national Associated Press. Tom had a strange job there. An atheist, he wrote the AP's religious features. He described Christians, but he had his eye on Madalyn Murray O'Hair, an American atheist activist fighting to end official Bible-reading in American public schools.

His pals favored martinis and nicknamed one writer "Hollow Leg" after he downed twelve martinis straight but never wavered when he rose and left. Or so they said. Tom, twelve years my senior, and I drank beer. He bought.

It was September 26, 1960, and we had gathered to watch the nation's first televised presidential debate: Senator John F. Kennedy vs. Vice-President Richard Nixon. America was ready for the show. By 1960, 88 percent of American homes owned TV sets, rapidly up from just 11 percent in 1950.

The TV program opened in gray tones; we had yet to see color. The moderator and the two debaters sat in simple straight-backed chairs on a large stage completely barren except for two spartan lecterns. Below the stage sat four reporters who asked questions, their backs to the camera.

Voters knew Nixon, Eisenhower's vice-president, much better than Kennedy, a young senator from Massachusetts. Nixon also had the advantage of experience in front of television cameras. In 1952, he had given an emotional sixty-minute speech—his famous Checkers speech—to the largest television audience of that time.

However, when the camera focused on Nixon, he looked pale and scrawny from a recent hospitalization; his suit hung on him. "My God," commented one wisecracker, "they've embalmed Nixon before he even died."

Kennedy's youth—he was forty-three to Nixon's forty-seven—and his Catholicism worked against him, but his calm, confident manner acted in his favor. He looked relaxed and handsome in his dark suit.

And so they jawed away, for sixty minutes, under glaring lights, their party labels entering their talk—Democrat for Kennedy and Republican for Nixon—as the Associated Press writers around me cheered or jeered. My buddy Tom, born and raised in Boston, favored Kennedy. And Dad, I knew, was rooting for Nixon.

Kennedy won the debate, a victory that would catapult him to the presidency. In the meantime, his presidential campaign went on, a ton of money poured into it, the straw hats, the buttons, the balloons, the Vote for Kennedy banners, the convertible rides, the hand outstretched to shake, Kennedy's promise not to put his Catholic religion ahead of the state, the slogans: On the Right Track with Jack.

But Kennedy wasn't the only one stumping. So was Jimmy Hoffa, crusading against that fuckin' Kennedy with everything the Teamsters Union had. He tried to scare his Teamsters as well as other labor unions to vote for Nixon.

"If that fuckin' Kennedy gets in," Hoffa blustered, "he'll investigate you just the way he's investigated me." He knew no one wanted that.

So Jimmy used issue after issue of the union magazine, *International Teamster*, to attack that motherfuckin' Kennedy. In speech after speech before labor groups he called Kennedy antilabor and blamed him for passing the Landrum-Griffin labor reform bill. Hoffa distributed bitter anti-Kennedy propaganda to his Teamsters, but many rejected Jimmy's mudslinging.

No wonder Jimmy ran scared. He knew that, as president, John Kennedy would hand Jimmy Hoffa's head on a platter to Little Brother Robert, and that fuckin' Bobby would do his best to nail Jimmy, jail him.

What's Good for America

On January 20, 1961, John Kennedy was inaugurated America's thirty-fifth, and youngest, president. He immediately appointed Bobby attorney general.

"Inexperienced," his critics claimed. "Unqualified." "Lacks experience in any state or federal court."

Which made the president joke, "I can't see that it's wrong to give him a little legal experience before he goes out to practice law."

Bobby said nothing. He just resumed his Hoffa investigations, carrying on the strongest attack on organized crime ever seen by the country, assisted by ample squads of "Get Hoffa" investigators. Bobby's new book, *The Enemy Within*, helped too. In it he described the Rackets Committee's "crusade" against Jimmy, "one of the most famous, consummate, and effective Senate investigations in modern Congressional history."

But not as effective as Bobby wished. In Miami Beach, the racket-ridden Teamsters reelected Jimmy general president for five more years, by acclamation.

The new Teamsters' president stood on the rostrum, speculating about the future. "What do you have to say," barked a young reporter, "about the attorney general's statement, 'the success of Hoffa is a reflection upon the morality of our time'?"

Jimmy whipped toward the reporter and snapped: "All I know is that our members used to take home two bent cans and $10 a week. Now they take home $125. That's what's good for America."

At least Barney Baker made more than two bent cans. Although he wore shabby clothes, he drove a brand new Cadillac. A sign on the back bumper read "Clergy." He arranged for the symbol. "Keeps me from getting tickets."

But it didn't keep him from getting hauled into court for shaking down a Pittsburg newspaper. In 1961, a federal court fined him $1,200 and sent him to jail in Sandstone, Minnesota, for two years.

WOOED BY SEMANTICS

Mama lay on the bed in my Hell's Kitchen apartment, recovering from the car ride from Nebraska to New York City. She turned up her nose at my working-class neighborhood, so I didn't mention that the Gambino crime family might be moving in next door. What did it matter? In a few more days, I'd be living uptown in Tom

Henshaw's apartment. As a married woman. My drinking buddy had turned into my fiancé, in the oddest manner: thinking I was pregnant by a cad who refused to marry me, I wept on my buddy Tom's shoulder. "I'll marry you," Tom said. What a relief! Until I discovered I wasn't pregnant. I fessed up, but Tom didn't care, and I was too polite to say I wanted out.

So that spring, Dad sat at the dining room table, figuring my income taxes for me: my federal taxes and my marriage ceremony fell on the same day: April 15, 1961. Except for taxes, I was ready. I'd made my simple wedding gown, blue. To wear white would be two-faced.

What really enthralled me wasn't matrimony but semantics. I'd breezed through S. I. Hayakawa's book, *Language in Thought and Action*, enlightened by the ways he explained how language shapes our thinking. Now I plowed through *Science and Sanity* by Alfred Korzybski, Hayakawa's teacher, known for saying, "The map is not the territory."

Once, while lecturing to a group of students, Korzybski stopped and pulled out a packet of biscuits wrapped in white paper.

"Excuse me," he opened the package, "I must have something to eat." He looked at the students on the front row. "Would you like a biscuit?"

Several reached for one.

"Nice biscuit, hmm?" Korzybski took a second one.

Before him, students chewed vigorously.

Suddenly, he ripped off the white paper, revealing a package labeled "Dog Cookies" sporting a picture of a dog's head.

Shocked students clapped their hands over their mouths, ran out of class to the toilet to vomit.

"You see," Korzybski told the remaining students, "I have just demonstrated that people don't just eat food, but also words."

I looked up from *Science and Sanity* to ask Dad, "That court case against Hoffa by you and Clark, whatever came of it?"

"You know how the courts are, honey, slower than molasses in winter. But the Teamsters indicated that they might settle out of court. So we're waiting. I'll let you know if anything happens." He shoved my completed taxes to me. "Sign it and drop it in a mailbox tomorrow and you'll be home-free."

OUT OF HELL'S KITCHEN

Tom had selected "the little church around the corner," a quaint Episcopal church, for our marriage ceremony. It was the "in" place in New York to exchange marital vows.

Our Saturday marriage ceremony proved uneventful, even though Tom and his best man, both three sheets to the wind, barely arrived on time.

Afterward, a wobbly Tom treated my folks to a nice restaurant meal, and

Tom Henshaw and I pose for our wedding picture.

we waved good-bye to them as they headed for Sidney, Nebraska, Dad happy in his position as city manager. He liked to talk about repaving streets, buying new police cars, tinkering with budgets, eating Chamber of Commerce dinners, and enjoying the crazy Shriners' circus.

Sunday we lugged my belongings from Hell's Kitchen to Tom's apartment, and that ended our honeymoon. Monday I returned to work at *Good Housekeeping*, and Tom went back to the Associated Press.

At the popular *Good Housekeeping* magazine, I had two jobs. From Monday through Wednesday, I worked as secretary for columnist Helen Valentine (a pen name); on Thursday and Friday, I read the slush. "Slush" referred to the dozens of manuscripts that piled up each week from writers who hoped to be published in the magazine. Each Wednesday evening, the post office guy brought me the slush piled high in three or four file-sized boxes. I had two days to find usable manuscripts.

I soon learned the fine art of skimming and of discrimination: if the manuscript was handwritten on tissue paper, forget it. I rejected "not right for *Good Housekeeping*" boxes of manuscripts, including some bylines I recognized.

Then, a few months after I started, *Good Housekeeping* fired me. Pregnant, I'd missed a few days due to morning sickness, and that was that.

My boss, Naome Lewis, the magazine's fiction editor, called me into her office. She was livid. "You can't expect to have a career in publishing, Marilyn, if you're going to have children." Her voice crackled across her carpeted office.

I stared at her, standing in her taupe suit. She was thirty-five years old, twelve years older than I, and she had sustained a long career in publishing. She'd worked on magazines since before World War II and held down jobs at *True Detective* and *Collier's* before she came to *Good Housekeeping*. More to the point, she had children, two quite young daughters that I'd met on the days she brought them to the office.

What did she mean?

IAN MICHAEL HENSHAW

On the dark evening of December 23, 1961, Tom hailed a cab and took me and my quivering body to the hospital.

"You're too early," the doctor said. "Walk around, see if you can hurry things up a bit."

I scooted clumsily to the floor and hoofed it up and down the corridor, but I didn't walk. I marched, puffing as I went. By the time the doctor saw me next, my water had broken, and he couldn't wait to get me into the birthing room.

My son, Ian Michael, beat midnight. The doctor called Ian, a full-term baby, premature because he weighed so little. Eventually I understood that my smoking and drinking caused that. Out of my womb, he gained rapidly.

Tom and I adored our playful baby. We hired a Spanish-speaking sitter so I could go back to work at *Home Furnishings Daily*, and I did, in my old job but with a new coworker, a smashingly tall, dark, and comical man who gave me the hots.

THE NASHVILLE CASE DRONES ON

On May 18, 1962, in Nashville, Tennessee, a federal grand jury accused Jimmy Hoffa of illegally accepting $1 million from a truckline to keep the Teamsters from stirring things up for the company. "A violation of the Taft-Hartley Act," the government claimed.

Federal Judge William E. Miller handled Jimmy's case. The government charged that Jimmy divided that illegal payoff with the late Owen Bert Brennan, a Teamsters' vice-president. It maintained that Test Fleet, Inc., owned by Jimmy's and Brennan's wives, handled the payoffs.

"I was told the arrangement was legal." Jimmy rubbed the back of his neck.

So day after day in the wood-paneled courtroom, the trial droned on. Then, on December 5, a laborer burst into the room. He wielded a pellet gun and claimed he heard voices. The first shot he took—at Jimmy—missed. Then the clomp of heavy boots disconcerted the laborer long enough for the bailiff to grab him and disarm him. Jimmy wasn't hit.

The next day generated some excitement, too, but not on the same level. Judge Miller disqualified three jurors.

He ruled out one, a Nashville insurance man, because Jimmy's buddies had offered him $10,000 to vote for Jimmy.

He eliminated another, Gratin Fields, seventy, a retired railroad worker, because two FBI agents warned Fields that someone tried to telephone him from Detroit, Jimmy's hometown.

He barred Mrs. James Paschal, the wife of a Tennessee state patrolman, because the Teamsters offered to help her husband get a promotion.

"The meeting," James told the judge, "was clandestine. A man I knew only as 'Mud' looked me up at home in November and told me to go to a certain crossroads and wait. I went, even though it was one a.m. and cold and rainy. Soon Ewing King, president of Teamsters Local 327, joined us. King said, 'How'd you like to get a promotion on your job?'"

Judge Miller disqualified no more jurors, so the nine remaining members began to deliberate about the third week in December. They hammered away for seventeen hours before they gave up. "We're hopelessly deadlocked," they said.

To a full courtroom, Judge Miller declared a mistrial. An estimated three-fourths of those present were members of Teamsters Union locals.

United States marshals blocked the doors to keep anyone from leaving or coming into the hushed courtroom while Judge Miller read his statement. "It's my duty to speak of the unfortunate events which have marked the trial from its beginning. From the very first as the jury was being selected there were indications that improper contacts had been and were being made with prospective members of the jury.

"I had to excuse one prospective juror after another when the jurors disclosed they had been improperly approached. After the trial started, I held two secret sessions to hear further evidence that Hoffa's labor union associates continued to try to influence certain members of the jury. As you know, I disqualified three more jurors."

With a flourish, Judge Miller signed an order to convene a federal grand jury to make a full and complete investigation of these attempts. He asked Bobby Kennedy, the attorney general, to present to the grand jury all the evidence it had uncovered during its investigation.

God, Bobby just won't let up. Jimmy brushed aside his son who tried to help him on with his coat. Reporters swarmed around him. *Leeches.*

Boy's Work

January 17, 1963, my phone rang. "Damn!" The cord had tangled into a wad. I could barely lift the receiver. "Hello."

Dad's warm voice rolled into my ear. "What's up, Junebug?"

"Hang on a minute." I lifted the phone high, dropped the receiver to the floor, and watched the cord unravel. "There. That's better."

"What are you doing?"

"Fixing the phone. Doing boy's work. Hey! Do you remember all those newspapers that wouldn't give me a job because I wasn't a boy?"

"Yes."

"Lucky I wasn't hired. Those papers have been on strike for more than a month, no end in sight."

Dad chuckled.

"And my new job's just as stupid. I can't write about washing machines because I'm not a boy. But forget all that. How's by you."

Dad hummed. "Happy. I've got good news."

"Tell me."

"You remember when Foy Clark and I sued the Teamsters and our lawyer said it couldn't be done?"

"You did it?"

"Yes, we did it. The International Teamsters Union settled out of court with us—and that was the first time the Teamsters had ever done that!"

"Wonderful." My throaty laughter hid the beginning of tears.

"You bet, wonderful. Foy and I really got back at that punk Jimmy Hoffa. The Teamsters agreed to triple damages: $61,200" (in 2017 dollars, that $61,200 would be worth nearly half a million dollars). "We're going to split it, fifty-fifty."

I whistled! "Whatever are you going to do with your thirty-thousand, buy Mama a red Ferrari?"

We laughed, remembering Mama's aversion to the red Chevy convertible Dad had given her. Outside my window, sunlight played along the Twin Towers.

"What *are* you going to do with it, Dad?"

"Invest it, honey. Invest it. Jimmy Hoffa's gonna buttress my retirement."

THE MOTORCADE SPED ON

I perched on a stool in a dark New York City tavern. My long-legged boss, Patricia "Pat" Chapman and I had run late, so we ordered beers and sandwiches. Our beers slid into place.

A blaring overhead TV depicted *As the World Turns*. Pat and I groaned at the low-class fare, then laughed.

Our sandwiches came. We munched down.

Above us, Thanksgiving provided a handy crisis for the TV soap when a CBS News Bulletin broke through. Walter Cronkite's voice said, "Three shots fired at President

Kennedy's motorcade in Dallas." My head snapped up. "Seriously wounded." I struggled to believe this.

Pat stood and fumbled with her purse. "Come on."

Cronkite continued: "Mrs. Kennedy jumped up and grabbed Mr. Kennedy. She called, 'Oh, no.' The motorcade sped on." I wanted to howl in protest, but I had no time. Pat slapped cash down. "Let's move it!" Our lunch stayed on the counter.

We ran and jogged back to our *Home Furnishings Daily* office, our handbags slapping our thighs. By the time we arrived, "seriously wounded" had changed to "dead." I felt glazed.

Pat divvied up the work, and we turned to our phones. I called manufacturers and importers of dinnerware, asking each the same thing: "How will the president's death affect your business?" I found the question difficult to ask, but jotting down answers proved even harder.

Our routine reporting seemed distasteful. Kennedy, to me, had been monumental, so asking how his death might affect business seemed crass and disrespectful. My body didn't stiffen, but inside, something congealed.

That night, my husband, Tom, called from the office. "We're putting together a book about Kennedy, all stops pulled. We want to be the first out with a hardcover, but we need copy editors. Can you come down?"

So I put my feelings on hold and worked around the clock with the AP guys to produce *The Torch Is Passed*. Heady with our achievement, whatever I might have felt about Kennedy's assassination disappeared.

Until I held the big wine-colored AP book. Flipping past large black-and-white photos, of the Dallas motorcade before and then suddenly after, of a slack-faced Lyndon

Johnson holding up his right hand, of Jacqueline refusing to change out of her blood-stained clothes, of her children, Caroline and John Jr., he with his famous salute, of the well-known shot of Jack Ruby killing Lee Harvey Oswald, of the casket and horses. But when I turned the page and saw Jacqueline, now dressed in black, a veil nearly obscuring her face, and beside her the familiar Bobby Kennedy, whose hand I once held, he holding her hand, then I wept.

WHODUNIT?

But who did it?

Oswald, of course, shot Kennedy but why?

Speculation soared. Tom brought home the latest from the Associated Press, and I compared it with the rumors running around *Home Furnishings Daily*.

Theories were rampant? KGB? CIA? Lyndon Johnson? Hoffa?

Many fingered the KGB, Russia's secret police. Wasn't Oswald a communist? Hadn't he lived in Russia? And the USSR had a motive for killing Kennedy: to gain revenge for its humiliation in the Cuban missile crisis.

The idea of the CIA as assassin also drew supporters for a complicated set of reasons: JFK's expected withdrawal from Vietnam, which the CIA opposed, the CIA's plan to invade Cuba and kill Castro, as well as the president's desire to "splinter the CIA into a thousand pieces and scatter it to the winds."

Lyndon Johnson's ambition to become president made him suspect too. So did his need to cover up his scandals, including one that could jail him and cost him his career.

Was there a reason Johnson had invited the president and Jacqueline to Dallas and suggested they ride through the city in an open-top car? Johnson would ride in the motorcade too. In a different car.

But the possibility that Jimmy Hoffa had engineered the assassination really caught my attention.

I ran that idea past Dad.

"Oh, honey, mobster that he is, I don't think he'd kill the president."

"Oh, I didn't mean directly. More likely he'd hire someone to do it."

Years passed before I could put the pieces together. They fit like this:

Sometime early in the spring of 1963, Jimmy Hoffa looked at Frank Ragano, lawyer for Jimmy and for Mafioso Trafficante, and said, "I tell you, Frank, I've got to do something about that son of a bitch Bobby Kennedy. He's on the brink of sending me down. I need some fuckin' Mob allies to help me get Bobby off my back. If necessary, by killing Kennedy."

"Killing Bobby, you mean."

"Hell, no. I mean John. When you cut down the fuckin' tree, the branches fall with it."

In July, Jimmy sent Ragano to New Orleans to meet mobsters Santo Trafficante, the Mafia boss at Tampa, Florida, and Carlos Marcello, boss of the New Orleans crime family, with plans to kill President John F. Kennedy.

"You won't believe this, gentlemen," Ragano told the pair in the Royal Orleans Hotel, "but Hoffa says we should take out Kennedy." Ragano thought Hoffa had been just kidding, so the lawyer delivered his message as a joke.

But Marcello and Trafficante didn't laugh. They looked at one other, without batting an eyelid. Ragano sensed that the idea was not new to them. Indeed, they seemed to take it seriously.

Certainly Ragano's "joke" was not news to Trafficante. A month earlier in the Scott Bryan Hotel in Miami, he'd complained about those Kennedy boys and their relentless attacks on Jimmy.

José Alemán, an FBI contact, replied, "But that Kennedy is going to be reelected."

"No, José," Trafficante shook his head. "He is going to be hit."

When José reported the warning to his FBI connections, they laughed. "That's nothing but gangland braggadocio."

But after Kennedy died, Jimmy turned to his lawyer. "I told you you could do it. This means Bobby is out as attorney general. He's just another lawyer now." He paused. "I'll never forget what Marcello and Trafficante did for me."

Marcello, on the other hand, told Ragano: "When you see Jimmy, you tell him he owes me and he owes me big."

JACK RUBY BOTCHED IT

Much later, when writers published books about the assassination, several held Hoffa, Trafficante, and Marcello, all close friends, responsible for Kennedy's death. Bobby's concerted attempts to destroy organized crime had angered the Mob bosses, who certainly shared Hoffa's well-known hatred for the Kennedys.

But what about that Dallas nightclub operator, Jack Ruby who supposedly killed Oswald to shut him up?

Who did Ruby talk to during those long-distance calls in the months before the murders? Mostly to organized crime gangsters, especially men associated with Marcello, Trafficante, or Hoffa, including Barney Baker. And Ruby talked a lot; he made 250 times more out-of-state calls than he dialed the previous year.

"I got nothing to do with the fuckin' assassination," Jimmy told reporters, "and nothing to do with Oswald's death."

But that's not what he told his Irish friend, Frank Sheeran, a high-ranking Teamster official and Mafia hitman.

"Ruby was supposed to coordinate some police officers to kill that fuckin' Oswald," Jimmy said, "but Ruby botched that. The cops told him 'Finish the job yourself or give up your life.'"

Hoffa Mourns

"John Kennedy was my president," Jimmy claimed, "just like everyone else's, so of course I felt sorry."

But on the afternoon when Hoffa heard the news of Kennedy's death, he had just finished lunch in a restaurant. When he heard, he climbed up on the table, stood and cheered.

Also that afternoon, Harold Gibbons, Jimmy's number one assistant in Washington, heard in the legendary Duke Zeibert's Restaurant that the president had been shot. He gobbled his lunch at a cloth-covered table. By time he got back to Teamsters' headquarters, news of Kennedy's death had flashed over radio.

Gibbons immediately ordered employees home, brought the flags down to half-mast, and sent a message to Kennedy's widow. Then he rang up Jimmy in Miami and reported what he had done.

Jimmy started screaming. "Why the hell did you do that for? Who the hell was he?"

Gibbons listened for a while, then said, "It was the best thing to be done, the right thing to do."

Jimmy interrupted. "I have no sympathy for that fuckin' Kennedy, either as a man or a president. Just because he got shot, that didn't mean we should close our building down or lower the flag. Doing that is just a matter of opinion. Go outside and pull those fuckin' flags to full mast."

"Listen, Hoffa, I don't have to take this shit from anybody. When you get back here, you can get yourself a new boy."

Gibbons's resignation, which terminated eleven years of his relationship with Jimmy, lay on his desk when Jimmy returned.

OF ORGASMS AND EGGS

Life normalized. "Larry," the tall, dark, comical coworker at my job, kept me quivering nine-to-five. I flirted as much as I dared. When he didn't ask me out, I propositioned him.

"You've got two strikes against you." Larry smiled and lowered his voice; we were in the office. "You work here, and I don't date coworkers, and you're married."

But the electricity sparked so strongly between us, Larry finally invited me to the theater. The cab from the theater to his bed steamed. The long-delayed roll in the hay bound us tightly.

Unlike most of my lovers, Larry didn't jump promptly on top. Instead, he strummed me, tuning me higher and higher until I exploded into orgasm. I flung my arms across the bed and screeched: "Oh, Jesus Christ."

He paused. "Don't ever do that again."

I'd forgotten that Larry was Jewish.

My orgasms arrived on such a regular basis, I asked Larry how he did it. He grinned. "It's all research. I read everything I could find on the subject. Experimented. Kept the best parts."

But what to do about Tom, who preferred his can of beer to a romp in the bed?

I did nothing except spend less and less time in our apartment.

One evening, when I came home about midnight, Tom had waited up for me. He stood in the middle of the living room, gazing at the floor. "You're seeing someone else, aren't you?"

I looked away from him. "Yes."

"You whore," he snapped and went to the fridge for another beer.

The only issue in our divorce was who should have custody of Ian. "I want a family," Tom argued.

"But would you agree not to move out of town?" He would not.

While Tom and I argued, life with Larry took an unexpected turn. He wanted me to pay for my orgasms. He wanted me to cook for him.

I refused. "I don't cook. I eat out."

"Come on. I'm only talking about breakfast."

"Coffee and donuts. I'm not kidding. I never cook."

But Larry just wouldn't let up. Finally one morning, my patience now thin, Larry opened the refrigerator, grabbed a carton full of eggs and shook it under my nose. "Come on, Marilyn. Anyone can scramble eggs."

My anger heated, but I spoke quietly. "I'll show you how I scramble eggs." I hurled the carton across the kitchen. It crashed against the far wall. We stood silent, watching a dozen broken yellow yolks stream down the white paint.

I soon lived alone in Greenwich Village, near Bleecker Street, in a tiny two-room apartment with shutters painted glowing raspberry. Coming home, I could see them from a mile away.

Larry was past tense, and Tom and I still had not determined who should care for Ian. We tried out joint custody. Ian lived with me for a week, and then with Tom. I liked this arrangement, but after a few weeks, I could see that Ian did not, so I knew a decision had to be made.

I considered the home Tom would provide Ian versus my home, with lovers running in and out. One-night stands. (More than twenty years would pass before I understood that my undiagnosed bipolar disorder caused my overheated sexuality.)

Knowing I couldn't provide Ian with a normal home, I gave Tom custody. He treated me to a round-trip to Mexico for our divorce. Then he moved back to Boston, his hometown.

NATIONAL TRIUMPHS

In the middle of December 1963, snow fell from the overcast sky as it had since dawn. I pushed open the heavy doors to my apartment house. Then I heard my fancy new push-button telephone ring. Of course I dropped my keys, but managed to tussle them back in time to enter and grab the receiver.

It was Dad.

"The *Saturday Evening Post*? You're going to be written up in the *Saturday Evening Post*?" I squealed. "That's terrific." The *Post* ranked as one of the most important national magazines. Mama subscribed to it, and as a teenager, I'd never missed reading the Hazel cartoon about the bossy maid on the last page of every issue.

But then our conversation turned.

"Remember that letter you wrote me from school just before I lost my business?"

My memory slowly shifted back: the run up my dorm stairs, the written and rewritten letter on the typewriter. "Yes."

"Well, the *Post* is going to publish it as part of the article." He sounded so excited, so pleased.

But I was not. "The letter was so gushy, I was so immature, I wasn't even a writer then, and it will be published nationally?"

My father's voice sounded thin. "If you have some problem with it, why don't you talk to the editor about it?" Dad gave me a name, a phone number, and hung up.

I felt like a turncoat, but I called the next day.

"We're not planning to publish the whole letter," the editor said.

Relief rushed over me.

"If you like," he said, "I can read you the part that we want to use, and you can tell me if it's all right."

"Okay."

He read: "Marilyn, our second oldest daughter, who was away at college and home only on weekends, wrote me a letter which I wouldn't trade for all the money in the Teamster treasury.

"'When we were little kids,' she wrote, 'and something went wrong, a zipper got stuck, a doll was broken, we'd always come running to you to patch things up. "Daddy fix" became sort of a motto around the house. I saw you this weekend really worried, and for the first time I realized this fight might be a losing one, that perhaps Daddy couldn't fix and that you might have to throw away a lifetime's work because of one bad spot. I'm glad you're not the sort of person who, when trouble comes along, takes the easiest way out. I want you to know how terribly proud of you I am.'"

I didn't feel terribly proud of myself then, having put my authorial fears ahead of my father's feelings. It helped that my language had held up over the course of seven years, and I could tell the editor, "Fine. It's okay as is," before I hung up full of mixed feelings about my first national publication.

A Dolphin on the Cover

In the week before the January 4–11 publication date, I kept my eye on the local newsstands, and sure enough, the latest issue of the *Saturday Evening Post* came out early. The flat magazine, big as a poster, featured a pet dolphin, "the new status symbol," over most of its blue cover. When I saw ONE MAN'S WAR WITH JIMMY HOFFA in the upper corner of the cover, I bought two copies, even though I no longer had a job.

I'd been fired from *Home Furnishings Daily*. Pat and I had spent a hectic weekend in Atlantic City, wiring breaking dinnerware news back to the office. In one of my stories, I forgot to capitalize the *m* in Melmac, a brand name for melamine dinnerware. One of our big advertisers, a Melmac producer, objected, and Fairchild Publications fired me the same day.

"Never mind," my boss, Pat, said. "Just go hit them up for unemployment benefits."

But I didn't qualify. Fairchild claimed I'd been fired for "intentional misconduct," and we were currently duking it out in the "courts."

Dad's story, on page sixty-eight, opens to a big picture of my father, his forehead high, his glasses plastic, and a smile under his little pyramid mustache. He holds an elongated photo of the many Coffey's Transfer Company trucks he used to own.

On the facing page, about half the size, Jimmy Hoffa and Barney Baker stand talking on the Senate Office Building stairs where I'd once met Bobby Kennedy.

"His courage cost him his business" opines the *Post*.

I dove right into the double-inch columns. The writing is just what I expected from a national magazine: clear, often clever, with a solid intro: "You didn't buck the Teamsters unless you were ready to risk everything." Then the writer marches his readers from 1947 when Dad met Jimmy until that day in 1956 when Dad closed his doors. My little letter became sandwiched in between.

One thing shocked me. The article, "My Private War with Hoffa," was written not by one of the *Saturday Evening Post* editors but "By Tom Coffey."

Both Mama and I knew how impossible that was. Why Dad couldn't even spell my name! He spelled it "Marylin." And he spelled my sister Margery "Marjorie." Of course, he did write an impressive "John Hancock," but after that, you'd never know he had a college education. Impossible spelling, bizarre sentence structure—no wonder he dictated his letters.

"How'd you do it, Dad? Did Mama check your spelling?"

"Do what, Junebug?"

"Write that *Post* story?"

He reached in his pocket, pulled out his silver dollar, and spun it in the air. "Gotcha!" he cried when it fell, heads, on the table. "Just my luck. I didn't write one word. I just told my story, and one of the editors put it all together smoothly and put my name on it."

As the days passed, my folks' enthusiasm for their national triumph grew. They received letters by the basketful from people all over the United States. The letters praised Dad for his courage and often shared similar stories. Mama read their favorites to Dad over again in the evenings.

"How many letters?" Mama said. "But Marilyn, I just stopped counting after a thousand." She still had boxes of letters squirreled away when I visited them. Those letters, perhaps the nicest part of the *Saturday Evening Post* article, salved the pain that both still felt.

By that time, I'd won my case against Fairchild Publications and collected my unemployment. The fact that *Home Furnishings Daily* had never filled my old job turned the case in my favor.

Better yet, I worked in a new job with a competitor, Haire Publications' *Gift & Tableware Reporter*. I'd been promoted from market reporter to associate editor. Some days it seemed as though I'd never stop writing about dinnerware.

TRIUMPH #2

The second triumph was Jimmy's, and a well-earned one too. At last he'd negotiated the nationwide trucking contract that he'd wanted to bag since his time with Farrell Dobbs in the late 1930s.

Jimmy had been in Chicago for days, going to the mat with representatives of the nation's trucking firms. They stared down Jimmy's barrel of possible strikes, coast to coast, set to start next midnight if they didn't yield. But with dawn came word that Jimmy had won a forty-five-cent wage increase.

On January 15, 1964, Jimmy signed the national contact between his Teamsters Union with its two million members and 15,000 trucking companies, the first such contract in US labor history and his greatest achievement as a labor leader.

The contract included that handsome wage increase, so good-looking that a reporter joked: "The Teamsters are so well paid now, they're suffering from high income taxes."

I couldn't wait to call my father. "Oh, Dad, he did it, didn't he? He really got a nationwide contract."

"I hate to think how that old humblebrag must be gloating." Dad sounded glum. "Damn glad I don't have to negotiate with him ever again."

The contract's package of wage and fringe benefit hikes would total $400 million over its thirty-eight months, enough to make a surge in freight rates "virtually certain," noted Jimmy's critics.

"That contract," argued the critics, "will give Mr. Hoffa a stranglehold over our economy. It puts him in the position to call a national truckers' strike."

"I'm not going to call a fuckin' nationwide strike," Jimmy said, even though now he could. "Why would I do that? A goddamn strike would take away my best negotiating weapon—playing the bastard employers off against one another by threatening to strike some while letting others go."

Congress evidently didn't believe Jimmy. It cooked up legislation to outlaw a national truckers' strike, just as it had curbed the railroads.

But Jimmy's glee at his achievement would be short-lived. From Chicago, he had to go to Chattanooga, Tennessee, to face federal charges of jury tampering.

CHATTANOOGA

When Jimmy's private plane landed at Chattanooga's Lovell Field on Friday, January 17, 1964, a crowd of more than a hundred whooping supporters greeted him. Banners flourished: Thanks for the Contract, Jimmy and We'll Always Be for Jo & Jimmy Hoffa. "Jimmy, Jimmy, Jimmy" his supporters chanted.

Ignoring the nippy temperature, Jimmy stopped to chat with reporters and to peacock for photographers. Then he climbed into the waiting Teamsters' Cadillac limo, which led a police escort and a forty-car caravan of Teamsters into Chattanooga.

Jimmy (and five codefendants) arrived in Chattanooga to be tried for attempting to fix a Nashville jury.

Federal Judge Frank W. Wilson held a pretrial meeting in the ornate third-floor courtroom in Chattanooga's federal building. Forty-seven-year-old Wilson, tall and soft-spoken, had been appointed a special judge for Hoffa's trial—by Bobby Kennedy.

The young-looking Wilson announced that the FBI had screened the prospective jury list of 200 people. Jimmy knew Wilson had done this to keep him and his gang from swaying the jury in Chattanooga. After all, they had tampered with juries three times on Jimmy's previous trials, and gotten away with it. Why would they stop at this one?

The court chose a "blue-ribbon" jury mostly of upper-middle-class people to judge the Teamster codefendants. Score One for Bobby's "Get-Hoffa Squad."

Hour after hour, day after day, the trial continued as James Neal, the federal prosecutor, trotted out one witness after another. He planned forty testifiers.

Neal, at eighty-one, had become one of the country's great trial lawyers. A short, cocky broad-chested former Marine, he knew how to charm a courtroom with a gallant manner and a rich Tennessee drawl. A natural storyteller, he rarely glanced at his notes. He whispered. He shouted. He glared. Sometimes he'd whirl dramatically and point at the defendants, Hoffa and his gang and their lawyers.

Jimmy, however, considered Neal vicious. The defending attorneys, earning their keep, leaped to their feet at each opportunity, crying out for a mistrial. They deliberately strained Neal's patience. Hoffa did his part by flashing obscene hand gestures at Neal, trying to get Neal's goat by giving him the finger under the table.

Soft-spoken James E. Haggerty, Hoffa's lawyer, grandfatherly with owlish eyes, kept his composure when objecting to Neal's actions, but not all the defense lawyers did. Harvey Silets conducted a vicious cross-examination that took all afternoon. And flamboyant Jacques Schiffer, admired for his free-swinging style, bounced up at every opportunity, screaming his objection. Once he objected fifty times in a single hour.

SPECIAL WITNESS #40

For weeks, a web of maneuvers and counter-maneuvers entangled the trial. But Jimmy, not mentioned by the prosecutor, became convinced of his innocence. He turned jaunty, worrying only that sitting so long in the courtroom would render him out of shape. He joined the local YMCA and worked out with barbells.

However, Neal had, although Jimmy didn't know it, a special witness, #40 on Neal's list, planned as a surprise.

This witness, a Teamster named Edward Grady Partin, had been hidden for days in a remote rental cabin on top of Lookout Mountain, near Chattanooga. Two US marshals guarded him.

Partin, secretary-treasurer and business agent of Teamsters Local 5 in Baton Rouge, Louisiana, also had acted as Hoffa's personal aide. The young Teamster, thirty-nine, had just been indicted for embezzlement in Louisiana, which made the "Get-Hoffa Squad" suspicious when Partin told them that Hoffa planned to murder Bobby.

"No, I'm not making it up." Partin drummed his fingers against his leg. "Hoffa called me into his office, and he said, 'Something has to be done about that little prick Bobby Kennedy. He'll be an easy target, always driving around Washington in that fuckin' convertible with that big black dog. All we need is some plastic explosives tossed in with him, and that will finish the fucker off.'" Then Jimmy asked him to get some plastic explosives for him. "Buy them far enough away from Washington so they can't be traced back."

"Did you buy them?"

"No." Partin, a former Marine dogged by a long trail of criminal activities including rape, forgery, and first-degree manslaughter, shook his head. "Breaking and entering is one thing, but killing the attorney general of the United States is another."

"Let's give him a lie detector test."

They did.

When Partin aced it, the FBI told Bobby to abandon his convertible.

At the mountain cabin, Partin rehearsed his testimony with Bobby's chief FBI investigator, Walter Sheridan.

"Don't say anything about Hoffa wanting to murder Bobby," cautioned Sheridan. "It's so inflammatory, it could backfire."

Partin, a big rugged guy, agreed.

Sheridan's voice sounded dogged. "Better to focus on the ways Jimmy tried to fix that Nashville jury."

"Right. Like the afternoon Mr. Hoffa told me he might want me to pass something for him. He hit his back pocket. 'I'd pay fifteen thousand, twenty thousand dollars— whatever it takes to get to the jury.'"

"That's a good one," Sheridan mused. "And what about that patrolman?"

"James Paschal? His wife was on the jury, and Jimmy talked some Teamster into offering the patrolman a promotion if he could sway his wife toward Jimmy."

"Did that work?"

"No, Paschal reported it. But other things worked, like Mr. Hoffa telling me, 'Don't worry. I have that colored juryman in my hip pocket.'"

When the time came to go to the courthouse, Partin and Sheridan left the cabin and drove down the mountain.

They parked at the federal building's back entrance and walked through the basement to an elevator. They rode the elevator to the fifth floor, two floors above the courtroom.

When they got a "coast clear" signal, they walked down the steps to a third-floor office. They entered and closed the door. So far, so good.

After lunch recess, Sheridan checked the lookout who waved an "all-clear" signal. Then he sneaked Partin into the witness room adjacent to the courtroom.

When Partin heard the call, "Next witness," at 1:50 p.m. on February 4, he stepped through the rear courtroom door and into the witness box.

Jimmy looked up, stunned. "My God, it's Partin!"

Jimmy never expected Partin to squeal. They'd known each other since 1957, and Jimmy had total confidence in the young Teamster.

In shock, Jimmy glowered at Partin, a deep penetrating expression of pure hatred, the sort the Teamsters' president once directed at Bobby.

Partin, unsurprised, shrugged, and took his oath. "I do solemnly swear, to tell the truth, the whole truth…"

DRUNKEN JURORS

When James Neal, lead prosecutor, stepped forward to introduce his fortieth witness, the courtroom exploded into an uproar. Jimmy's defense lawyers flew all over the place. The bailiff hustled the jurors into a back room, and Neal met separately with the lawyers.

"Mr. Partin turned to the FBI for help when Mr. Hoffa asked him to procure explosives to kill our attorney general,

Robert Kennedy." Neal waited for the clamor to subside. "This is not part of this trial. The FBI reported the threat to the proper house committee, the one that will determine if Mr. Hoffa had a hand in assassinating the president."

When the jury, the lawyers, and the spectators—about a hundred strong—came back into the courtroom, Partin opened his testimony. With Jimmy prodding his nine defense lawyers, they made a frantic effort to suppress Partin.

Jimmy's soft-spoken lawyer, Haggerty, led the pack. "The government's case is a foul and filthy frame-up designed by the 'Get-Hoffa Squad.' This tramples on Hoffa's rights."

But Judge Wilson disagreed.

The defense lawyers grew abrasive. "You're biased in favor of the government," they shouted at mild-mannered Wilson. "The Justice department has been stealing Teamster documents!"

That evening, outside the courtroom, the FBI aces eyeballed the Teamsters while Jimmy's boys spied on the feds. They bugged rooms, tapped phones, entered rooms and stole files. Jimmy hired armed guards. His defense lawyers, afraid to talk in his room or a lawyer's room for fear of being overheard, went outside and bought Coca-Colas in order to find a place to discuss strategy for the next day.

Here was their strategy. The defense lawyers for Jimmy and his codefendants filed a motion for new trial.

Their reason?

The jurors had been drunk during the trial. The defense lawyers showed signed statements from four bellhops at Reed House Hotel. They swore that they'd delivered liquor to the jurors and saw some of them drunk.

"I am flabbergasted," the jury foreman told reporters. "It is ridiculous. We were most circumspect, because we realized the importance of our assignment. That is terrible—just terrible."

But other bellhops at the hotel said they'd been bribed for false statements but refused to give them. One displayed a briefcase full of cash. "The more information you give, the more cash you can have." He stood wide-eyed. "It don't matter if it's true or false as long as it helps Hoffa."

The mistrial was not granted.

The hotel fired the bellhops who had signed a statement, but they didn't cry for long. Instead, Atlanta Cabana Motor Hotel in Atlanta, Georgia, hired them. You know the Atlanta Cabana. Built with Teamsters' pension fund loans.

THE BETRAYAL

Jimmy's defense lawyers fought vigorously to the end of the trial. Schiffer continued to display his free-swinging style. As the trial closed, he hurled coins at the government prosecutors.

"I say to the Washington prosecutors, take these thirty pieces of silver and share them—you have earned them."

Schiffer knew his listeners would remember that Judas Iscariot had been paid thirty pieces of silver to betray Jesus.

But if Partin's Judas Iscariot, that makes Hoffa a Christ figure. The reporters' eyes widened. That's a hard sell to even the most sympathetic juror.

US Marshals later counted the coins. They totaled only twenty-one for a total of $2.50.

The jury deliberated for five hours. On March 4, 1964, it found—of Jimmy's five codefendants—two not guilty, three guilty of one count of attempted jury tampering. It found Jimmy guilty of two counts. When he heard, the color drained from his face.

Sheridan bolted out of the courtroom, located a phone, and called Bobby.

"Guilty—two counts! We made it!" Sheridan reported.

"Nice work," Bobby said.

Bobby ordered a plane to bring Sheridan, Neal, and the others back to Virginia for a party at Bobby's Hickory Hill home. Bobby had plenty to celebrate, but he looked subdued, sour even. His brother's assassination still grieved him.

Outside the courtroom, surrounded by reporters, Jimmy snapped, "Of course I'll appeal. What do you think? The whole trial was a fuckin' railroad job, a farce of American justice."

When I called Dad, he'd already heard. I couldn't resist. "Don't you wish you could have been a mouse in that courtroom to watch when that Mr. Partin stepped into the witness box?"

"A mouse? Me? A mountain lion, maybe."

I turned pragmatic. "Oh, no! A lion's too big. You'd dominate the courtroom. You don't want that. Think small. Maybe a spider in the corner."

He laughed. "Have it your way. Oh, wait a minute. How about one of the lizards that can walk across the ceiling. That small enough for you?"

I agreed, and just before we hung up, I heard Dad chuckle. "Well, I'll say this. It sure couldn't-a happened to a nicer fellow."

AN ANIMAL IN A CAGE

On April 27, 1964, two months after his Chattanooga conviction, Jimmy stood trial again, this time in Chicago. The federal government charged him with helping himself to $20 million in Teamsters' funds, giving it to real estate developers, and profiting from the deal.

Jimmy frowned and refused to discuss money with reporters. "I don't want to hear about it. Don't give me any razzle-dazzle."

Thirteen weeks later, the court found Jimmy guilty on four of the twenty counts against him. Judge Richard B. Austin sentenced him to five years imprisonment on each count, to run at the same time but after he'd served his eight years for jury tampering, for a total time in jail now of thirteen years.

"Are you going to appeal the conviction?" a newsman asked.

"What do you think?" Jimmy snapped. "This verdict's a fuckin' railroad job."

Appeal he did, in every way he and his attorneys could imagine. He even produced sworn statements from prostitutes who said they'd had sex with jurors and government witnesses. One whore turned over a tape recording of a heavy breather: Judge Wilson, she swore.

The appeals weren't working, and Jimmy knew he would be jailed. Riding the edge of a nervous breakdown, he lay on the floor and yelled, "I'm not gonna go!"

But he also took care of practical matters. He designated forty-one-year-old Charles "Chuckie" O'Brien as his foster son. That had some truth in it. Since he turned six,

Chuckie and his mother, Sylvia Pagano, famous Detroit moll and Josephine's close friend, had been part of the Hoffa household.

In the early thirties when Sylvia and Jimmy had been lovers, she connected him with Detroit's mobsters, including her former lover Frankie "Three Fingers" Coppola, nationally known for his heroin ring. Later, Sylvia moved to Kansas City where she married Chuckie's father, a driver for a gangster-politician type. Coppola became Chuckie's godfather.

Claiming Chuckie as Jimmy's foster son had a practical twist: Chuckie would have visiting privileges as a family member. Jimmy could use his foster son, also a Teamster, to take messages to the Marble Palace, for Jimmy intended to continue to act as general president in jail.

When the Supreme Court refused Jimmy's appeal, he called Frank Edward Fitzsimmons to the Baltimore hotel for instructions. The two had known each other since 1935 when Fitz, a truck driver and a tough street fighter, had joined Jimmy's local 299 in Detroit.

Fitz worked his way up the Teamster ladder, despite ridicule. A chubby, passive, inarticulate man, Fitz blushed easily when embarrassed. Jimmy often made Fitz go for coffee or hold chairs—Teamsters called him Jimmy's shoeshine boy—but Fitz proved to be a sharp manager and negotiator.

Remember debonair Harold J. Gibbons? Jimmy's number one assistant in Washington who lowered the flag when John Kennedy died and quit his job when Jimmy told him to "pull those fuckin' flags to full mast."

Fitz took over Gibbons's position, and during the four years that followed, he became Jimmy's strongest supporter.

So that night, in the Baltimore hotel, Jimmy said, "Fitz, I'm going to jail, and I want you to take over my fuckin' duties."

Fitz blushed. "When you get out, Jimmy, the keys will be right here. You come right back, don't worry about a thing."

THE VENDETTA VICTIM

At 8:20 a.m. March 7, 1967, on a gloomy, drizzly Washington day, the doorman telephoned up to Jimmy. "There's a swarm of reporters waiting for you in the lobby," the doorman cautioned. "Why don't you leave through the back entrance?"

"Thanks for the warning," Jimmy said, "but no. They have an assignment to complete, the same as me."

He rode the elevator down. Looking glum, he told reporters, "I'm a vendetta victim from tangling with that son of a bitch Bobby Kennedy."

Later that morning, when Chuckie O'Brien drove Jimmy to the federal building to surrender to the marshals, Chuckie warned, "There's going to be a mob of media folk at the front door. Let me drive you around back."

Jimmy refused. "I never ran away from anybody, and I'll be damned if I'm gonna start now. Drive this son of a bitch right up to the front door."

At the formidable entrance, he stood in the rain facing microphones and cameras. "I know you all have a job to do for which I hope you're getting paid union wages, which I doubt if most of you are." He paused, then continued, "This is a very unhappy day in my life." After he griped about the government, he entered, with his four lawyers, the big granite-faced building to be taken into custody.

There the marshals prepared Jimmy for his trip to the federal penitentiary near Lewisburg, Pennsylvania, 192 miles away. They handcuffed his wrists, put him in the backseat of a dark blue Pontiac, and chained his legs to the floor. He covered his humiliation with his raincoat.

A marshal sat on either side of the Teamsters' president, and a caravan of government vehicles full of marshals followed them to Pennsylvania.

"The cuffs, the caravan. That feels a bit like the fuckin' capture scene from *Bonnie and Clyde*," Jimmy observed.

The Headline

On Tuesday morning March 7, Janet Niebruegge, a staff reporter for the Fort Collins *Coloradoan,* rang my dad.

"Did you know that Jimmy Hoffa's on his way to jail right now?"

"Yes, I know. I've anticipated this day for a long long time."

Janet's voice sounded bouncy. "And how do you feel about that?"

Dad took a deep breath and proceeded to recite what he'd composed during restless nights. "'I would be less than honest if I were to say that I had not looked forward to today when the prison gates closed behind James Riddle Hoffa.'"

"That's a mouthful." Janet paused. "Maybe something shorter?"

"Okay. How about this?" Dad's voice lightened. "I will sleep a little sounder tonight."

"That's great! Thanks, Tom." And the short version became Janet's headline that afternoon.

But even Janet's news story didn't express the glee my father felt knowing that Jimmy had been locked up. "Served him right, that punk."

LIFE IN THE "BIG HOUSE"

In the federal penitentiary, the staff photographed Jimmy, fingerprinted him, gave him a regulation blue denim prison uniform and a number: 33-298. Jimmy stripped, took a delousing shower, and retreated to his cell for twenty-four hours.

His cell, a far cry from Jimmy's office in the Marble Palace, measured roughly seven by ten feet. It contained a cot, a toilet, a wooden chair, and a clothes locker, leaving Jimmy not much room to pace. The labor leader tried to humanize his cell by posting pictures of his family: Jo, of course, their children, Barbara and Jim, and grandchildren, Barbara Jo, and eventually Jim's two, David and Geoffrey, born during Jimmy's time in prison.

Among the prisoners, Jimmy spotted his old buddy Tony "Tony Pro" Provenzano, with his big grin, his dark eyebrows, and his mop of curly white hair. Tony, now forty-nine, had already served ten months of his four years for extortion.

"Here, have a seat." Tony patted an empty chair at his own four-man dining table. Jimmy sat gratefully. Tony had status. Eating with him meant a better grade of food than the often unfit, sometimes maggot-invaded general meals. It also meant protection. Tony and his buddies screened Jimmy, when he worked out, from unwanted invasion by prisoners. More importantly, Tony and his gang protected Jimmy from violence, including rape, always a threat in prison.

Every day, as required, Jimmy reported to the mattress shop to unstuff and restuff old mattresses. He also watched out for his Teamsters, and they watched out for him. When he'd been imprisoned two weeks, a local Teamster offered a bribe to a prison official to give Jimmy preferential treatment. The official declined. Other Teamsters busily offered cash to Partin if only he'd recant his Chattanooga testimony and help get Jimmy out of prison. "Name your price," they told Partin, but he declined the offer, even though threatened.

Then Jimmy saved Tony's life. Tony, hit by stomach problems, wasted to ninety-five pounds, but the authorities wouldn't let him go outside the prison for treatment. Jimmy threatened bad publicity and a lawsuit if Tony weren't let out. Within hours, the staff drove Tony to a local medical center for surgery.

After Tony recovered, he asked Jimmy to cream some money off the top of the Teamsters Pension Fund for him.

"No," Jimmy said.

Tony insisted.

"It's because of people like you," Jimmy tapped Tony on the chest, "I got into trouble in the first place."

Soon they shouted, then jostled until the guards broke them up. Afterward, Tony became Jimmy's tenacious enemy.

Jimmy could no longer count on Tony's protection, but he hesitated about joining the prison's other mobster, formidable Carmine Galante. Galante didn't look threatening; he stood five and a half feet tall and weighed 160 pounds. However, diagnosed with a psychopathic personality, Galante could be vicious. New York's Police Department suspected him of committing eighty murders.

On the other hand, Jimmy did need protection, and Galante functioned as top dog in the jail. He'd already served five of his twenty-year sentence for importing massive amounts of heroin into the United States from Montreal.

So Jimmy made a prison pact with Galante by sitting at his table.

And there the Teamsters' president lived. He stuffed mattresses, he worked out, he devoured books, and he never stopped being a labor leader. When he heard the guards complain about their working conditions, he offered to unionize them.

But he had no illusions about jail with its "bad guards, bad food, and bad everything. You're just an animal in a cage and you're treated like one."

"THE TIMES THEY ARE A-CHANGIN'"

With one too many slugs of cognac, I hoped to quell my jittering heart as I stood before a small New York City audience in March 1967 and read a few of my poems. I'd written poetry for not too many months, but I was on a roll.

Then jazz musician, Alan Surpin, picked me up by convincing me that he was from Canada. It took almost a week for Alan's accent to wear so thin that even I could hear it. A strange lover, he had a body like an ironing board.

Alan played reeds—saxophone and clarinet—and I loved to read my poetry, so we performed together. Alan

Alan Surpin and I combined music and poetry in our Sound Forms.

dressed in black; I wore a multicolored psychedelic dress. We called ourselves Sound Forms and tried to erase the barrier between words and music.

Gifted at finding gigs, Alan placed us in art galleries and churches, but our highlight came when we performed for the American Ethical Culture's Society in New Jersey. Also on the program was Louis "Moondog" Hardin.

Alan and I had seen the blind musician around town. Who hadn't? A tall, genial man with flowing gray hair and an even longer beard, Moondog dressed in full Viking regalia: sweeping robes, tall spear, fur helmet sporting steer horns. This forest spirit apparition stood stock still on a busy Sixth Avenue sidewalk, begging for his living.

Louis "Moondog" Hardin in his Viking regalia.

In New Jersey, when Moondog walked on the New Jersey stage, I saw that his regalia made my psychedelic dress look "off the rack." I listened to him play his drums and keyboards, recite his poetry: "She bought a cover to cover the seat; but the cover was so nice, she bought a cover to cover the cover; and now it's covered twice."

I liked Moondog's simple poems. Musicians like Philip Glass and Charlie Parker praised the Viking's music.

Alan moved to Canada, but I kept on reading—at Eagle Tavern and Cummington Community of the Arts, on the radio in New York and Houston and on TV in Woodstock, I read at a medical center in New Orleans, at galleries, and at many colleges.

I had a good time, but I missed Alan's pizzazz.

Downright Tumultuous

The gooseneck lamp made a pool of light on my desk about 3 a.m., June 5, 1968. Pencil in hand, I drafted a poem until someone pounded on my apartment door.

Who could that be at this hour?

When I opened the door, tall skinny Bev, my upstairs neighbor in our tenement building, cried, "You've got to come up! They've shot Bobby Kennedy!"

My hand trembled as I remembered the warmth of Bobby Kennedy's hand when he shook mine, and I could still hear the funny way he pronounced, "Nice to meet you."

"Come on." Bev grabbed my elbow. "I've got a news channel on."

I couldn't afford a TV. I taught now, at Pratt Institute in Brooklyn, but only part-time with no summer income, so I followed Bev upstairs.

On Bev's TV, I saw the classic image of that night: Robert Kennedy, dressed in his black campaigning suit, sprawled flat on the kitchen floor, his limbs jutting out as though they didn't belong to him.

"Oh my God!" Bev shook her fist at the TV. "I can't believe this! I can't believe this! Martin Luther King only two months dead, and all that rioting, looting, attacks everywhere, thousands arrested, and who know how many shot!"

"The rioting, it's everywhere, even Omaha. I read that kids there trashed businesses and cars, cops shot at them, wounding some and killing a black kid. It's the same all over!" I said.

"And now this." Bev sat down heavily, and we turned to the TV.

Bobby, still alive, asked, "Is everybody okay?" And a few moments later his voice changes as he says, "Everything's going to be okay."

Bev reached for a tissue. Then we saw Ethel, Bobby's wife, bending over him, him turning toward her. Then we watched the medics take him away.

After that, the TV repeated the same old story, over and over.

"And it isn't just race riots." Bev walked me to her door. "It's more and more anti-Vietnam protests. It's getting downright tumultuous!"

"Maybe we aren't going to overcome."

"Oh, don't say that!"

We wouldn't know until the next day that Bobby had died.

The Kennedys flew his body to New York where it rested in that huge St. Patrick's Cathedral for two days, but I didn't go see it. I couldn't. I felt too sad.

I called Dad.

"Yes it is sad," Dad's voice dropped, "first John and now Robert. Old Man Kennedy must regret pushing those boys into politics."

"I keep thinking about our trip to Washington, DC." I pushed a couple paper clips around on my desk.

"Me too." Dad laughed. "Boy, that Robert was young. In his early thirties, and me already fifty-one. He looked so clean-cut with that expensive suit of his."

"Yes, but you could tell what a rebel he was by that mop of hair he wore." I closed my eyes to savor my memory.

"Right! You know, I didn't think much of Robert at first, what with Curtis saying what a spoiled brat Bobby was, engaging in shouting matches instead of building solid legal cases."

Dad kind of clucked, "But he was smart, the way he lined up those questions he asked me, in perfect order. I couldn't have told my story better. I credit him as being as responsible as I was for creating that Landrum-Griffin Act."

I rolled my eyes. "But Bobby couldn't have created that act without your story."

"That's what the historians say."

"And with Bobby dead," I stifled a giggle, "now nobody's left to beat that tricky Dick Nixon."

My Republican father scoffed. "What you want to beat Nixon for? He's the best man we got going."

Unbelievable, Baby

"We've got to go in there and I mean really go in." President Richard Nixon's face flushed. "I don't want gunships, I want helicopter ships. I want everything that

can fly to go in there and crack the hell out of them. Is
that clear?"

Nixon's intent to invade Cambodia angered National
Security Advisor Henry Kissinger, but he notified the military.

"We should keep that campaign as low-key as we can,"
advised army General Creighton Abrams, who commanded
the military operations in Vietnam, but Nixon disagreed.
He modeled himself on his favorite movie, *Patton*, a
portrayal of a controversial general that the president had
seen five times.

So on Thursday, April 30, 1970, President Nixon
announced his decision on all three US TV networks.
Staring ahead, he declared, "Our will is being tested tonight.
The time has come for action."

His campaign to invade Cambodia began the next
day. It ignited a firestorm of antiwar protests in some 400
colleges, as students beefed up their rallies.

Students at Kent State University in Ohio initially held
peaceful protests, but later that balmy spring night, they
heaved beer bottles at police cars. About midnight, a mob
of students rampaged through town, shattering windows.

Saturday night, Kent State students firebombed the
rickety old ROTC building on campus. The mayor called
Governor James Rhodes who declared martial law and sent
900 National Guardsmen to the campus. "We will eradicate
the problem," he promised.

Sunday remained quiet, but Monday, May 4, students
gathered for a noon rally. Five times a campus policeman
called for students to scatter. They ignored him.

Finally, guardsmen, carrying loaded rifles, submachine
guns, and pistols, moved forward.

"They've got guns now. You don't throw rocks against guns," a student voiced.

Barrages of tear gas pushed the crowd up a knoll. The students hurled rocks, chunks of concrete, and the troopers' own burping gas grenades at the guardsmen. Several times, troopers kneeled in what looked like firing positions, perhaps to frighten their attackers.

The hail of rocks and cement continued. So did the guard's gas barrage, until no gas grenades remained. Then the sound of gunfire deafened.

"My God! They're killing us!" a student shouted.

"This is no accident! This is butchery."

Four students lay dead. Ten wounded.

"Unbelievable, baby, that they shot. This isn't Berkeley or Columbia."

GETTING DAD'S GOAT

Aging can change a person. It did Dad, who became more of what he was, the top dog.

I noticed this one summer when Dad, Mama, me, my sister Margaret and her husband, Wade Dent, went on summer vacation. Wade had been born and raised in the little cowboy town of Ten Sleep, Wyoming, where a lad learns to ride, shoot, and hunt. He wooed Margaret in Denver, when both were students. Now he ran a commercial plumbing business and would soon be a millionaire.

That summer we traveled in two cars, Wade's and Dad's. Before we left that morning for Yellowstone, Dad laid out our plans; he would lead and Wade would follow. He made sure Wade understood the places we would stop.

We got in our cars. I jumped in Wade's backseat. "Wanna watch me get his goat?" Wade grinned. Margaret and I cheered him.

So, instead of waiting for Dad to hit the road first, Wade pulled out ahead, with a great squealing of tires, driving fast enough so Dad couldn't easily pass him.

Eventually we stopped at an unplanned place, and Dad pulled out of his car, taller than any one of us. He seemed stiff, his face had turned red, and he lit into Wade.

We all listening politely until Dad ran down, but back in Wade's car Margaret and I broke into giggles. Wade had made his point, so he didn't take the lead again.

Colorado Bound

When I spoke to the folks in the fall of 1965, I found them in the midst of packing to leave Sidney, Nebraska. Dad had accepted a city management job in Fort Collins, Colorado, a town twice as big as Sidney.

"So how come you're leaving Sidney? Did they run Dad out of town?" I snorted.

"No, no, not at all." Mama sounded indignant. "City managers are like preachers; they don't last long. Five years is typical, but your father's been working here for seven and a half years, and nobody wants to see him go."

"They were going to run me out of town," Dad's voice crackled across the line, "but they had to lock me up first, and nobody could catch me."

"Oh, Tom, it wasn't like that at all. Everybody's sorry to see him go, Marilyn, and they said the nicest things about him." Mama read some newspaper articles to me.

"'He appreciates honest difference of opinion. He solves complex problems with ease. He's a man who stands above the crowd.'"

Dad broke in. "You better not listen to your mom any longer. I'm going to owe her a pretty penny."

BLOOD ON THE WAR MEMORIAL

When Dad accepted a job in Fort Collins, he moved into an unusually conservative town experiencing a growth boom. From 1950 to 1970, the population of Fort Collins almost tripled. New industries moved into town and buildings rose rapidly.

In 1965, after Dad became city manager, Fort Collins encountered turbulent times. National unrest over the Vietnam War and the civil rights movement penetrated the town, especially on its Colorado State University campus. Although "White Trade Only" signs no longer hung in storefront windows, prejudice against Mexican Americans and blacks ran deep.

Student and faculty activism became intense at Colorado State in the 1960s and '70s. On March 5, 1968, several hundred antiwar protesters marched from the campus to Fort Collins' downtown War Memorial. There they wiped blood on a placard tied to the memorial.

This upset townspeople who heckled and harassed the marchers. A man tried to drive a truck into the protesters.

When townsfolk blocked the marchers' return to campus, police had to use Mace to break up the crowd.

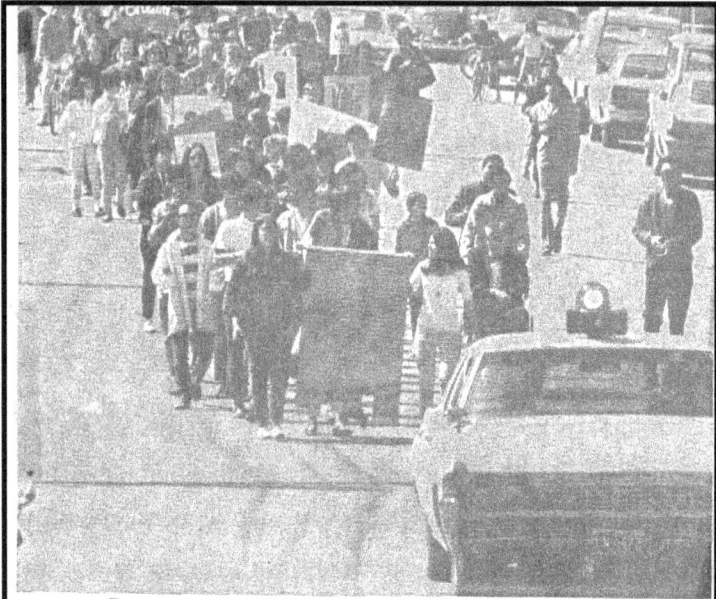

Demonstrators march on city hall

Shouting cries of "Chicano Power," a group protesting alleged police brutality marched on city hall today. Students from Colorado State University and the University of Colorado met memebrs of the League of United Latin American Citizens (LULAC) at the former Grant Avenue Presbyterian Church leased to LULAC to begin the march. Police escorted the delegation, composed mainly of young persons, to City Hall where a protest was to be lodged with the city council. (Coloradoan photo by Joel Draut)

Mexican-Americans march in protest against Rains

4-9-70

Mexican Americans march on Fort Collins city hall. From the Fort Collins' Coloradoan.

SGT. TERRY RAINS

Around April 1, 1970, Sgt. Terry Rains, a Fort Collins police officer, arrested Spanish-speaking Joe Serna, twenty-three, and charged him with drunkenness and resisting arrest.

"Chicano Power" bellowed some 300 Mexican Americans and college students. They marched to city hall April 9 and demanded Rains be fired.

The next day, still insisting that Fort Collins fire Rains, 150 marchers jammed into the town's fifty-seat council chamber. As city manager, Dad made all decisions to fire, hire, or discipline city employees. He refused to fire Rains, but agreed to "relieve" Rains of active duty, an action that wouldn't go on his record.

"Police officers carry around stereotyped images of Mexican American citizens and disregard their rights— utterly," said Ernest Andrade, president of LULAC, a Latin American league in charge of the protest. He pushed for "immediate suspension with no pay."

But Dad refused to yield. "To suspend Rains with no pay would be punitive since he's convicted of nothing." Dad waved his hand. "Besides, there's no reason to penalize his family."

My father expected that he and the police chief would investigate the Rains case as required by the city charter. But no. Five city councilmen and six Mexican American reps decided to investigate—until the district court halted them. "The Chicano reps have no official connection with city government," the court held.

When told that the investigation must be handled through administrative channels and that Dad would be in charge, LULAC President Andrade broke off communication with the council. Before he left, he said, "How can Coffey be in charge, he keeps saying he's sure that Rains is innocent. How can you have a hearing when a man is innocent before anything is brought forward?"

Someone in the audience shouted, "We don't want Coffey, that's what it is. It's as plain as that."

When the group marched back to LULAC headquarters, Dad, the police chief, the assistant city attorney, and Mayor Karl Carson followed them, feeling it essential to reestablish communications "with these people." While there, Carson suggested they'd accept an outside, independent investigation.

And so on April 20, Fort Collins hired Colorado State University law professor William Rentfro to hold an inquiry about the Rains charges. All parties agreed to this.

Old Main on Fire!

Friday evening, May 8, 1970, Colorado State student protesters met outdoors to hear Nixon speak. The good-natured crowd listened quietly to Nixon's press conference, and sometimes laughed.

Then the students, 1,600 strong, headed into the field house to warm up. There they held a rap session, both for and against continuing to strike to protest the Vietnam War. When they voted, two-thirds chose to continue the strike.

Late that night, a campus police sergeant making his rounds saw smoke billowing from the basement of Old Main, a landmark classroom and office building on the university campus. He heard two explosions.

A few minutes after Fort Collins fire engines and firemen arrived, a window broke, letting oxygen combust. The fire burst out of control.

A column of smoke rose, turning from gray to glowing orange. People ran toward the blaze. Flames mounted higher and higher. Shabby walls of the building collapsed.

The firefighters lacked plentiful water. "Without water," the fire chief said, "there is no way we can stop the fire." They managed to contain the spectacular blaze, but they could not halt it. It burned for five hours, its flames visible for miles.

Officials suspected arson, but evidence of it lay buried under five feet of pungent rubble—all that remained of the ninety-two-year-old building.

When Dad heard about the fire Saturday morning, he and Mayor Carson drove to the campus and met with the Colorado State University president who glared, his cheeks red. "If arson caused that fire, it's bound to be the act of a sick person, someone trying to shut this university down by terrorist tactics."

He and student leaders called for rational actions by all university residents. Dad and the mayor joined them, urging rational actions by all Fort Collins citizens too. Reporters snapped pictures.

Then May 28, Dad received "findings of fact," which acquitted Sergeant Rains of all but two charges levied by LULAC.

"The charges brought by LULAC on the whole," Dad said, "are not substantiated. I see no pattern of conduct to justify disciplinary measure. The sergeant has been under suspension with pay for seven weeks. That seems a stronger disciplinary action than the facts in this case warrant. I have, therefore, ordered Sergeant Rains reinstated to duty effective at three p.m. this afternoon, at the time his shift goes on duty."

And so a "get Coffey" movement started. The next night, LULAC members held a press conference to denounce Dad's action in reinstating Rains. Their condemnation wouldn't fully manifest itself for another year and a half.

"Retire? I'd Go Crazy"

Dad started his sixth year as city manager of Fort Collins September 30, 1971. He was sixty-four and not talking about retiring until John Gagnon, reporter for the local *Coloradoan,* dropped by in December.

Gagnon regarded my casual father tilted in his big office chair.

"So when you going to retire?" Gagnon raised an eyebrow.

Dad stretched out his legs. "Retire! Me? I'd go crazy."

"But you'll be sixty-five next June." Gagnon had done his research. "City rules say employees must retire at sixty-five."

Dad's chair dropped noisily forward. "Not all employees. Not city managers." Privately, he intended to work until he tuckered out.

After Gagnon left, Dad called his pal, the mayor, Dr. Karl E. Carson. "What the hell am I supposed to do," Dad cleared his throat, "if I want to keep on working?"

Carson investigated and called back. "You've got to ask the council—sometime between now and your birthday— to let you continue as city manager. I think they will, but a couple said they hadn't given it much thought, but I think it will be satisfactory," Mayor Carson murmured. "There's no particular reason for a change."

However, in a surprise move, reporter Gagnon interviewed council members.

J. W. N. Fead said the council should take "a long, hard look at the choices of enforcing retirement at age sixty-five and getting a new man."

Mable Preble said she'd be in favor of extending Dad's tenure, but William Lopez favored retirement at sixty-five.

"The advantages and disadvantages of age versus youth are relative," Mayor Carson said. "You have to judge each individual's performance."

"Age is on my side," Dad told Gagnon. "I know my way around in political circles. Like the $1.2 million in federal funds we got for the Soldier Canyon plant. Getting that took all my political savvy. Savvy like that, invaluable to the city, takes experience, which comes with age."

At the next council meeting, Andy Anderson showed up. Dad winced. He had no use for the little guy, nothing but a publicity hound supported by his wealthy wife. A pipsqueak rabble rouser.

"I've lost all faith in Coffey." Andy gave Mayor Carson a petition demanding that Fort Collins retire its city manager at age sixty-five.

"Citizens can no longer rely on Coffey's word." Andy's face reddened. "I don't have any complaints personally, but I have become a kind of 'father confessor' to other citizens, including students."

He gestured to the cluster of Colorado State University students he'd brought with him. Gary Kimsey, editor of the university's *Collegian*, stood. He turned his back to my father. "Coffey couldn't even resolve a conflict over distributing our newspaper at the Municipal Building. The council instructed Coffey to do everything he could to solve the problem, but meetings with Coffey weren't productive."

"You can see Coffey's gross inability," Andy flapped a hand in dismissal, "to cope with, let alone solve, today's complex problems."

Then, in response to Andy's petition, council member William Lopez offered a plan to set a mandatory retirement age of sixty-five years for the city manager. Lopez, a high school teacher, looked out over the rims of his glasses. "I've received forty-eight phone calls, most in support of this idea. It provides for an orderly transfer of the job."

After a long, detailed discussion of Lopez's plan, council members voted it out, 4 to 1, much to my father's relief.

Then, by a unanimous vote, the council raised Dad's salary from $20,500 to $21,525.

Andy stood to leave. "We only need 449 signatures on this petition to force a special election on retiring at sixty-five. But we've got such tremendous support, I'm planning to get a thousand signatures."

Several weeks later after Andy's petition for an election had circulated widely, Dad called a press conference to announce his retirement effective March 31, 1973. He stood behind his desk, his fingers splayed out on his desktop.

"This is a reversal of my feeling to date. I previously indicated that I wanted to remain city manager until my health failed."

"Did Andy's petition influence you?" Kimsey of the *Collegian* exchanged a knowing look with the other reporter.

"I have no comment on Andy Anderson," Dad narrowed his eyes, "but I'm not trying to forestall an election, if that's what you mean."

"Will you retire sooner if more public pressure is forthcoming?" Gagnon, reporter for the *Coloradoan*, poised a pencil above his notebook.

"No way!" Dad shook his head. "I'm not hired by the public but by council; I'll abide by the wishes of the council. They hire and fire city managers." Dad slowed down, became calm. "I've had this March date in mind for some time. I didn't talk about retirement because it's difficult for a lame duck city manager to operate. With this March date, I'll have time to tie down the JWR water system, Fort Collins capital improvement program, and the Northside Park along the Poudre River."

Gagnon called Andy. "What do you think about Coffey's announcement of a March 31, 1973, retirement date?"

"Oh, that?" Andy chuckled. "It's nothing but a stalling tactic on Coffey's part to save face."

FREE AT LAST!

Then suddenly Jimmy's jail time ended; he walked out of Lewisburg federal penitentiary December 23, 1971, a free man. Well, almost a free man. To earn his pardon from President Richard Nixon, Jimmy had to agree not to "engage in direct or indirect management of any labor organization" until March 1980, the end of his thirteen-year prison term.

Jimmy, being Jimmy, fought that ridiculous restriction.

Not that he needed to earn money. The Teamsters had given him a $1.7 million pension in a single payment. No, Jimmy wanted power. He hoped to return to leadership.

So he accused John Mitchell, Nixon's attorney general: "You took away my rights when you came up with that agreement."

Mitchell denied it.

Then Hoffa turned to the courts, but he lost that battle too. He couldn't even win points with his parole board.

Jimmy didn't know it, but his lap dog, President Frank Fitzsimmons, initiated that restriction. Indeed, he'd pushed it for years. He didn't want Jimmy to get his old job back.

Now Fitz could function as the real Teamsters' president instead of waiting for Jimmy's messages from jail. Now Fitz could run for president in the Teamsters' upcoming election without bumping into Jimmy.

Nixon told Mitchell: "Fitzsimmons has been damn good in all of his private, ah, he's, you know, he's, he's, I know, he's done some things privately that are very helpful."

Such as sending large cash payments from the Teamsters to Nixon's 1972 reelection campaign. The Teamsters also endorsed Nixon's reelection bid, even though Nixon was a Republican and the Teamsters almost always endorsed Democrats. Plus the Teamsters helped Nixon control anti–Vietnam War demonstrations by providing experienced thugs to clobber antiwar protesters.

Ted Kennedy's possible reaction troubled the president.

"Hoffa is a great symbol," Nixon noted. "He cuts into the Kennedy mystique, even though Bobby's major accomplishment as attorney general was putting Hoffa in jail. So Teddy Kennedy will come roaring out and kick the hell out of us for letting Hoffa out of jail. So what?"

Jimmy's release made page-one news all across the nation. Tons of editorial writers filled their columns with suspicion.

I couldn't wait to hear Dad's take. I caught him at home, part of his holiday celebration.

"Dad, what did you think when you heard Hoffa was released?"

Dad's laugh shimmered along the phone line.

"What did I think? I thought 'Jiminy crickets, that's almost enough to turn me into a Democrat.'"

WHO'S GONNA RUN THE CITY?

Late that February, reporter Gagnon called Andy again.

"Yes, it's true," Andy laughed, "now 450 people have signed the age-limit petition. And signature numbers are mounting. Only 449 are needed, so I already have enough to force a special election. But I hope to have a thousand when I present the petition to the council March 2.

"And yes, that's true, also. I am trying to force Coffey out of office. He lacks decent contact with the public. He seems to have a general attitude that 'we're going to run the city the way we want to.'"

Dad's supporters stepped forward:

"This petition drive is an almost hysterical effort to limit the age of our city manager to sixty-five. It's true that Coffey is tough, but this is not a job for Mr. Milktoast. Since the council can fire the city manager on sixty days' notice, to change this would be like adding a set of dentures when one's own teeth are perfectly good." —Harry Troxell, Colorado State University professor

"From what I can determine, no other Colorado city has such a policy." —Mayor Karl Carson

"Evidently this is intended to hurt Tom Coffey, but on the contrary it would be a tremendous detriment and loss for the people." —A. J. Mason, retired businessman

April 1, 1972, the Fort Collins council decided to hold an election Tuesday, May 23, to decide if city managers must retire at sixty-five.

The ballot read, "Shall Section 4 of Article III of the City Charter which now provides for removal of the City Manager by majority vote of the City Council be amended to add additional causes for removal as follows: (a) majority vote of the electors at an election to be held every four years and (b) his attaining age sixty-five, effective with the incumbent city manager." A yes vote is yes to both (a) and (b).

Glen, Baby of the Family

My phone rang unexpectedly Friday April 10, 1972. It was Mama. She sounded as if she'd been crying. "We're getting ready to drive to Omaha."

"Why are you doing that?"

"Well, your father can't take time off for the funeral—it's on Wednesday—but he wants to see Mary." Mama's voice cracked.

"Funeral? What funeral?"

"Oh, I meant to call you earlier—let me find a tissue—but then I had to pack. Glen, honey. He died today."

My hand flew to my chest. "Uncle Glen?"

"Yes." Mama blew her nose. "Mary found him. On the sofa in their house."

"Oh, my God!" My muscles stiffened. "But he's so young!"

"Fifty-three. Baby of the family, and first to go."

I slumped into a chair. "How did he die, Mama?"

"Blood clot to the brain, we think. Like your grandpa Coffey. One moment alive, the next dead." She sniffled.

I squeezed my eyes shut. "How's Dad taking it?"

"Hard. You know what Glen meant to your father, the two of them working together through that awful Hoffa strike." Mama hiccupped. "Dad just crumpled up when he heard it. Almost as bad as when he saw his own father lying dead. Then Dad flung himself on the bare wooden floor, beat his fists against it, and howled until his brothers pulled him away."

TOO OLD TO CRY

Dad read the headline in the Fort Collins *Coloradoan* May 18, 1972: The answer should be 'No.'

At least reporter Gagnon is on my side, he thought. And Dad read what he knew, that voters, next Tuesday, will decide if he should leave office at age sixty-five.

"Don't expect a big turnout of voters," Gagnon wrote. "And don't make your decision on the popularity of sixty-five-year-old City Manager Thomas Coffey or political gadfly Andy Anderson. Today's election is far too important for that. It could have far-ranging consequences for our community. This issue deserves a resounding 'no' from voters."

Dad didn't usually drive by the university on his way home, but today he'd been cutting the ribbon for a new business in the neighborhood, so he spun by.

He slowed down when he saw a horde of students caper around a larger-than-life-size figure of a man dressed in a business suit. Many held "Vote YES" signs.

Dad pulled to the far curb and stopped when he saw the figure's face: it was his, a large black-and-white photo of his mug. The students had labeled the figure *TOM COFFEY*.

Then he noticed the rope around "his" neck. He watched students elevate his figure toward an overhanging tree branch. "Damn," he said. "They're hanging me."

He didn't wait to watch his effigy twirl in the air.

On May 24, 1972, 30 percent of Fort Collins's citizens turned out for the election. Most voted in favor of making city managers retire at sixty-five. The amendment passed by 927 votes.

"Short-sighted" read the *Coloradoan*'s headline the next day.

"As a lawyer, I am ashamed of a legal system that will permit a group of eighteen-year-old college students to have something to say about amending our charter," Maurice O. Nelson wrote. "Then they leave town and we are stuck with the change."

Dad's interview sounded formal. "The people have spoken, and I'll abide by their wishes."

Later, a few friends gathered at Dad's house, "The Coffey Grounds."

"In one way it has to be a relief for you," banker Allan Anderson patted Dad on the back, "not to receive the antagonizing phone calls and libelous attacks on your character."

"Well, as Abe Lincoln said, after he lost an election, 'I'm too old to cry, but it hurts too much to laugh.'" Dad's voice slowed to a whisper. "I've been beat before."

By the final council meeting June 9, Dad sounded more chipper. "I am not fond of the way I'm leaving, but I've lost elections before. I won't kill myself."

"Don't you feel bitter?" Mayor Carson asked.

"No, I can't be bitter." Dad's chest puffed out. "This town has been good to me. I'd much rather leave by other circumstances, of course, but I learned long ago that to tear a building down it takes muscles, not brains." Dad glanced at Andy sitting in the audience. "But to build it takes somebody who's pretty smart."

Dad chuckled. "All on earth that's happened to me is that I retire a few months before I intended to."

The council gave Dad three months' severance pay. "That's forty-five days longer than the charter requires," the mayor said, "but we considered it fair, just, and honest in view of your forced early retirement."

Carson picked up a plaque and read: "In appreciation of your six-and-a-half-year stewardship of city administration. For your dedication, loyalty and outstanding contributions to the city of Fort Collins." The plaque showed Dad's dates of service, 1965–1972.

The mayor flipped the plaque over and read a long Teddy Roosevelt quote, which Carson said was appropriate in view of the election. It partly reads: "It is not the critic who counts— not the man who points out how the strong man stumbled. The credit belongs to the man who is actually in the arena; whose face is marred by dust and sweat and blood."

To my dad's satisfaction, he saw Andy squirm.

"You know," Dad grinned, "I've worked like a dog all my life, so I plan to do a little fishing now, but not in Colorado. I'm not going to fish for your nine-inch trout here. I'm going to Nebraska to catch some pike so you know there's something on the end of your line."

HOFFA'S LAST STAND

Beer-bellied Chuckie O'Brien, Jimmy's foster son, carted the twenty-pound coho salmon, caught in Lake Erie, to the maroon car. He'd mooched the car, a long, low-slung 1975 Mercury Marquis, from his friend Joey Giacalone.

Chuckie, now forty-one, fancied long sideburns, a wide-collared paisley shirt, and scads of gold chains on his neck. He popped open the Mercury's door and plopped the fish down on the backseat. The fucker was packed in ice, inside a plastic bag, and in a box, but it oozed salmon juice just the same.

Always one to take the easy way out, if he could find it, Chuckie left the dripping fish on the seat. *Nothin' I can do about it now; I've got places to go and people to see.* He revved the Merc up.

Chuckie didn't mind being an errand boy delivering the salmon as a gift from a Teamster bigwig to Bobby Holmes, himself a Teamster vice-president. He'd been with Jimmy since their strawberry days.

Holmes didn't answer the door, but his wife did, their baby on her hip. "Bobbie's gone. Oh, that's for us?"

Chuckie deposited the big coho salmon on her kitchen counter.

He and the wife shot the breeze. Time passed. When he looked at his jewel-encrusted watch, it was already half past one. *Shit. Too late to join Uncle Tony Jack at his athletic club. Looks like I might be late to pick up Dad too. Well, he can just wait.*

As Chuckie turned to go, he noticed the fish leaking blood and slime down the counter door. He shrugged and left.

"Should I Stay or Go?"

Jimmy Hoffa looked normal early on the morning of July 30, 1975, as he worked in his yard at his Lake Orion home. But Josephine knew better.

The date Jimmy had finally agreed to, after a third phone call from that Detroit gangster, seemed to make him uncommonly nervous. And no wonder. He'd be meeting the two Tonys, "Tony Jack" Giacalone

Natty dresser Anthony Giacalone.
The FBI arrested him later in 1975.

from Detroit and "Tony Pro" Provenzano from New Jersey. Both ranked high in the Mafia, and Tony Pro had a tick up his ass. He never forgave Jimmy for, as Tony Pro put it, stiffing him when they were in jail. Tony Pro had wanted just a nice chunk of Teamsters' pension money for himself, but Jimmy refused to donate it.

However, that was all yesterday's worry. Giacalone swore that Tony Pro wanted to bury the hatchet, so the three would get together today to shake hands.

No wonder Jimmy looked a bit stretched.

But when he came out of the bedroom wearing sunglasses, a dark blue short-sleeved polo shirt, black trousers, white Gucci loafers and, of course, his white socks, he looked chipper enough.

"I'll be home late afternoon," he told Jo. And he jumped into his dark green 1974 Pontiac Grand Ville and left, a little before noon. He did feel better. He had a plan.

"Louie the Pope"

A third of the way to Detroit, Jimmy detoured to Pontiac, Michigan, to see his close personal friend, Louis "Louie the Pope" Linteau. They'd been buddies for better than two decades.

Round-faced Louie had boxed as an amateur in Canada for five years. Then Jimmy named Louie business agent for the Pontiac Teamsters Local 614. After he rose to president, an embezzlement conviction landed him in jail, but he still could count on his salary. Jimmy saw to that.

Out of jail, Louie received enough cash from Jimmy to start Airport Service Lines, his airport limousine business. Louie prospered. So did Jimmy, thanks to his stake in the business.

As he pulled into the parking lot, Jimmy beamed, certain that Louie would help him. But when he entered the lobby, he didn't spot his buddy.

"Looking for Mr. Linteau, Jimmy?" The big dispatcher Elmer Reeves frowned.

"Yeah. Is that little rat fink here?"

"Naw. He left for lunch just minutes ago." Elmer turned back to his keyboard.

"Damn!"

So the Little Guy hung around and chatted with employees. "He seemed nervous," one said later. Time slipped by.

"Think the old thwacker will be gone much longer?" Jimmy asked Elmer.

"Hard to say. He doesn't really run by a ticker."

"Dammit! I'm fuckin' on my way to a joint about fifteen miles north of Detroit. The Machus Red Fox Restaurant. You know it?"

"That classy eatin' place that caters to Teamsters? Along Telegraph Road?"

Jimmy nodded. "I want Louie to go with me."

Elmer's eyebrow shot up.

"Well, listen to this fuckin' Mob lineup I'm meeting. Tony Pro Provenzano. Know him?"

Elmer shook his head. "Never heard of him."

"Well, he's a fuckin' boss in New Jersey *and* Florida."

Elmer's eyes widened.

A car pulled up. Jimmy looked at the parking lot, but still no Louie. "How about Tony Jack Giacalone?"

Elmer nodded. "I know that name. Detroit boss, isn't he?"

"Yeah. A fuckin' natty dresser, but tough. He's bringing his heavy-duty kissin' cousin, Little Lenny Schultz."

"Wow! Some lineup!"

"Yeah." Jimmy grumbled, "I was counting on bringing Louie with me."

Elmer nodded. "I can see why."

Shortly after, Jimmy drove off.

STEPS SHORT BUT RAPID

A stickler for punctuality, Jimmy arrived at the Red Fox right on time for the 2 p.m. meeting. He parked his dark green Pontiac in a nearby shopping mall and waited. He had a half hour to wait for the two Tonys, due to show up at 2:30, but Frank "The Irishman" Sheeran said he'd be here at two. What the hell for, Jimmy didn't know. Probably with a message from legendary crime boss Russell "McGee" Bufalino, Frank's mentor. He was something, one of the nation's biggest Mafia leaders, cunning, rational, ruthless. But an odd one, a squat aging man who wore exquisitely tailored suits and talked only in whispers and nods.

At ten past two, Jimmy got out of the Pontiac. *I'm going to get all stoved up if I just sit there.* He began to walk, short steps but rapid.

What the hell could be keeping Frank? Jimmy remembered when they met. The Irishman towered over me, almost a foot taller. *I knew Frank whacked men for McGee, so when he introduced us, I said, "I hear you paint houses." Frank grinned and nodded. To paint a house is to kill someone, and I knew that Frank, a hitman, had painted a dozen houses for Russell. Never caught. After I mentored Frank, he began to paint houses for me too.*

At twenty past two, Jimmy stopped walking. He cracked his knuckles and glared, his famous knock-down stare he'd perfected for Bobby Kennedy. Frank a no-show and the others not here yet. He had spotted a phone booth outside a nearby hardware store. Too early to call anyone. He didn't want to sit in the cramped car. He didn't feel hungry, so no point going to the restaurant. So he walked and walked and walked, growing more furious with each step. At 2:40 he called Jo.

"Tony Jack hasn't shown. Did he call? Where the hell is he?"

"Nobody's called, Jimmy."

"Well, I'll wait a little longer and come on home. I should be there by four. I'll grill us some steaks on the barbecue for dinner."

He waited longer, walked around the parking lot again. Then he went back to the pay phone and called Louie.

"The bastards are late! They've put me on ice. I been here since two and it's now…wait a fuckin' minute. Maybe that's them. That maroon car. Sure looks like Joey's Mercury. And Chuckie's driving it. Oh, it's for me all right."

"Drop by the Airport Service when you get finished."

"Will do."

Jimmy hung up. It was 2:48. The Mob, by design, had made him wait, knowing it would make him nuts. And it had.

Jimmy walked to the maroon Mercury, planted his feet wide apart, and glared at Chuckie.

"Sorry I'm late, Dad."

"What the fuck are you even doing here?" Jimmy yelled. "Who the fuck invited you?" He jabbed his finger at Chuckie.

Jimmy swirled and stared at Salvatore "Sally Bugs" Briguglio, a short, skinny middle-aged guy with thick curly black hair and fat Coke-bottle eyeglasses. He sat in the backseat behind Chuckie. "Who the fuck is he?" Jimmy's eyes narrowed.

"I'm Tony Pro's right-hand man."

The answer relieved Jimmy. The two Tonys must have sent Sally Bugs, along with Chuckie, a Tony Jack ally, to pick up Jimmy for the meeting, but he just frowned and yelled. "What the fuck is going on here?" He scowled at Sally Bugs. "Your fucking boss was supposed to be here at 2:30."

"People are staring at us, Jimmy." Sally Bugs pointed at Frank. "Look who's here."

Tall Frank Sheeran.
Photo credit on copyright page.

In the front passenger seat, Jimmy's habitual spot, sat Frank Sheeran. Jimmy bent down, looked across Chuckie at Frank, who turned and waved.

"His friend," Sally Bugs spoke low, "wanted to be at the thing. They're at the house, waiting."

Frank's "friend" was Russell "McGee" Bufalino, Jimmy knew. *McGee, Tony Pro's mobster superior, might be the only person who could keep that fuckin' Tony Pro in line. Russell must have come down to Detroit from Pennsylvania. That would explain the change of plans. McGee's very private. He would never meet in a public spot like the Red Fox or my Pontiac. He's somewhere in a house, sitting at a kitchen table, waiting for us.*

Jimmy dropped his hands down and stood squinting in the July sunlight. Then, somewhat embarrassed at his outburst, he scurried around the car and opened the back door.

"Watch out for that wet seat." Sally Bugs swept his hand across Jimmy's seat.

"Thought it might be wet," Sally Bugs said, "But it's dry now."

Jimmy sat down behind Frank and closed the door.

"Mine was wet when I sat down." Sally Bugs took out a handkerchief and wiped his hands.

Chuckie upped the AC and pulled out of the parking lot, narrowly missing a truck. "I had a frozen fish. Had to drop it off for Bobby Holmes."

"A fish." Sally Bugs mused. "How do you like that?"

But Jimmy wasn't in the mood for small talk. He tapped Frank's shoulder. "I thought you were supposed to call me last night. I waited in front of the restaurant at two for you. You were going to be sitting in my car with me when the Tonys showed. I was going to make them get in for the sit-down."

"I just got in." Frank turned his head. "We had a delay in plans. McGee had to rearrange things so that we could do this meeting right. Not sitting in a car."

Jimmy, satisfied, turned to look at Sally Bugs. "Who the fuck is Pro? Sending a fucking errand boy."

"We'll be there in two minutes." Chuckie, as usual, tried to make peace.

Jimmy ignored him. "I called Jo," he said to no one in particular. "You could have left a message."

Frank answered. "You know how McGee is about the phone when it involves his plans."

"Somebody could have told me." Jimmy's face reddened. "At the very least. With all due respect to McGee."

"We're almost there already." Chuckie cleared his throat. "I had to run an errand. It's not my fault."

Jimmy turned to watch them pass a footbridge and pull up in front of a two-story brick house with brown shingles, a high backyard fence, and a detached garage in the back. Nearby stood houses but not on top of one another. Everything looked normal for a meeting.

To the left of the house, a long driveway ran from the street to the detached garage. Two modest cars, a plain brown Buick and a dusty gray Ford, neither flashy, were parked in the drive, just the sort of nondescript cars the two Tonys would drive when they don't want to be noticed. Jimmy could see that they and McGee no doubt waited inside.

The two parked cars left room for Chuck to pull in the drive, almost to the house's front steps, which he did. Everyone but Chuckie got out; Sally Bugs, not important enough to stay for the meeting, got in the front passenger seat. Chuckie backed out and headed the way he'd come in.

Jimmy and Frank walked toward the house, Jimmy taking the lead, as usual. Even though his steps were short, he was fast, his white Gucci loafers tapping down the sidewalk and up the half-dozen steps of the front stoop. By the time Jimmy opened the front door, Frank caught up to him. They entered the house's vestibule and Frank, towering over Jimmy, shut the door behind them.

The quiet house felt empty. No one came to greet Jimmy. He understood what that meant, and he would have grabbed his piece, if he'd had it. But he didn't. It was still in his Pontiac, forgotten in the frenzy of waiting for the Tonys.

But Jimmy didn't feel frightened; he had Frank as his backup. Jimmy turned so swiftly he bumped Frank hard. When he saw the gun in Frank's hand, he felt relieved that Frank was prepared to protect him.

Jimmy took a quick step around Frank to get to the door. Frank judged the distance between them. Too close and Jimmy's paint would spatter Frank's clothes red. Frank shot twice, at decent range. Two shots in the back of Jimmy's head just behind his right ear. That's where you shoot if you're killing a friend. That way you guarantee your friend doesn't suffer.

Frank didn't look at Jimmy on the floor. He looked back down the hall and listened. He wanted to make sure nobody was going to come out and take care of him. Then he dropped his piece on the linoleum in the vestibule; in the silence it sounded like a shot fired.

THE PATHOLOGICAL LIAR

When Chuckie learned that Jimmy had gone south, he went a bit berserk. Scared to speak for fear the Mob would silence him, he vanished for a few days. When he turned up at Lake Orion, he told Jimmy's kids, James and Barbara, "I never laid eyes on Dad, didn't see him anywhere at all July thirtieth."

James shook his head. "We won't believe you unless you pass a lie detector test."

"I'll have to check with my lawyer first." Chuckie ran out of the room.

Panicked, he went to Memphis to see his new bride and her three children, then to Washington, DC, to consult with his boss, Fitzsimmons.

When he heard that Tony Pro had come to Washington looking for him, Chuckie dove under a friend's bed and refused to come out for two days. He surfaced to find himself a laughingstock.

"Go back to Detroit," Fitz told Chuckie, so he did.

He returned to find the FBI investigating Jimmy's disappearance. Its prime suspect: Chuckie.

"I never drove Joey's car," he protested. But when investigators dusted the inside of the maroon Mercury, they found, among countless fingerprints, Chuckie's on some paper and a 7UP bottle.

"Okay, okay, I did borrow Joey's Merc," Chuckie told the agents. "But I only took it to the car wash to get rid of salmon slime on the car seat. I never drove Dad in Joey's car. In fact, I didn't see Dad anywhere at all July thirtieth. Never laid eyes on him. I just wasn't there."

"Well, where were you, Chuckie?" The agent's eyes narrowed.

"At the car wash."

When no one at the car wash remembered Chuckie, he said, "No problem. I used my Standard Oil credit card to pay for the wash."

But he couldn't find the receipt.

"Then after I washed the car, I went to Southfield Athletic Club and met Uncle Tony Jack."

But no one at the club remembered seeing him.

"Well, I didn't go *in* the club. I just met Tony Jack in the lobby. It was about 2:15. He gave me a hundred dollars for my kids' birthdays coming up.

"And then I spent the afternoon at Bobby Holmes's house helping his wife cut up a forty-pound frozen salmon into steaks." Forty pounds? Not twenty? That salmon, just like Chuckie, made itself bigger than it was.

However, Mrs. Holmes did vouch for him.

So did his Michigan lawyer, James Burdick. "Chuckie didn't know what happened," Burdick told the FBI. "He's such a notorious big mouth, he never could have kept quiet."

The FBI reported that Chuckie gave them so many inconsistent accounts of where he was and what he did on July thirtieth that the agency considered him "a pathological liar who borders on being totally incompetent."

The Two Tonys

And where were the two Tonys on July 30, 1975? Grooming their alibis.

All that afternoon they had been visibly elsewhere.

Tony Jack Giacalone hung out at his health club, Southfield Athletic Club in Detroit, getting a massage and a haircut (and giving money to Chuckie whose now dead mother had been Uncle Tony Jack's girlfriend).

Tony Pro Provenzano kept busy, but not in Detroit. He lingered in Union City, New Jersey, in local 560's union hall, playing Greek rummy with several business agents.

"What meeting at the Red Fox?" Neither Tony knew anything at all about a 2:30 meeting there with Jimmy Hoffa.

FRANK SHEERAN

Frank stepped around Jimmy's body and left the house, lowering his head to reduce his height. When he opened the gray Ford in the driveway, the keys lay on the floorboard, as expected.

Inside the house, Frank knew, those two good-looking Italians, Tony Pro's boys, would be cleaning up. They'd take off Jimmy's jewelry, put his body in a bag, and pick up the linoleum. Then they'd cart his remains to a nearby crematorium. It shouldn't take long. They wouldn't want to linger with such a high-profile body on their hands.

Frank drove to the Pontiac airport, ditched the car, and walked toward McGee's private plane. He noticed that the pilot made a point of not looking at him. And off they went.

He hadn't expected to feel anything about offing Jimmy, and Frank didn't. "I couldn't afford to feel much. That builds nervous tension. Confuses you. You might even act stupid.

"No matter what I did, Jimmy would be just as dead, and if I'd said no to McGee, no doubt I'd be dead now too."

The US Army had taught Frank, during his 411 days of combat duty in World War II, how to kill with no remorse. He had plenty of practice. He didn't know how many men he'd eliminated, more than he could count, all those mass slaughters plus rubbing out numerous German POWs. By the time the army discharged Frank, at age twenty-four, he had learned not only how to shoot to kill, but also how to be callous about it.

By 1975, a professional hitman, he'd whacked a couple dozen for McGee, and for his friend Jimmy. Frank and Jimmy *had* become friends (thick as thieves some folks said).

Frank never felt much about shooting Jimmy, but the memory stuck with him. It persisted for twenty-three years. Then he felt the need to come clean.

Raised a Catholic, Frank went to confession and told the priest. *That felt better, but it wasn't enough.* Two years before he died in 2003, he confessed to his lawyer, Charles Brandt. Together they wrote his story in a book that bore, as its title, the first words Jimmy spoke to Frank, *I Heard You Paint Houses. That felt better.*

Frank read and okayed the full manuscript, then died two days later, eighty-three years old, with his conscience as clean as the killer of Jimmy Hoffa could be.

WHERE'S JIMMY?

It's June 2013, and the FBI is at it again: searching for Jimmy Hoffa's remains. This time the agents bring in a bulldozer, a backhoe, and shovels. They dig and dig in a field of waist-high grass where a barn used to be. They're looking for the spot where a couple of thugs supposedly buried Jimmy alive almost thirty-eight years ago.

The agents are so certain they'll find the famous ex-Teamsters' boss that they bring in cadaver dogs to sniff out his decomposing body and they hire Michigan State forensic anthropologists to identify his remains.

But on the third day of the excavation, the FBI agents give up.

Where is Jimmy? They don't know.

Nobody knows but ideas abound.

He was ground into dog food.

Run through a wood chipper.

Obliterated in a fat-rendering plant.

Sealed in a compacted fifty-five-gallon drum in Japan.

Scorched in a crematorium's trash incinerator.

Chucked in a toxic waste dump.

Tossed in a Florida swamp or in Michigan's Au Sable River.

Buried under a horse barn.

Laid to rest in the foundation of General Motors headquarters.

Hidden in a car's trunk and crushed in a compactor.

Dismembered with a power saw.

Mixed in the concrete that built the New York Giants' football stadium.

Although all these possibilities have been suggested, still no one knows where Jimmy is. No one has even proved who killed him: The Mob? His labor union rivals? FBI agents?

That's my favorite tale: two FBI agents snatch Jimmy, drive him to an airport, give him a ride in a small airplane, and heave him out over one of the five Great Lakes.

Dad's Fondest Wish

Dad called from Alma. He and Mama had stayed in Fort Collins for a while after his forced retirement. Then they moved back to Alma for the summer and snowbirded to Arizona for the winter.

Dad called in the afternoon, not even waiting for a cheaper evening rate.

I bit my lip. "Is Mama okay?"

"Oh, yes, she's fine, we're both okay." His words tumbled all over each other. "Have you heard that Hoffa's missing?"

"Missing." That sounded like something you'd say about a toddler, not a grown man. "What do you mean, missing?"

"Well, nobody's seen him or heard anything from him since yesterday afternoon." Dad rushed his words. "Carl Curtis called to tell me."

"They don't know what happened to him? To superstar Jimmy Hoffa? That sounds incred—"

Dad cut me off, his voice louder than mine.

"Curtis says that the FBI thinks that the Mob did him in. They've looked all over for him. Curtis thinks they won't find him, not even a body. The FBI agents haven't a clue, he says.

"Oh, Junebug, you know what this means." He whooped. "If he's dead, and Curtis seems pretty sure he is, then my fondest wish has been granted: I've outlived that punk Jimmy Hoffa!" Dad roared with laughter.

I could almost see him, eyes snapping, jowls quivering, belly shaking.

TIME MARCHES BY—BOSTON AND NEW YORK

I moved to Boston so I could be close to my son, Ian, then eight years old. I found a home, a commune, in Quincy, Massachusetts, on the bay. Tom and Ian lived in Braintree, Massachusetts, about four miles away. I picked up Ian for the weekends and returned him to Tom for the school week. I hadn't seen Ian since he left New York, so I felt awkward in my new role as a mother.

The first night Ian slept over, he woke upset about a nightmare.

"Mama." He clutched the blanket. "Will you wait for me in heaven when you die?"

Ian's question floored me. Heaven! I hadn't believed in heaven since my sophomore year in college. So instead of replying, I knelt by the side of the bed, stroked Ian's cheek, and tucked him in again. I didn't think any more of it until the next weekend, when he woke in terror asking the same question. This time I said something indirect, such as, "Well, if there were a heaven, I'd wait for you there."

I thought that had settled the matter, but the next weekend, in the middle of the night, I heard the same question. This time I decided not to be so wishy-washy, so I said, "I can't wait for you in heaven because there is no such thing as heaven."

I thought surely that had quieted him, but no. He woke again, and asked again. Exasperated, I threw all my religious unbeliefs aside, and lied, "Yes, Ian, I'm going to wait for you in heaven when I die."

He never asked again.

I smile at Jon Powell, who later became my husband.
Photo by Ralph Stephenson.

About this time, I met John "Jon" R. Powell III, an artist, dancer, and yoga instructor, celebrating his twenty-first birthday. That made him twelve years younger than I. I kneed him under the table as Elmer, Clara, and I, housemates, drank the pink champagne I'd given him.

Jon was gay, the sort of gay I'd call a "fairy," willowy and feminine. Actually he was bisexual, which I discovered about a week later during our introductory night. The next morning, for our first date, we set out in my VW Bug on a 4,500-mile journey, from Quincy, Massachusetts, to Alma, Nebraska, to Lander, Wyoming, and home.

In Alma, we stayed with Mama's oldest sister, a spinster, Faith Kemper. I took copious notes on buildings all around town, part of the research for my novel, *Marcella*. I showed Jon the Methodist church basement where, in my teens, I'd tried to kill myself.

Jon stiffened. "Why did you do that?"

"I was such a tomboy. I knew I could never be the good girl Mama wanted me to be." My shoulders slumped.

Jon embraced me, pulled me to the floor, and we made love on the carpet there.

A barrel full of used clothes stood in one corner, and we pawed through it. We each chose a flowing evening gown, donned it, and paraded up and down Main Street.

Back at Faith's house, my aunt looked truly quizzical. "Why are you wearing those old clothes?"

"Just for fun."

But Faith looked concerned at the sight of Jon swishing around in a dark blue gown.

In Lander, Jon and I arrived expecting to stay with my sister Margaret and her husband, Wade Dent. We arrived at dusk and found their house locked and unlit. A neighbor stopped us. "You might find him down at the Elks Lodge." He told us the way.

Wade, sitting high on a stool, looked down on us. "Ain't no unmarried folks going to foul the sheets in my house. You better get out of town."

We left, but I turned back. "Where's Margaret?"

"She went to visit your folks." I nodded. Faith must have called her.

Jon and I, both shell-shocked, jumped in the VW and headed out. By the time Jon tired of driving, we'd left Wyoming and were moving through the desolate Sandhills of Nebraska. We decided to camp out for the rest of the night. Jon pulled into a cornfield. Not bothering to set up our tent, we tumbled into our sleeping bags and conked out.

The sun felt hot on my face when I woke. "Jon," I shook him. "That sounded like gunfire." I sat up. A big farmer, who waved a rifle over his head, rode on his tractor right through the cornfield toward us. He shot over our heads. I scrambled out of my sleeping bag, grabbed it, and headed toward the car, Jon right beside me. The farmer didn't shoot again, but he waved his gun and shouted terrible things about our mothers as we entered the VW. The clodhopper stayed right behind us, his big old tractor breathing down our necks until we pulled out of the cornfield and onto the highway, heading east.

WALLS THAT BREATHE

On the weekend before second semester classes at Boston University began, Jon and our two housemates invited me to drop some LSD with them.

"Oh, I can't. Classes begin Monday." I taught full-time at the university; its pay sure beat Pratt's part-time paycheck.

Jon laughed. "Monday's a day and a half away. You'll be down by then."

"A sure thing?"

"For certain." All three chorused "yes."

I loved puffing on the little white sticks of marijuana Jon or Elmer brought home, so I decided to give acid a whirl.

Unprepared for the swift initial rush of the hallucinogen, I panicked, but the others calmed me. I retreated into the bathroom. I sat there for eons, marveling at the beauty of a Tampax I'd just extracted. When I came out, I saw Jon, Elmer, and Clara relaxed in a circle in our living room.

"Come on over, honey." Jon patted an empty chair. I hesitated, charmed by the walls breathing around me. And the music, it rushed up and down in colors. Finally I floated into the living room and sat down.

"You're a teacher." Elmer beamed his silly lopsided grin and tapped a pencil against his writing tablet. "Help me figure out this one: How much LSD would you have to feed a 12,000-pound whale to get it to trip?"

I never knew. It was Wednesday when the walls stopped breathing. I'd missed, with no notice, the first three days of classes.

Boston University did not renew my annual contract that spring; I didn't ask why. I found a low-level job writing captions for a Volkswagen service manual. It nearly drove me batty. So did Boston, so often behind the times compared to New York.

I wanted to go back to the big city, if only one of my friends could find a pad for Jon and me. I didn't like to leave Ian, but I knew I could always come visit him. Tom agreed that our son, now twelve, could come visit me.

In the meantime, the Women's Liberation Movement swirled all around me in Boston, as it had in New York. Some half-dozen women and I formed a consciousness-raising group. It met regularly in my communal home by the bay.

"The Personal Is Political" became our motto as, at each meeting, we took turns speaking about a topic related to women's experience: husbands, dating, economic independence, having children, and many more. At each meeting, we "told it like it is" by sharing examples from our personal lives. Over and over we saw how what seemed merely personal became political when shared.

By the time Jon and I returned to New York in 1974, I had become a feminist although not of the vintage of

S.C.U.M. (Society for Cutting Up Men). Jon listened patiently to my rants about men.

A Full-Time Position

New York seemed bigger and busier than ever. I learned that Pratt Institute, breaking its "men only" precedent of eighty-seven years, had hired two women full-time in its English department.

Wanting a full-time job teaching English again, I caught the subway to Pratt. The current chairperson, Carl Craycraft, started teaching as a part-timer a year or two after I'd started. Shortly after I mentored him, he rose to full-time and was now department chair, leapfrogging ahead the way men did at Pratt.

I'm in my classroom at Pratt.

Carl seemed pleased to see me.

"We can offer you a part-time position, but there are no full-time positions open. They've all been filled by now," he lied, although I didn't know that then.

I told Carl I'd taught full-time at Boston University, but that didn't change his mind, so I accepted the part-time position.

Shortly after, I joined another consciousness-raising group, this one for professional women. At one meeting, we brought our resumes. Mine, like most of the others, looked pretty skimpy.

"That's because, as women, we've been taught not to value our work." Andrea Dworkin, dressed as usual in a black T-shirt and big black overalls, shook her tousled black hair. "We think our achievements are not important. Well they *are!*"

Her assignment: bring in resumes that listed *everything*.

Andrea spoke so zealously, her energy buoyed me, so I spent hours flipping through papers and scanning notebooks. Some things I remembered easily. Like *Marcella*, my first novel, a coming-of-age story featuring masturbation, that I'd published in 1973 with a big New York house. Australia and Denmark had reproduced part of it, as had *Ms.* magazine. I'd made enough money to fly Jon and me to Europe for several weeks. Amsterdam, Scotland, England, Wales, Ireland—and Paris.

I also remembered with ease seeing my article, "Badlands Revisited," published by the *Atlantic Monthly*. When I picked up the prestigious magazine, I nearly flipped. *Atlantic* hadn't just mentioned "Badlands Revisited" on its cover, it devoted the whole cover to my article about mass murderer Charlie Starkweather.

I even remembered my 1968 free lunch with Ted Solotaroff, editor of *New American Review*. He'd bought my poem, "Wordlessly," for his prestigious magazine, published in New York, Toronto, and London. "Write about what you know," Solotaroff advised. He thought I should move back to Nebraska. Fat chance. Being 1,400 miles away from my mother's sharp tongue suited me just fine.

But these recent publications only tipped the iceberg. If I listed everything, I'd have to detail

- Nineteen poetry readings

- Eight poems published

- Four features syndicated nationally

- Six publications in well-known magazines

- Several hundred news features, columns, articles and editorials in national business publications

- Promotion to editor of a national business magazine

And that didn't include my work in Denver on that liquor publication or in Nebraska for the university paper, the *Lincoln Journal*'s copy desk, or the *Hastings Daily Tribune*. So I added those too.

When I finished typing, my new single-spaced resume ran five pages long. Even I felt impressed.

Walking the Picket Line

I took my five-page wonder to Pratt and asked Carl to look it over before I handed it in. He sat behind his desk on his round wooden chair, his body now and then dipping backward as he read. He hadn't finished the first page before he started exclaiming, "Oh, Marilyn, I didn't know you'd done all of this."

When he plowed his way through all five pages, he laid my resume on his desk and looked at me. "How would you like a part-time job as affirmative action director."

Of course, I would. "But if I'm teaching half-time and directing half-time, that makes a full-time job, doesn't it?"

Carl's face dropped. "Well, technically, no."

I took the job anyway.

As affirmative action director, I had access to privileged materials. The first thing I did was check the English department's hiring papers. Just as I suspected, two male instructors had been hired, full-time, after Carl told me all full-time jobs had been filled.

Then, wondering what Dad would think, I joined the teacher's union, the United Federation of College Teachers. I even walked in the picket line. The founder and president of the union, Estelle Horowitz, a strong, feisty woman, encouraged me. When I told her that Carl had lied about available full-time jobs and wouldn't hire me full-time even though I worked two half-time jobs, she said, "Sue the blockhead." So I did.

When I called home, I chatted with Dad a while to see what sort of mood he was in. Then I gambled. "Hey, Dad. You'll never guess what I did."

"Quit smoking?"

"No. Joined a union."

He fell silent, then erupted with a roar of laughter, a big guffaw. After he wound down, he said, "Well, you're right. I never would have guessed it." He fell quiet again, then said, "Don't tell me you joined the Teamsters Union."

"No, I couldn't do that. This is just a teachers union. They don't hire thugs." I paused. "And there's something else."

"I'm afraid to ask what."

"I'm suing Pratt Institute." And I told him the whole story.

After he'd heard me out, Dad said, "I want you to know, I'm proud of you. Do you have a lawyer?"

"Yes, a good one, I believe."

"Good. Well, keep me posted."

I had joined a class action suit, so when we won, I gained a full-time position. I felt deliriously happy. Not only would my salary more than double, but I'd receive all sort of perks including a town house on campus.

That night, Jon skipped around our almost empty living room, decorated with a couple of beanbags. "Marilyn, listen." He stopped and looked at me. "I'm not going to ask this again." He bounced on his toes. "Will you marry me?"

The question stunned me. Early on, we'd agreed just to live together. Why this now?

Slowly it dawned on me. Jon had complained to me, over and over, that he couldn't get a decent job because he had no education beyond high school. My perks, as a full-timer, included a bachelor's and a master's Pratt Institute education for my family, including my married husband.

"Of course."

He beat a rapid tattoo, and we began to plan the summer wedding.

Perfect for the Party

Elmer and Clara no longer lived in the Quincy commune. They'd moved to a farm in Maine, and yes, they'd love to host the wedding for us. Elmer even found some hippie preacher, professional on the paperwork but light on the Bible-thumping.

I went shopping and came home with the perfect wedding dress, long with a Byzantine look, highly colorful in hot shades of oranges and yellows. I tried it on for Jon. He pursed his lips and looked. I turned around. He clapped his hands. "Perfect for the party afterwards, but not for the wedding. For the wedding, you'll wear white."

I croaked, and recited the now hundreds of reasons that I wasn't a virgin. I ranted, I raved. Jon heard me out. When I stopped, he kissed my cheek. "Nobody will arrest you, sweetie. No law says only virgins wear white."

I started up again, but he tapped two fingers against my lips. "I'll help you find something."

Jon came home with the perfect dress, white, of course, long-sleeved and floor length. Instead of the ugly satiny fabric I associated with wedding dresses, Jon had chosen a delicate see-through cotton.

I became alarmed when I tried the dress on. Its low-cut neckline revealed bigger boobs than I knew I owned. I clapped my hands over them.

"Ahhh!" Jon delicately lifted my fingers. "Try this." He worked some magic with his hands. "Better?"

"I don't know, are you sure?" I whirled to the mirror. The diaphanous gown moved easily with me, its fabric a gentle hug.

I examined the neckline. Surely a clip here, a clip there, would resolve the matter.

Jon nodded and smiled. "Yellow and white for the flowers. What do you think? Clara wants to give them to you."

The Wedding

Our wedding day dawned clear; the temperature rising gently toward the seventies. Food cooked in the primitive farmhouse—a turkey, roast beef, and a ham in the ovens. Around the house, a big yard spread out in all directions, lush and green. Plenty to hold the fifty or so people we expected.

Jon had chosen the spot for his dance. His huge papier-mâché bull's head waited in one of the bedrooms.

About noon, we began, the preacher in patched overalls hearing our vows. (I was lovely in white.)

Elmer cleared the "dance floor," Jon donned the bright red bull's head and danced. I'd never seen him dance better. His body turned into the bull's body, and in the silence, his movements spoke.

We lined up for food, and I changed to my bright Byzantine dress. White papers rolled around marijuana, and I began to toke and chatter with the many guests. Someone broke out a guitar.

When the sun lowered toward nearby hills, I dropped down on the grass and stretched out. Only a dozen or so people stayed.

"Mom! Mom!" I turned to see Ian running toward me. "The ham!"

"The ham? What's with the ham?"

"It's still in the oven. We never ate it."

Ohmylord. "Get Clara." I ran toward the house to find the ham shrunken, its juices barely bubbling.

DAD'S LAST REVENGE

Early that April 1977, the folks packed their big Airstream trailer and pulled out of Mesa, Arizona, heading for a summer in Alma, Nebraska, a 1,300-mile journey. Dad planned to lay over in Fort Collins, Colorado, to see old friends.

My dad loved to drive, and he loved his Airstream. "Most of those trailers I saw were just big square boxes, built with a brick wall in front," he told me. "But not my 'silver bullet.' Those round aluminum ends let the wind flow over the trailer. So easy to drive."

Easy? I wondered. He'd bought the biggest Airstream made, thirty-one feet long. It couldn't be *that* easy.

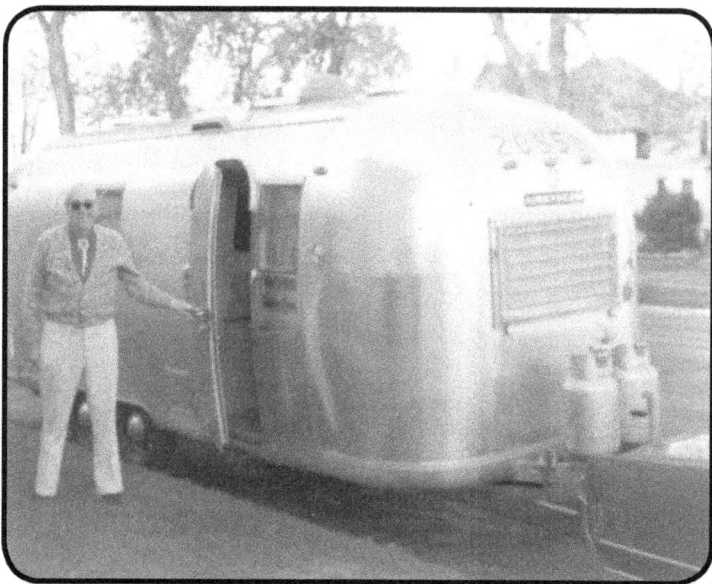

Dad shows off his Airstream, his "silver bullet."

Although maybe it was for a man who drove loads of cattle that danced the hootchy-kootchy.

Thursday afternoon, April 7, Dad and Mama had just driven through Denver with about fifty miles to go to Fort Collins, when Dad pulled to the side of the highway and stopped. Mama watched him search in his shirt pocket for his nitroglycerin tablet. He found the pill box, took out one, and put it under his tongue.

After the pill dissolved, he asked, "Pete, honey, can you drive us in?"

"Tom," her voice quavered, "you know I can't. I've never driven anything bigger than a car."

He leaned back. "Well, let me rest a bit."

After he'd taken a second and a third pill, he pulled himself together and drove straight to the Poudre Valley Memorial Hospital's emergency room in Fort Collins.

I heard about it Friday morning when Mama called. "Don't bother to come out. He's got some color back, and the doctors think we'll be out of here day after tomorrow." So I didn't go.

The next day, Saturday, Mama heard people clattering down the hospital hall, laughter spiking. "They didn't have an ounce of decorum," she told me. "They sounded like they were in a bar, not a hospital."

When they piled into Dad's small room, Mama recognized his brothers and their wives from Denver, most in their sixties. Vic and Ray, Dad's brothers who looked like identical twins, brought their wives who were sisters, Rose and Anna Piper. And Dad's little brother Lyle, after a solo life, was packing a girlfriend, Mique. Mom said she looked seven feet tall, but a couple feet might have been her straw-colored beehive hairdo.

When Mama saw them, she smiled, nodded briskly, and skedaddled. Often called a "lady," Mama couldn't bear Dad's low-class loud-mouthed brothers, and their cheap wives. That Tom came from such smutty rowdy people embarrassed her. She knew their shared childhoods as dirt-poor, scruffy-haired, dirty-faced, barefooted, ragged-pants kids had bonded them, but she couldn't understand why they never grew up like Tom had or why Tom still shared their vulgar humor.

Mama fidgeted on a bench in the hall and tried to ignore their lusty voices, their cascading laughter, Tom's voice loud among them.

What did they find to laugh about? she wondered. Probably the same ancient stories. Laughing at the ornery streak Lyle had as a kid. One time in grade school he turned into a wild bull, chased kids on top of the schoolhouse, on top of the toilet, on top of the bell house, mad about who knows what. Wouldn't say what made him mad. Never did.

Or maybe they're hashing one of their favorites. Mama wished she hadn't thought of it, it was so disgusting, but she couldn't get it off her mind. Vic liked to be sneaky. One day he and Ray were shucking corn when Vic had to honor Mother Nature's call. As he put it. He was a ways ahead of Ray in the corn rows, so he squatted. Then he spotted this great big ear of corn over in Ray's row. Vic pulled the stalk down, grabbed the ear, peeled the husk back. Then he squatted down and did his business on the corn. Afterward, he pulled the husks back and kind of stood the heavy ear up a bit. He knew Ray would be sure to grab such a big ear.

Mama could remember Vic's shoulders shaking as he said, "Well, and you know how you shuck corn." And laughing. Those laughs of his somewhere between a hoot and a holler. Of course, Ray grabbed the ear and let out a cuss so loud it started Vic's team of horses running, so Vic jumped in his wagon and Ray lit out after him.

Finally Tom's relatives stopped carrying on. Mama smiled politely at their greetings as they filed past.

She rose to go sit beside Dad again, but stopped when she heard the clatter of a table on wheels being rushed by two attendants sprinting past her and into Dad's room.

Just after, as she heard the attendants curse, she froze.

"The doctors said a blood clot to his brain killed him," Mama bawled into my phone. "But that's not what killed him. His own blood relations killed him, carrying on like that, the way they got him all worked up. Didn't they know better than to make him whoop like that?" She collapsed into tears.

The Embalmer

Jack Russell picked me up at the airport and drove me to his funeral home, Russell Funeral Chapel in Fort Collins. I liked Jack. He was one of Dad's best friends, the only one to continue playing poker with Dad after he studied how to win. Everyone else had given up, Dad won so often.

Jack's round face had lit up when he spotted me. I smiled, too, remembering his sharp sense of humor. He wasn't just Dad's friend, he was a family friend, and we'd be staying in his funeral chapel until we left for Alma.

I couldn't sleep that night, so I didn't bother. Instead, I went into the basement where Dad's body, embalmed and suited up, lay. I pulled up a chair. I had with me a sheath full of poems, mine and some favorites, so I read to him and laughed. I never could get him to sit still and listen to a poem while he was alive, so this provided a perfect opportunity. I wondered if he knew what I was up to. If he did know, I felt pretty sure he wouldn't mind.

The next morning I asked Jack. "Did you embalm Dad?"

Jack rubbed the back of his neck. "Yes."

"Oh!" I clapped. "I'm so glad it was you!"

Jack stared at me. "Well, it didn't make me that happy."

Startled, I walked over to him and grabbed one hand. "Oh, Jack, I'm sorry. I just felt relieved that a stranger didn't cut him up."

Jack tousled my head and went back to the papers he had been sorting.

DAD'S SILVER DOLLAR

"Where's Dad's lucky dollar?" I asked Jack.

"Your mom has it. I gave her all his things."

When I entered Mama's room, I felt happy to see her sitting by the window, reading a book. I asked her if she had Dad's silver dollar.

"Yes, I do, and I don't know what to do about it. It seems like a sacrilege that it's not in his pocket."

"Well, let's put it there."

Mama looked out the window and back, her eyes moist. She handed me the silver dollar. "Good idea. You'll have to ask Jack."

"Let me see what I can do," I said, unaware of how much I sounded like my father.

On the way out, Mama called, "Here. You might want these."

I turned. In the palm of her hand lay Dad's "two front teeth."

"He still had them?" I picked them up, marveled at them, and stuffed them in my pocket.

Mama nodded. "He kept them in his pocket with his dollar."

I found Jack in his display room, readying my dad's casket. He turned and smiled. "What's up?"

"This." I held up Dad's skinny dollar.

Jack took it. "Look at the thing. Thin as a wafer and blank on both sides."

"I know. Dad wore the liberty head off one side and the eagle off the other, just flipping the thing."

Jack handed it back.

"No." I waved my hands. "I don't want it. You take it and put it in his pocket."

"That's against the rules, Marilyn. Putting personal items in the casket."

"But Jack, he's had that dollar in his pocket since 1929, almost fifty years. That's where it belongs. It would be a sacrilege [I quoted my mother] if you didn't."

We had a stare down. Jack shifted his eyes first. "Okay." He put the dollar in his pocket. "This all right with your mom?"

"Yes." I punched his shoulder. "And I better not find that silver dollar in *your* pocket after you put him in his casket."

Jack grinned and punched me back. "Don't worry."

The Fort Collins Motorcade

Tuesday, April 12 we dressed for Dad's funeral service. When I finished, I went to Mama's room to see how she was doing. When I opened the door, Mama stood in the middle of a modern bedroom decked out in a dress I loved. Its soft maroon and white fabric draped around her still curvy figure.

"Mama! You look so beautiful!" I wanted to hug her, but I restrained myself.

She looked up, as though I'd jarred her out of a reverie. "That's what your father always said."

"The Denver crowd's here."

Mama flinched. Her eyes narrowed, her nose wrinkled, and her lip curled. "Well, I'm not riding in the same car with any of those butchers."

I could see she meant it, so I left to tell Jack.

As I crossed the waiting room, I saw Dad's relatives standing in a row: Vic and Rose, Ray and Anna, and Lyle alone. When Aunt Rose turned and held out her arms to me, I stumbled across the room and plunged, howling, into her embrace, able to weep for the first time since Dad's death.

Later, Mom, my sisters, and I piled in Jack's car and waited. Behind us, in a separate car, rode the Denver gang. Then came two police cars to lead the way, but Jack didn't move his car until after the motorcycle motorcade, at least a dozen police officers, roared in and followed the police cars. We pulled in behind them. What a magnificent rumble! Cars drew in behind us, Dad's friends and acquaintances, forming a line longer than I could see.

The air in the First United Presbyterian Church, where Dad had been an elder, felt cool. I stepped on the red carpet that led us to our seats and flowed under Dad's coffin, poised on its gurney as though on a pedestal. Sunlight, filtered by an enormous stained-glass window, lit my father's large white casket, sparkling its golden hardware. The coffin lid could not be seen. Dozens of fresh red roses smothered it.

People poured into the church. As I waited, surrounded by music, for some odd reason, I thought of Jimmy Hoffa and my dad, how different their deaths had been. In the two years since Jimmy's disappearance, no one had found his body and no funeral had been held. Not only did my father outlive Jimmy, even Dad's exit proved superior. This is not simply a funeral for Dad; this is his last revenge.

The Huge Rectangular Slab of Concrete

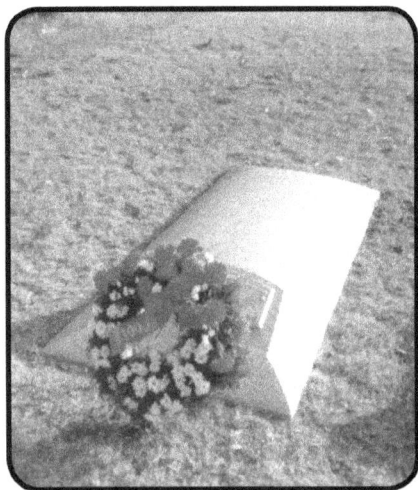

Dad's concrete coffin.
Photo by Mabel Coffey.

On Thursday, April 14, we gathered for Dad's burial in the Alma cemetery. Our group consisted of Mama's family and a surprising number of friends. We stood by the open hole; Dad's big sealed coffin lay alongside it. I looked at the huge rectangular slab of concrete. Dad had chosen it from among many options because he wanted a leak-proof box. "I don't want those worms playing pinochle on my snout."

Mama, on the other hand, felt claustrophobic, and begged him to choose standard wood for them. But Dad refused.

As I stood looking at the big concrete coffin, Mama touched my elbow. "I gave in to him." She patted me. "I'm going to be

My son, Ian, displays his catch.

buried in a concrete coffin too. It'll look better."

Then it was my turn to read a poem, "The Waking" by Theodore Roethke. Mama had cautioned me against reading. "Are you sure you can do it?" I guess she thought I'd break down, but by that time I had become a pro as a reader, so I ignored her. "Don't worry, Mama. The poem's short." Short but superb. I never could have written it, a villanelle with so many things to count: five stanzas of three lines followed by one stanza of four lines for a total of nineteen lines.

I'm not sure why I chose it. I knew Dad wouldn't "get" it. Its last line, "I learn by going where I have to go," spoke more to me than to him.

Then the service was over and my fifteen-year-old son, Ian, stopped me. "I'm going to watch him buried."

"Okay. Let me know when you're finished."

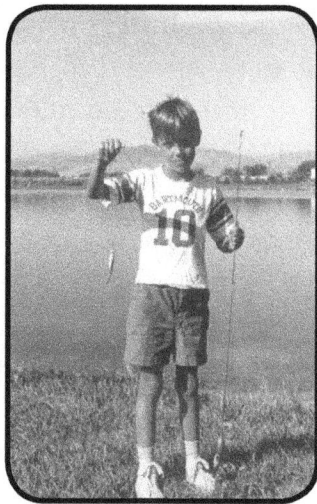

Later, Ian and I walked back to the cemetery together, down the gravel road, across the railroad tracks, past huge fields that would mature into wheat. The afternoon's heat had decreased, and the cemetery trees cast shadows. I showed Ian where his great-grandparents, the Kempers, lay alongside a small stone marked "Baby."

"Is this where you'll be buried?" he asked.

"I suppose. I'm in no hurry."

Then we stood again at Dad's grave, the concrete casket just above earth now. The sun began to set. Ian leaned over the tomb, then turned. "Look at this, Mom. That's not his name."

"Really?" I leaned over and squinted:

June Thomas Coffey
1907–1977

"No. That's his name."

"June?"

I laughed. "Oh, you didn't know his mother wanted a girl so bad she named him June, did you?"

"No," Ian said.

I elbowed him. "See? There are worse names than Ian."

Ian grinned and fooled around with a stick he'd found somewhere.

I smiled. "I'm really proud of your granddad, you know. The many ways he beat Jimmy Hoffa. That bundle of money Dad won from the Teamsters, and the laws that were changed after he testified in Washington and in Lincoln. Plus the publicity—good for him but bad for Jimmy. The Chicago booklet that printed 250,000 copies. And who knew how many the *Saturday Evening Post* sold. But you know what pleased him most?"

"What?"

"That he outlived Hoffa. I'll never forget the way he whooped when he called me."

I leaned over "June's" concrete tomb. "Hey, Dad!"

"What you doing?" Ian stopped fiddling with the stick and looked at me.

I hollered, "The FBI still can't find Jimmy."

"Mom."

I turned to my son. "Can't you hear Grandpa? That big old belly laugh of his. He's tickled pink that he's bested Jimmy one more day."

"Go on." Ian tossed the stick away and turned to leave, but I leaned a little closer. I swear I could almost see Dad, eyes snapping, jowls quivering, belly shaking, fingers rubbing his silver dollar. And I swear I heard him say, "Nobody knows where Jimmy is, but I know where I am: right where I'm supposed to be, dry and safe from everything but time."

Epilogue: The House That Hoffa Built

Dad invested the money he won from Jimmy, and it grew. He didn't touch it; he had plenty of retirement funds for him and Mama to live on. So when he died, the Jimmy money went to Mama plus everything else Dad owned. She didn't touch the Hoffa money either.

In 1984, Mama noticed that her osteoporosis had limited her life to a predictable pattern of fall, break bones, hospital, physical therapy, back to her retirement home, fall. She couldn't stand the monotony, the predictability, so she refused to eat and died.

Jimmy's money, then, came to us three girls.

I invested most of my share. With some, I bought a sturdy car and a Scamp trailer with rounded corners like Dad's Airstream. Then my dog and I took off for the Midwest.

Our summer route took us alongside the Missouri River from

I pose with my traveling companion, Phebe.

Missouri to Montana, following the tracks of the Astorians who, in turn, had followed Lewis and Clark. I planned to write about these early explorers. I even flew to England on a grant to research an Astorian in London and Liverpool. I filled dozens of tablets, and acquired even more books, but I never wrote the Holy Rainbow series I planned.

Instead, in 1986, I sobered up, took lithium for my bipolar disorder, and eventually left New York.

By this time, Jon had earned his bachelor's and master's degrees at Pratt Institute and worked as an art therapist. Then he left me for a good-looking well-to-do Israeli guy. AIDs caught up with Jon and killed him. Miraculously, it never touched me.

After living in Harlan County, Nebraska, in Hays, Kansas, and in Charlotte, North Carolina, I decided in 2004 to settle down in Omaha, Nebraska. Ian, now forty-two, still lived in Braintree, Massachusetts, with his

The House That Hoffa Built where I live in Omaha.
Photo by David L. Loyd.

father. When my son visited me in Nebraska, his Boston accent made him sound like Bobby Kennedy.

In Omaha, I scouted for a modest house to buy. Then my financial advisor pointed to my funds, my Jimmy Hoffa money, and said, "Why don't you use a chunk of this to make a sizable down deposit?"

So I did.

I now live in the big House That Hoffa Built, a more palatial home than I had expected, twelve rooms, a double garage, and a huge backyard.

Regularly I thank my dad for suing Jimmy.

I'm happy for the federal and state laws Dad helped change. I'm pleased about the national write-ups he received. But most of all, I'm delighted that Dad and Clark sued Jimmy Hoffa, and that Jimmy, in an unprecedented move, decided to settle out of court.

So here I sit, in the big House That Hoffa Built, and write. Haven't decided yet how to spend the rest of that Teamsters' money. Maybe another research trip. They say the Bahamas are pure heaven. Or I might take a Fiji submarine ride, browse Kenya's rare book collection, stalk birds, butterflies and crocodiles in Mozambique, or just go modern in Dubai.

BIBLIOGRAPHY

BOOKS

Brandt, Charles. *I Heard You Paint Houses: Frank "The Irishman" Sheeran and Closing the Case on Jimmy Hoffa*. Hanover, NH: Steerforth Press, 2005.

Brill, Steven. *The Teamsters*. New York: Simon & Schuster, 1978.

Clay, Jim. *Hoffa! Ten Angels Swearing: An Authorized Biography*. Beaverdam, VA: Beaverdam Books, 1965.

Curtis, Senator Carl T. with Regis Courtemanche. *Forty Years against the Tide: Congress & the Welfare State*. Lake Bluff, IL: Regnery Gateway, 1986.

Dobbs, Farrell. *Teamster Power*. New York: Monad, 1973.

Dobbs, Farrell. *Teamster Rebellion*. New York: Pathfinder, 1972, 2004.

Franco, Joseph (Joe) with Richard Hammer. *Hoffa's Man: The Rise and Fall of Jimmy Hoffa as Witnessed by His Strongest Arm*. New York: Prentice Hall Press, 1987.

Hoffa, James R. with Oscar Fraley. *Hoffa: The Real Story*. New York: Stein & Day, 1975.

Hoffa, James R. with Donald I. Rogers. *The Trials of Jimmy Hoffa: An Autobiography*. Chicago: Henry Regnery, 1970.

James, Ralph C., and Estelle Dinnerstein James. *Hoffa and the Teamsters: A Study of Union Power*. Princeton, NJ: D. Van Nostrand, 1965.

Kennedy, Robert. *The Enemy Within: The McClellan Committee's Crusade against Jimmy Hoffa and Corrupt Labor Unions*. New York: Harper & Row, 1960.

Moldea, Dan E. *The Hoffa Wars: Teamsters, Rebels, Politicians and the Mob*. New York, NY: Paddington Press Ltd., 1978.

Moldea, Dan E. *The Hoffa Wars: The Rise and Fall of Jimmy Hoffa*. New York: S.P.I. Books, 1993.

Mollenhoff, Clark R. *Tentacles of Power: The Story of Jimmy Hoffa*. New York: World, 1965.

Neff, James. *Vendetta: Bobby Kennedy versus Jimmy Hoffa*. New York: Little, Brown, 2015.

Pratt, Bill. *Omaha in the Making of Nebraska Labor History*. Joe D. Seger (ed). Omaha, NE: Ad Hoc Committee for Study of Nebraska Labor History, 1981.

Schlesinger, Arthur M. Jr. *Robert Kennedy and His Times*, Vols. I and II. Boston: Houghton Mifflin, 1978.

Sheridan, Walter. *The Fall and Rise of Jimmy Hoffa*. New York: Saturday Review, 1972.

Sloane, Arthur A. *Hoffa*. Cambridge, MA: MIT Press, 1991.

Zajicek, Len. *Local 554 History* (unpublished manuscript). Omaha: Local 554 archives.

GOVERNMENT SOURCES

SENATE

Congressional Record - Senate, 25 April 1958, pp. 7379–7380; 28 April 1958, p. 7505.

Hearings before the Select Committee on Improper Activities in the Labor or Management Field, Eighty-Fifth Congress, Second Session. Part 41, 19–20 Nov, 1958, pp. 15624-15757. Washington, DC: USGPO, 1959.

NATIONAL LABOR RELATIONS BOARD (NLRB)

Case No 17-RM-91, Coffey's Transfer Co & IBT Local 554, AFL; "Official Report of Proceedings," "Petitioner Exhibits" and "Board Exhibits," Alma NE, 25 Oct 1955. National Archives, Washington, DC.

Decisions & Orders of National Labor Relations Board. Washington, DC: 1956, 1957, 1960.

International Brotherhood of Teamsters v. NLRB. US District Court Civil Case # 550-'56; NE District, Civil Case # 074, 1956. National Archives, Washington, DC.

NLRB vs. Local No. 554 International Brotherhood of Teamsters. Federal District, Court Civil No. 080, Omaha NE, 1956. Answer, 6 Feb. 1956; Findings, Hearings, Memorandum, Order, Petition, Stipulation, Transcript 2 Feb.- 30 July 1956.

NEBRASKA STATE LEGISLATURE

Introducer's Statement on LB 509, LB 510, LB 560, Nebraska State Legislature.

Legislative Bill 560, Secondary Boycotts, Session Laws, 1959: 806-811.

Legislative Journal of the State of Nebraska, 69th Session, 6 Jan.-27 June 1959.

Minutes, Labor and Public Welfare Committee, 4 March 1959.

Srb, Hugo F., Clerk, compiler. *Legislative Journal of the State of Nebraska, Sixty-Sixth (Extraordinary) Session.* Lincoln, NE: Joe Christensen, Printer, 1954.

Weinberg, David D. "An Analysis of Legislative Bill 560...69th Session."

NEWS MEDIA

NATIONAL NEWS MEDIA

Coffey, Tom. "My Private War with Hoffa." *Saturday Evening Post,* 4-11 Jan. 1964: 68-70.

"Senator Carl T. Curtis, 94, Staunch Nixon Ally," *New York Times,* 26 Jan 2000.

The Unionist, an American Federation of Labor paper published in Omaha in the 1930s.

State and Regional Media

Midwestern Trucker and Shipper

"Coffey Is State Purchasing Agent." May 1956: 18.

"Coffey Transfer Closes Because of Strike." March 1956: 1.

"Glen Coffey Now with Ford Van Lines." April 1956: 19.

"Hoffa Subpoenaed to Give Testimony in Grand Jury Probe…" June 1956: 28.

"Truck Union Is Called 'Unfair' by Examiner." August 1956: 4.

Nebraska Farm Bureau Federation

Marshall, Charles. *Nebraska Farm Bureau Federation Statement on LB 510.*

Local Media

Harlan County Journal

"Burlington Buys Coffey Franchise," 22 March 1956, p. 1.

"Burlington Truck Lines to Begin Operation Tuesday," 26 April 1956, p. l.

"Coffey Transfer Ceases Operation This Wednesday," 1 March 1956, p. 1.

Lincoln Journal

Burnham, Dave. "Stalling by Teamsters Delayed NLRB Rule," 20 Nov. 1958.

Burnham, Dave. "'Teamsters Put Us Out of Business,' Nebraskan Asserts," 19 Nov. 1958.

"Law Tactics of Teamsters Attacked," 21 Nov. 1958.

"On Boycotts: Coffey's View Is Requested," 13 Nov. 1958.

"Seven Are Called to Testify," 11 Dec. 1957.

"700 Attend Hearing on Boycotts," 4 March 1959.

"'Teeth in It': Coffey Praises Anti-boycott Bill," 7 May 1959.

Lincoln Star

"Anti-Boycott Bill Praised…by Tom Coffey," 9 May 1959.

"Coffey to be Witness," 22 Oct. 1957.

"Nebraskans to Appear in Rackets Probe," 8 Nov. 1958.

Person, Betty. "Secondary Boycott Bill Is Advanced; 750 at Hearing," 5 March 1959.

"Senate Labor Probers Call 7 Nebraskans," 15 Nov. 1958.

"Truckers Tell of Sabotage and Boycotts," 20 Nov. 1958

Omaha World-Herald

"Boos, Jeers Mar Secondary Boycott Hearing," c. 3 March 1959.

"Coffey Hails Law Curbing Boycotts," 7 May 1959.

"Coffey to Testify About Boycotts," 14 Nov. 1958.

Jarrell, John. "Boycott Quiz State Issue," 30 Aug. 1957.

Jarrell, John. "Coffey Case Lag Cited in Probe," 20 Nov. 1958.

Shasteen, Don. "No-Boycott Bill Sent to Floor, 4-2," 5 Mar 1959 AM ed.

Sidney [NE] Sun-Telegraph

Denney, James. "Ex-Trucker: Man Who Defied Hoffa Sidney's City Manager," c. Jan 1964.

ACKNOWLEDGMENTS

My thanks to the many who helped me research, write, and produce this book. Foremost should be Dr. Cliff Edwards, chair, Fort Hays State University, who encouraged me to write about my father and Jimmy Hoffa.

Rhonda M. Hall, who suggested the title *That Punk Jimmy Hoffa*.

Lee Bachand and Lorraine Duggin for reading my manuscript in its entirety and making valuable recommendations for revision.

Also to members of NightWriters, my writers' group who critiqued sections of my manuscript, namely Gina Barlean, Sue Bristol, Gleenobly Butterworth, Terri Chappell, Sheryl Fawcett, Jen Floyd, Therese Guy, Jack Loscutoff, Bruce Shedd, Charlie Vogel.

To Dan Reynolds, an enthusiastic advocate of my Hoffa book.

To Carl Curtis for his backing of my father and my work.

To Omaha Teamsters Local 554, for information and images from its archives.

To David L. Loyd, for photos and for technical assistance (use of a record player).

To those supportive of my Hoffa book: colleague, Denise Cassino; friends, Kira Gale, Dorothy Lund Nelson, Marilyn

Ray, Floyd "Bub" Schippert, and my family, sister Margaret Dent and son Ian Michael Henshaw.

To those who helped me transform my manuscript into this book: Sandra Wendel, editor and owner of Write On, Inc., and President Lisa Pelto, Ellie Pelto, Sarah Knight and Rachel Moore, designer, all of Concierge Marketing in Omaha.

Although I express my deep gratitude to all those who helped me research, write, and produce this book, any mistakes are solely mine.

ABOUT THE AUTHOR

A best-selling, national prize-winning, internationally published author of poetry and prose, Great Plains writer Marilyn June Coffey has written several thousand poems and prose pieces, and nine books, many set in the Great Plains.

Her most popular book, *Mail-Order Kid: An Orphan Train Rider's Story*, is an Amazon and Kindle best seller. This biography, "a new and unusual look at the Orphan Train experience," tells Teresa Martin's story. She was one of 250,000 children relocated from eastern cities to most US states during 1854–1929. Teresa's story is celebrated today with a statue near the Concordia, Kansas, library. A national prize, the National Orphan Train Complex's Special President's Award, honored *Mail-Order Kid* in 2011.

Coffey's *Thieves, Rascals & Sore Losers: The Unsettling History of the Dirty Deals that Helped Settle Nebraska* is often comic. "I laughed till I cried," wrote critic Bonnye Reed Fry. Midwest Book Review called the book, "An extraordinary and consistently compelling read from beginning to end, history as it is never taught in a classroom."

Coffey's most famous poem, "Pricksong," won a national 1976–77

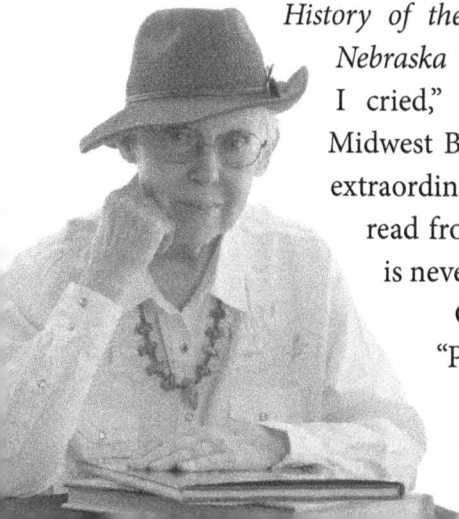

Pushcart Prize in New York. The *Los Angeles Times* called the winner "a wry poem about an obscene houseplant." It is the title poem in Coffey's libidinous book, *Pricksongs*, a collection of tart poems from the turbulent sixties.

Some of Coffey's poems, and those of her lover, Jack Loscutoff, appear in their book, *JackJack & JuneBug: A Love Song in Poems and Posts*. Their poems and Coffey's posts tell a story of love, aging, and grief that George Lauby, editor, *North Platte Bulletin*, calls "heartwarming." Paula Wallace illustrated the uncommonly beautiful book. It won the third national prize, a 2016 Pewter Award from Gold Ink Awards, for its print artistry.

Charterhouse published Coffey's controversial coming-of-age novel, *Marcella*, in New York in 1973; Quartet Books in London brought it out in paperback in 1976. Excerpts then appeared in Australia, and Denmark serialized her book, making Coffey an internationally published author. *Marcella* also broke a world's record; it's the first novel written in English that features female autoeroticism. Feminists praised it. Gloria Steinem called it "an important part of the truth telling by and for women" and published a chapter in *Ms.* magazine. A 40th Anniversary Edition of *Marcella*, paperback, was released in 2013.

Coffey is a trained journalist (BA, University of Nebraska, 1959) and creative writer (MFA, Brooklyn College, 1981). For thirty-four years she taught (Boston University, Pratt Institute in Brooklyn, and Fort Hays [Kansas] State University) earning tenure twice. Now retired, Coffey lives in Omaha, Nebraska.

INDEX

OTHER BOOKS BY MARILYN

Mail-Order Kid: An Orphan Train Rider's Story

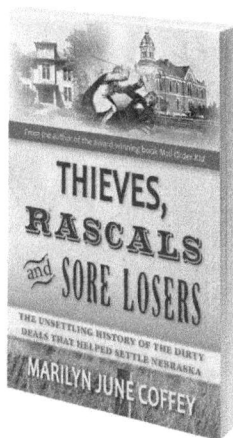

Thieves, Rascals, and Sore Losers: The Unsettling History of
the Dirty Deals that Helped Settle Nebraska

TO SEE MARILYN'S ENTIRE COLLECTION GO TO
WWW.MARILYNCOFFEY.NET

www.ingramcontent.com/pod-product-compliance
Lightning Source LLC
Chambersburg PA
CBHW031458270326
41930CB00006B/140